D1353442

Visio® 2013

ABSOLUTE
BEGINNER'S
GUIDE

Alan Wright and Chris Roth

800 East 96th Street,
Indianapolis, Indiana 46240

Visio® 2013 Absolute Beginner's Guide

ISBN-13: 978-0-7897-5087-7
ISBN-10: 0-7897-5087-2

Library of Congress Control Number: 2013936235

Printed in the United States of America

First Printing: July 2013

Trademarks

All terms mentioned in this book that are known to be trademarks or service marks have been appropriately capitalized. Que Publishing cannot attest to the accuracy of this information. Use of a term in this book should not be regarded as affecting the validity of any trademark or service mark.

Warning and Disclaimer

Every effort has been made to make this book as complete and as accurate as possible, but no warranty or fitness is implied. The information provided is on an "as is" basis. The author and the publisher shall have neither liability nor responsibility to any person or entity with respect to any loss or damages arising from the information contained in this book or from the use of the programs accompanying it.

Bulk Sales

Que Publishing offers excellent discounts on this book when ordered in quantity for bulk purchases or special sales. For more information, please contact

> U.S. Corporate and Government Sales
> 1-800-382-3419
> corpsales@pearsontechgroup.com

For sales outside of the U.S., please contact

> International Sales
> international@pearson.com

Associate Publisher
Greg Wiegand

Executive Editor
Loretta Yates

Development Editor
Susan Hobbs

Managing Editor
Kristy Hart

Project Editor
Andy Beaster

Copy Editor
Barbara Hacha

Indexer
Tim Wight

Proofreader
Dan Knott

Technical Editor
John Marshall

Publishing Coordinator
Cindy Teeters

Interior Designer
Anne Jones

Cover Designer
Matt Coleman

Compositor
Nonie Ratliff

Contents at a Glance

Table of Contents

About the Authors

Alan Wright has worked professionally in and around IT for nearly 10 years. He has provided enterprise-level support in the Detroit, Michigan, area and continues to provide software and hardware support for small business and residential users. He holds several certifications from CompTIA and Microsoft and enjoys working with technology and teaching others how they can make technology work for them.

Alan has been the technical editor on other books from Que Publishing, including *Using Windows 8* and *Microsoft Project 2013 In Depth*. When not working with computers, he enjoys working on projects in his cabinet shop. Alan lives in northern Michigan with his wife, Pam, and their two children, Joshua and Jonathan.

Chris Roth has always enjoyed creating pictures of any kind and absolutely enjoys the combination of computer technology with graphics. He has been working with Visio since The Beginning in 1992, when he was part of the Visio 1.0 team at then-extant Visio Corporation. Since then, he's continuously been busy helping customers incorporate diagrams, drawings, and visualizations into their daily business and to develop custom graphical solutions based on Visio.

A Microsoft Visio MVP since 2002, he has presented sessions at several Visio conferences and has written more than 250 articles about Visio for his "Visio Guy" website (www.visguy.com), which he launched in 2006.

Originally from Seattle, he currently lives with his wife and baby daughter in Munich, Germany. Away from family, laptop, and relaxing Bavarian beer gardens, he plays trombone with the TT Orchestra and the wind ensemble Pullacher Blasmusik.

Dedication

To my loving and very patient wife, Pam; you will never know how glad I am to have you by my side.

—Alan Wright

Acknowledgments

Over the years, I have worked with and learned from many quality people who make technology and software enjoyable for me. Tim Scott and Scott Gaines are a couple of managers I have enjoyed working with and who have supported me over the years. Seth Melton, Tammy Mays, Nick Abughannam, and Shawn Elliott are a few other underappreciated IT professionals I have had fun working with.

Chris Roth has been a great source of Visio tips and how-to information for many years and has earned his Visio MVP recognition many times over.

I especially want to thank Visio MVP John Marshall, who has been a very knowledgeable and supportive technical editor on this book. As someone who has seen Visio develop since the beginning, he has a wealth of knowledge that he enjoys sharing.

I want to thank Loretta Yates, Andy Beaster, and everyone at Que Publishing who has helped to bring this book about.

Finally, I would like to single out and thank and acknowledge the support of J. Peter Bruzzese, who has been a great friend and likely shares some of the blame for where I am today.

—Alan Wright

We Want to Hear from You!

As the reader of this book, *you* are our most important critic and commentator. We value your opinion and want to know what we're doing right, what we could do better, what areas you'd like to see us publish in, and any other words of wisdom you're willing to pass our way.

We welcome your comments. You can email or write to let us know what you did or didn't like about this book—as well as what we can do to make our books better.

Please note that we cannot help you with technical problems related to the topic of this book.

When you write, please be sure to include this book's title and author as well as your name and email address. We will carefully review your comments and share them with the author and editors who worked on the book.

Email: feedback@quepublishing.com

Mail: Que Publishing
ATTN: Reader Feedback
800 East 96th Street
Indianapolis, IN 46240 USA

Reader Services

Visit our website and register this book at quepublishing.com/register for convenient access to any updates, downloads, or errata that might be available for this book.

INTRODUCTION

Nervous, excited, frustrated, giddy, exhausted—maybe one of those words captures how you feel right now as you look at this *Absolute Beginner's Guide*. Learning how to use a new piece of software or getting up to speed on a new version is not always fun. On the other hand, you likely enjoy learning new things when you see new possibilities and feel the benefits. Visio may be a mystery to you now, and you may feel some trepidation, but rest assured this book was designed to quickly get you comfortable with this amazing program.

Visio is all about visualizing ideas and information. You can create amazing diagrams to show how processes work and how things interact. You can create floor plans and layouts with relative ease. Visio is used more often than you probably realize, from web content and org charts to advertising and business presentations. It has been said that a picture is worth a thousand words, and Visio allows you to speak volumes, which is why it has become an integral tool for businesses that put a premium on communication.

Visio has been around since 1992 and has gone through some big transformations to keep pace with the demands of technology. If you have used it in the past, you'll find some new features worth getting excited about. If you have never used it, prepare to be amazed. You will love how easy it is to create diagrams using templates and to preview changes using themes. Using Shape Data, you will find new ways to display information that are limited only by your imagination.

Despite the complexity and overwhelming potential that Visio presents, it is all built on basic concepts and tools that you will quickly grasp. If you have an artistic side, you will enjoy how satisfying Visio makes it to visualize and present information and data.

The *Visio 2013 Absolute Beginner's Guide* will assist you as you explore this application and consider ways to change and improve your ability to communicate ideas and concepts to others. We'll encourage you to poke around, try different things, and we will alert you to some best practices and tips. Above all, enjoy learning about Visio.

What This Book Covers

Visio is a communication tool used everywhere by people of all backgrounds and all types of organizations. Because of this, we have tried to keep to the basics and provide essential tips and suggestions to help you save time and give you the knowledge needed to make you a power user, no matter how you use Visio.

Although you may feel like an absolute beginner, we will quickly have you creating diagrams and working with Visio's tools, and you will feel your confidence grow. You can follow along using different templates, and where more advanced concepts are considered, you will see the steps you can follow. At times we may only point out that there are more complex options or that more can be learned than we have space to develop.

Because Visio 2013 comes in three versions, we principally consider information that is practical to any user of Visio. We will try to point out anything that may be unique to specific versions along the way. A few chapters have content aimed at users with Professional or Pro for Office 365 versions, and we warn you when this is the case.

With this book you will be able to do the following:

- Create your own flowcharts, org charts, and network diagrams using a variety of shapes and connectors.

- Create and manage customized shapes and arrange your own stencils.

- Organize and arrange your diagrams using a variety of tools, such as containers, callouts, and layers.

- Utilize SmartShape features and shape data to create more powerful communication tools.

- Print your diagrams efficiently using an array of settings and tools to control what prints and how it will appear.

- Export Visio content for use in other applications in different formats.

- Share your Visio drawings with others through a variety of tools, including email, SkyDrive, and SharePoint.

How This Book Is Organized

This book is arranged in three parts, which are broken down into chapters:

Part I, "Visio 2013 Basics," helps you get familiar with the tabbed interface used in Visio 2013. You will become familiar with the components of a basic diagram, including Page Backgrounds and Themes. You will create drawings using Templates and understand the ins and outs of Shapes and Stencils.

Part II, "Customizing," will deepen your awareness of additional features to be found in Shapes and Connectors. You will get to know tools that help you work better with content in your drawings using Containers, Layers, and Text. Editing, Duplicating and Formatting options are considered and you will dive into SmartShapes and Shape Data. You will learn all about Printing in this section.

Part III, "Advanced," introduces you to the many ways you can share and export your diagrams into other formats. You will see how to use special Touchscreen menus and learn about other unique situations here. How to collaborate with other Visio users and where to find more Visio content and information will be considered. You will learn about more complex ways to use and work with Data, including data that is maintained outside of Visio. Finally, you will look at unique features and get some tips for working with specific templates and diagram types.

Conventions Used in This Book

Most terms specific to Visio will be explained as we go along in the book. However, there are a few terms and standards that we had in mind while preparing this book that we should explain at the outset.

Working with Visio Tools and Menus

When the book describes labels or titles that you can see on the screen while working with Visio, they will be capitalized. Instructions to press a specific key or keyboard combination will also be capitalized, like this:

1. Select the Design tab.

2. In the Page Setup section, click the Page Setup button or press Shift+F5.

3. Review settings on the Page Size tab and click OK.

Because of touchscreen interfaces, we generally use the term "select" rather than "click" to describe the process of activating a button or menu item, so feel free to click, tap, or press the indicated item to carry out the action. When there is a need to activate a button to continue to another step, "click" tends to sound better and has been used for that reason.

Using Screen Illustrations

The screen illustrations used throughout the book as figures are a valuable reference tool. Generally, illustrations will show you the step being discussed in the text. Some illustrations are cropped to focus attention on details, whereas others show the whole Visio window to help you get familiar with how things are laid out. Look around and notice tabs and features that are not being discussed, just to get a feel for where things are located. Occasionally, we may include callouts or combine multiple elements in a single illustration so that you can compare menus or layouts.

Web Addresses

You may see web addresses referred to in the book. These are offered as points of reference in examples, or they may point to additional information or resources. They will appear in this format:

http://www.microsoft.com

Throughout this book you will see the words "drawing" and "diagram" used almost as synonyms. Both are words used in the Visio interface, and they tend to be interchangeable. Technically, a *diagram* refers to a more conceptual drawing, whereas a *drawing* conveys the idea of a more finished product with measurements and details. In practice, some types of templates tend to be considered as diagrams, whereas others are more often referred to as drawings. Don't think you need to read into the way these terms are used in this book.

Special Elements to Watch For

As with all books in this series, *Visio 2013 Absolute Beginner's Guide* includes special items that provide additional information that will add to your understanding:

 TIP Tips indicate a useful time-saving step, shortcut, or a way for you to easily get better results.

 NOTE Notes provide additional background information or related material about the task or topic being considered. It's not information you absolutely *need* to know, but it may provide you with a clearer understanding of the topic.

 CAUTION Cautions alert you to potential undesirable results and point out items or choices that could cause problems if misunderstood or accidently used.

Although you could read this book from beginning to end, you will likely find it practical to jump around, and we have included references to subjects that are considered more in depth in other places in the book. Feel free to go back and forth as you get familiar with specific tasks and topics.

PART I

VISIO 2013 BASICS

IN THIS CHAPTER

- What is Visio?
- How can I use Visio?
- How are Visio 2013 versions different?
- What is new in Visio 2013?

1

GETTING TO KNOW VISIO 2013

Allow us to introduce you to Visio 2013. We are confident that you will be excited to learn all about this application. This chapter briefly considers ways that you can use Visio; you even create your very own diagram in the first few pages. This chapter also shows you some of the differences between versions as well as the improvements included with Visio 2013.

What Is Visio?

People who have never used Visio often ask what it does. Even those who have used Visio over the years may have a hard time explaining what Visio is because they use it for only one or two very specific tasks. Visio is an application that allows you to create visually distinctive and professional diagrams that can be used in a variety of settings, subjects, and professions.

The idea behind Visio is to provide standardized tools that enable you to easily *assemble* drawings or diagrams using basic building blocks or *shapes*, so you do not need to be an artist or even know how to draw. This approach to diagramming makes it possible for anyone to create amazing charts and diagrams by putting shapes together from groups of shapes called *stencils*. *Templates* make this even easier by providing you with a basic starting point that determines formatting and which stencils are used. You start working by dragging and dropping shapes into a drawing.

Create a Basic Flowchart

Visio will quickly make sense to you as you follow the examples and create some of the sample diagrams in this book. Many tools will be intuitive, and you will see a layout similar to other Microsoft Office applications that you may already be familiar with. We progressively explain in detail what all the buttons and menus are for through later chapters. You do not need to be an expert before you start making Visio diagrams; in fact, you can start right now with a simple flowchart.

Follow these steps to create a basic flowchart:

1. Open the Visio application.

2. To the left you see a list of the most recent drawings you have opened. As you work with Visio this grows, even if it is now empty. To the right where you see a list of drawing types, select Basic Flowchart as shown in Figure 1.1.

3. A smaller window appears, labeled Basic Flowchart. Click the Create button for now.

4. To the left you see a few shapes with different names. Look for the Start/End shape and drag it over to the drawing window by selecting it and dragging it. Drop it toward the top of the page, as shown in Figure 1.2.

5. While the shape is still selected, type the words **Start flowchart** and then press the Esc key on your keyboard when you are done. The shape is still selected, and the words "Start flowchart" are now centered in the shape.

FIGURE 1.1

Choose a basic flowchart to start a new diagram.

FIGURE 1.2

To begin making a diagram, drag a shape onto the drawing window.

6. Position your mouse pointer over the shape for a couple of seconds to see four faint blurry arrows. Move the mouse pointer until you hover over the arrow pointing down. A group of four shapes appears; select the left-most rectangle with a click, as shown in Figure 1.3.

7. A rectangle is placed below your start shape, and a line with an arrow connects the two shapes. With the rectangle selected, type the words **Add shapes to identify steps in the flowchart** and press Esc again.

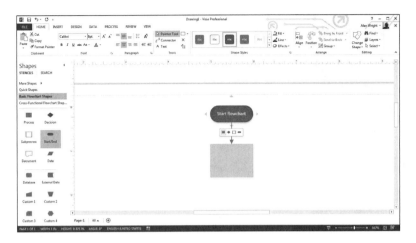

FIGURE 1.3

Add additional shapes using your mouse with a hover technique.

8. Hover your mouse pointer over this rectangle and then the arrow pointing down, as in step 6. Select the right-most oval shape as an end shape for your flowchart.

9. With this end shape selected, type in the words **End flowchart**. Press Esc when finished.

Your flowchart should look like the one in Figure 1.4. Congratulations! You have created a simple but complete flowchart that summarizes the nine steps just completed.

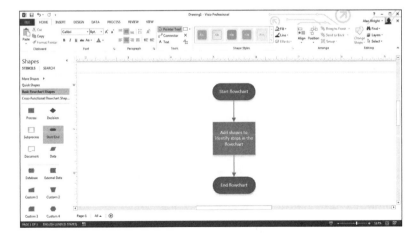

FIGURE 1.4

Text can be added to shapes to make steps in a flowchart easy to follow.

What Else Can I Make?

Visio is known for many other diagram types besides the flowchart that you just created. Out of the box, Visio Standard 2013 includes the 26 types of templates shown in Table 1.1; the Professional version includes 76 templates. Many are new and improved with the Visio 2013 versions.

To see which templates you have, open Visio and scroll through the templates listed in the template gallery as shown in Figure 1.5. You learn more details about templates in Chapter 3, "Working with Basic Diagrams."

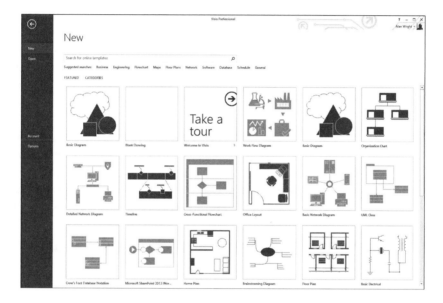

FIGURE 1.5

The template gallery offers many choices of drawings. These are a few of the templates that you can choose from in Visio Professional 2013.

TABLE 1.1   The 26 Templates Included with Visio 2013 Standard

Audit	Work Flow (3D)
Brainstorming	Basic
Cause and Effect	Block
Charts and Graphs	Block with Perspective
EPC (Event-driven Process Chain)	Directional Map
Fault Tree Analysis	Directional Map - 3D
Marketing Charts and Diagrams	Office Layout

Organization Chart	Basic Network
Organization Chart Wizard	Basic Network - 3D
TQM (Total Quality Management)	Calendar
Basic Flowchart	Gantt Chart
Cross-Functional Flowchart	Timeline
Work Flow	PERT (Program Evaluation and Review Technique) Chart

Although these templates are included to provide the basic tools specific to a variety of fields and situations, you are not limited to these choices. Chapter 13, "Unique Needs: Touchscreens, Custom Templates, and Complex Printing Concerns," looks at how you can create templates of your very own. Chapter 16, "Additional Visio Resources," also suggests recommendations for websites that offer downloadable resources like templates.

To help you make sense of the way some of these templates are used, consider a few common examples:

- Connected diagrams include flowcharts, network diagrams, brainstorming, org charts, database diagrams, and many types of engineering schematics that use lines to show how elements of the chart relate to one another or a correct flow for processes. Figure 1.6 shows an org chart that uses lines to show hierarchy.

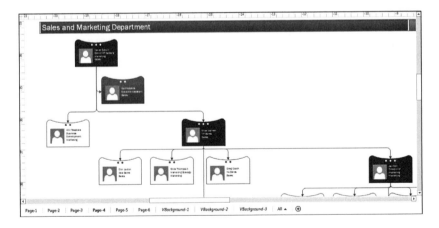

FIGURE 1.6

Connected diagrams like this organization chart use lines to show relationships.

- Block diagrams are often used to show concepts and illustrate relationships without using lines. Instead, shapes, colors, style, and the position are used to communicate how shapes and ideas relate to one another. Figure 1.7 shows a basic block diagram where smaller shapes represent components of a computer.

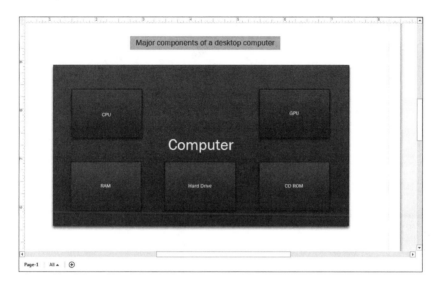

FIGURE 1.7

Block diagrams use positioning, color, size, and other visual cues to explain the relationship between shapes.

- Measured drawings include plans, maps, layouts, and views that rely on scale and measurements to communicate to the viewer. These are often used for planning and design and can be used to present ideas to clients. Figure 1.8 shows a floor plan with an assortment of dimensions that can be hidden or displayed as needed.

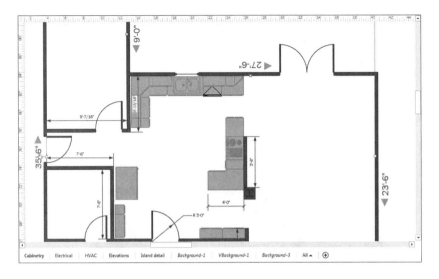

FIGURE 1.8

Measured drawings use measurements to accurately capture the position and size of drawing elements such as walls, doors, and windows.

Which Edition Should I Use?

There are three versions of Visio 2013 that you can choose from, and each provides unique features and advantages. Which one is for you? The answer depends on how you use Visio. Compare the basic features to get a better idea as to which fits your needs:

- Visio Standard 2013 is designed to work with basic business diagrams, organization charts, basic flowcharts, and multipurpose drawings. Table 1.1, shown earlier in this chapter, lists the 26 templates that are included. Some of the more advanced features are not included in this edition, such as importing external data and SharePoint integration.

- Visio Professional 2013 includes 50 more templates that allow you to create more advanced types of drawings, such as advanced process diagrams, engineering schematics, floor plans, logical network layouts, software mapping, and database and modeling. Enhanced tools for collaboration and many tools for linking data to your drawings are included.

- Visio Pro for Office 365 is a completely new subscription-based offering that includes the features of Visio Professional 2013. A person with an active subscription can install Visio Pro on up to five computers. Additionally, with an active subscription you can use Visio on Demand temporarily from *any* computer you happen to be using while logged in to your Office 365 online account, even if you are not the administrator or do not own the computer. You can save your work as you would with other Visio versions. Because it does not install onto the temporary computer, it simply is gone when you close the application.

What Is New in the 2013 Editions?

Microsoft recognizes that the way people and organizations work have changed. As a result, there are many new features in Visio that have been influenced by evolving needs and changing technology. People are more mobile, which creates challenges to collaboration and sharing; tablets have become more common in the workplace, which in turn has influenced the Visio interface.

Visio 2013 boasts updated and modern shapes and stencils. Many stencils have been improved with new shapes (see Figure 1.9), and new stencils have been created. Regarding shapes, the capability to change a shape has been added without the need to redo work or data when you decide a different shape would be appropriate.

FIGURE 1.9

Visio 2013 includes updated stencils with modern shapes. Here the shapes in the Department stencil are shown.

For Visio Professional, drawings can be shared to a SharePoint server and then, using SharePoint Services, individuals without Visio can view Visio drawings from a SharePoint server. Multiple individuals can work on the same Visio drawing simultaneously, and even communication tools have been improved for collaboration from within Visio.

Improved Touch Support

Windows 8 and touchscreen-enabled devices have brought about a dramatic redesign of the ribbon interface and menus that make it much easier for you to use touch to work with Visio drawings. Figure 1.10 shows the Touch-mode-enabled ribbon interface.

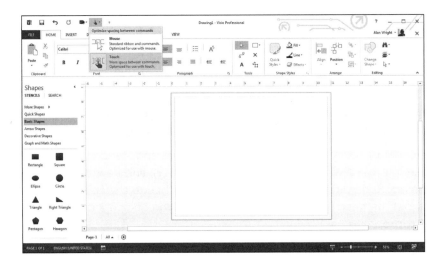

FIGURE 1.10

Enable Touch mode to increase the spacing around your menus when using a touchscreen.

➜ To learn more about using touch controls, see page **246**.

Streamlined Layout

Work has been done to make tools easier to find and keep the drawing window at the focus of your work experience. Visio has so many tools to assist us that the interface can become cluttered, and you might forget where tools are located. To reduce this screen clutter, many tools appear as needed when you use a right-click to bring up the context menu, as shown in Figure 1.11.

Another area that has been improved by this streamlining effort is the print preview. Shown in Figure 1.12, the Print Preview pane is a print-what-you-see live preview tool. You look closer at how to use this tool in Chapter 11, "Printing Visio Diagrams."

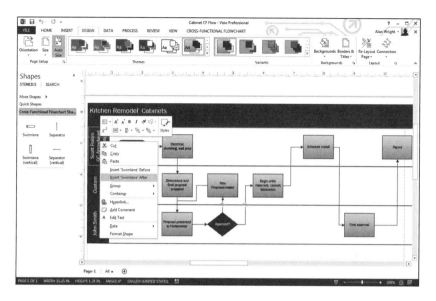

FIGURE 1.11

Visio makes good use of context menus that offer tools only when needed.

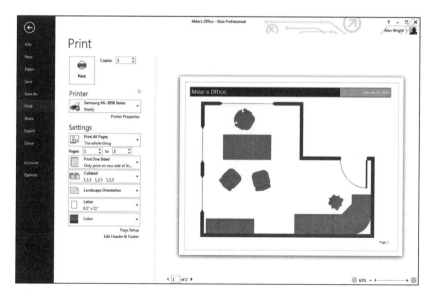

FIGURE 1.12

You will really like the improved Print Preview pane.

The New VSDX File Format

Visio 2013 saves drawings to the .vsdx file format, which uses XML and brings Visio up to the standard that has been established for all the Office applications. This brings benefits such as smaller file sizes and easier data recovery, and third-party tools can work with XML to extract data saved to this format.

Drawings that have been created and saved to the older 2003–2010 drawing format can be converted to this new format, allowing you to take advantage of new themes, styles, and tools like co-authoring. You learn more about this format in Chapter 3.

THE ABSOLUTE MINIMUM

As you learned in this chapter, creating Visio content using shapes and stencils is easy; all you need to do is experiment and practice. As you get comfortable adding shapes and labeling your shapes with text, you quickly imagine ways to put these tools to work.

Consider which version of Visio satisfies your needs. If you work with more advanced types of drawings and schematics, or need to work with external data sources, you need to use Professional. For basic flowcharts, diagrams, and org charts, Standard should make you very happy. If you travel a lot and often use computers that are loaned at a worksite or in hotels, you may find Pro for Office 365 a nice option.

New features improve your touchscreen experience by keeping tools readily available and providing touch-friendly contextual menus.

FINDING YOUR WAY AROUND THE INTERFACE

If you have ever been lost and consulted a map to get your bearings, you already understand the concept of this chapter. This chapter shows you where things are located, and you become aware of various menus and tools that might otherwise escape your attention. Notice how things are referred to in this chapter because that makes it easier to follow the steps and recognize these features throughout this book.

You may already know or understand some of the features presented here; just skim through to make sure you haven't missed any critical information. The same as with a map, you can come back to this chapter occasionally to get your bearings, if you need to.

The Ribbon

Microsoft introduced the Fluent User Interface (Fluent UI) with Office 2007, and it has been a feature in Visio since 2010. Undeniably, the horizontal *ribbon* of *tabs* is the most noticeable feature of the Fluent UI, which also provides a *backstage* area, a status bar, and a Quick Access toolbar (see Figure 2.1).

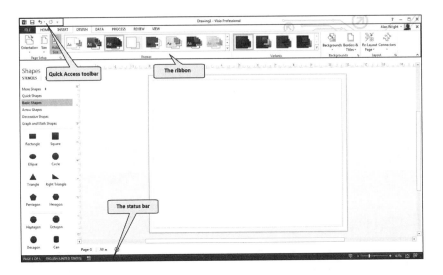

FIGURE 2.1

Visio 2013 includes the standard Office interface elements such as the ribbon, status bar, and the Quick Access toolbar.

If you have not used this type of interface before, you may be initially perplexed by the way menus are grouped into tabs. This is an efficient and intuitive way to access the many tools included in Visio.

Embrace the Tab

In Visio 2013, notice the tabs for File, Home, Insert, Design, Review, and View. Professional also provides you with Data and Process tabs.

Tabs are tools that have been grouped together based on tasks; tools are grouped together even further on the tab itself. When you want to insert a picture or text, you find those tools on the Insert tab. When you change the appearance of a drawing, you find common tools for this task on the Design tab, and so on.

Tabs contain many straightforward tools and quite a few unlabeled controls that reveal additional options that you may not need to see as often. Figure 2.2 shows some of the types of controls available on a tab:

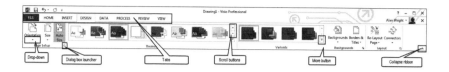

FIGURE 2.2

Tabs present a streamlined array of tools to suit a task and still provide many ways to access additional tools as needed.

- Drop-down arrows indicate the presence of a menu with additional tools. Selecting this expands down to reveal the drop-down menu.

- Dialog box launchers open a small window referred to as a dialog box. This contains additional options and tools.

- Tabs allow you to quickly jump from one tool set to another based on the task at hand.

- Scroll buttons are used with galleries, and they allow you to browse right from the tab.

- More buttons expand a gallery and provide access to additional menus.

- Collapse ribbon hides the ribbon from view, allowing for more screen to be used in the drawing window. Selecting a tab reveals its contents temporarily.

Contextual Tabs

Contextual tabs refer to tabs that appear only as needed. They contain tools that are unique and are needed only when working with special templates or when special tool sets are used. Often these appear simply because of a shape that has been selected. Figure 2.3 shows the Picture Tools Format tab. This tab is visible only if an image file is selected.

Following are contextual tool tabs you may encounter:

- Picture Tools

- Ink Tools

- Container Tools

- ShapeSheet Tools

FIGURE 2.3

Contextual tabs appear as needed, such as this Picture Tools tab.

Template Tabs

Many templates are so unique that they have special tools grouped into their very own tab. Open one of these templates and the tab appears automatically. Figure 2.4 shows the Org Chart tab, which contains unique buttons related to org chart shapes, spacing, size, and contents.

Following are some of the template-specific tabs you may see:

- Brainstorming
- Cross-functional Flowchart
- Plan
- Org Chart
- Gantt Chart
- Web Site Map

Customizing the Ribbon

As you can see, the ribbon is practical. Imagine trying to find space to work if all the buttons and tools were always visible. It is possible to create custom tabs and tool groups where you can collect selected tools all in one place.

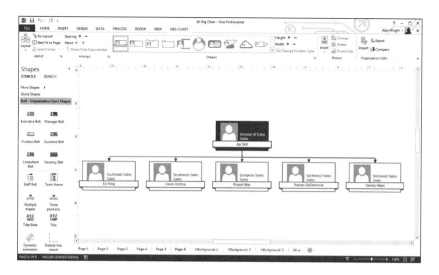

FIGURE 2.4

Many templates have their own tabs, like this Org Chart tab.

Customizing the ribbon is done from the Visio Options dialog box, shown in Figure 2.5. Notice that there are two lists—the first shows commands that exist and the second shows locations on tabs where commands are or can be located.

The first list, Choose Commands From, defaults to the Popular Commands option. You can select in the drop-down list from a few other options to refine the list of commands shown. For example, All Commands lists every command Visio includes, whereas Tool Tabs lists only commands currently located on the four contextual tool tabs.

The second list, Customize the Ribbon, enables you to show the All, Main, or Tool tabs. Based on the selection, you can expand a tool group using the plus sign (+) to see the tools located in the group or collapse a tool group using the minus sign (–). Check boxes enable you to hide or make visible individual tabs.

Selecting commands from either the Choose Commands From or Customize the Ribbon lists allows you to use the Add and Remove buttons in the middle to change the contents of custom tabs and custom tool groups. You can also rename tabs, add new groups and tabs, or reset the commands and tabs to their original configuration.

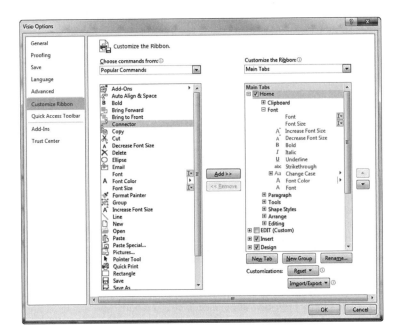

FIGURE 2.5

Use the Visio Options dialog box to customize the commands located on a tab.

To customize the ribbon and add a couple of commands, follow these steps:

1. Select the File tab and then select Options at the bottom of the left-side vertical menu.

2. Select Customize Ribbon from the vertical list of tabs on the left.

3. Below the list to the right, select the New Tab button. This adds a new tab and a new tool group to the list of tabs.

4. Select the new tab you just created and then select the Rename button. Type in the display name for your tab using all uppercase letters in the Rename dialog box that pops up so that your tab name will match the default tab name uppercase formatting. Click OK.

5. Select your new tool group and then select the Rename button again. In the Rename dialog box shown in Figure 2.6, type in a display name for your group and click OK. (You can see symbols listed here, but they appear only when you rename a command, at which time you can assign a symbol to replace the displayed icon.)

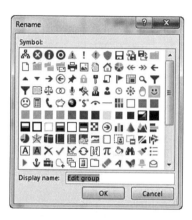

FIGURE 2.6

The Rename dialog box allows you to rename tabs, tool groups, and even assign icons.

6. Using Popular Commands to display commands in the left-side list, select Pointer Tool and then select the Add button. The Pointer tool is now listed in the new group you just created.

7. Select the Connector command from the list of popular commands, and select Add to add it to your custom group. Figure 2.7 shows the new tab named Edit and the new group named Edit Group. Both have (Custom) following the name to alert you to the tab being customized, but it does not appear on the actual tab.

8. Click OK on the Visio Options dialog box to close it and apply the changes you have made. Visio pauses as it updates, and then your tab appears as shown in Figure 2.8.

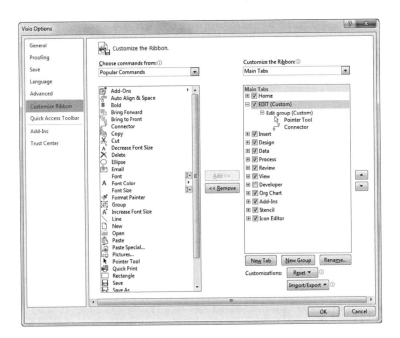

FIGURE 2.7

Adding commands to tabs that you have created is an easy undertaking.

FIGURE 2.8

You use custom tabs to bring tools that you choose to a single place.

Where Did That Command Go?

As Visio has evolved, some commands have dropped from usage, or they have moved. You might get frustrated when you're unable to find a command that you know used to be in a certain place. Use the Visio Options dialog box to help you locate those commands. To open this, select the File tab, select Options, then select Customize Ribbon.

To locate a command, select All Commands from the drop-down list located under Choose Commands From, and scroll through the alphabetically organized list. You can hover over commands in this list to see where they are located on the tabs, as shown in Figure 2.9. In this image, Bold is shown in the All Commands list as being located on the Home tab, in the Font tool group. The list of the Home tab contents off to the right verifies this.

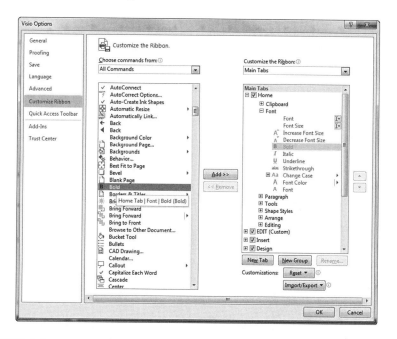

FIGURE 2.9

Find commands using the All Commands list from the Customize Ribbon tab of Visio Options.

In some cases a list is not used on any tab. Figure 2.10 shows how you can also select the Commands Not in the Ribbon to reveal commands that are not located directly on any tab. Notice in this figure that the All Caps command has been found and added to a new custom group.

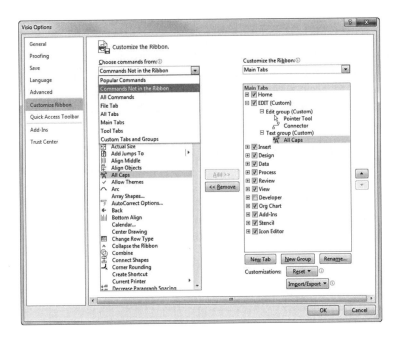

FIGURE 2.10

Checking the list Commands Not in the Ribbon may be useful when trying to locate commands that seem to be missing.

Important Features of the Visio Application

Besides the ribbon, you should know a few other tools when you're working with Visio that are part of the Fluent UI, which is used across the various Microsoft Office applications.

The Quick Access Toolbar

The Quick Access toolbar allows you to place commands that will always be visible in the upper-left corner of the Visio window (see Figure 2.1). Basic commands are located here by default to save, undo, and redo actions. You can also customize the toolbar by clicking the More button, which reveals the drop-down list shown in Figure 2.11.

If you select More Commands from this list, it enables you to pick specific commands from the Visio Options dialog box similar to the way you found and added commands to tabs in the previous section.

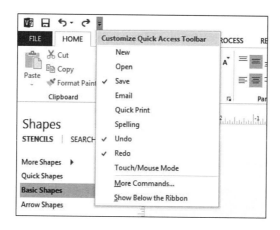

FIGURE 2.11

You can customize the Quick Access toolbar to keep the commands you use often always visible.

Context Menus

Context menus are sometimes called right-click menus, and they are used the same way in all Microsoft products. They provide basic functions that allow you to cut, copy, and paste, as well as tools to format text and perform editing. In Visio, context menus are valuable tools when working with shapes and text. Some shapes display hidden abilities when examined using the context menu. Figure 2.12 shows the results of right-clicking a door on a floor plan. In the context menu, notice this shape can reverse its orientation with a simple click.

The Backstage

Of all the tabs, the File tab is truly distinctive with its dark blue color, meant to emphasize its uniqueness. Unlike other tabs, this tab takes you behind your drawing to the Backstage area, where you can open additional drawings, create new drawings, save your work, print, share, and export drawings. It also provides access to settings for the Visio application.

Shown in Figure 2.13, the Backstage area does not display the other horizontal ribbon tabs; instead, a vertical list of tabs is found off to the left. To return to where you last were, select the large arrow pointing off to the left at the top of this vertical list.

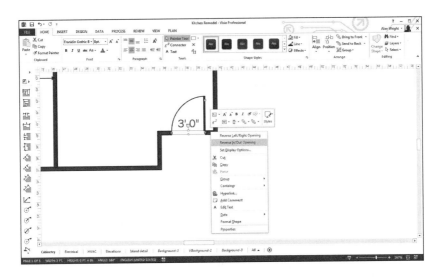

FIGURE 2.12

Context menus provide valuable tools that may be unique to a particular shape like this door shape.

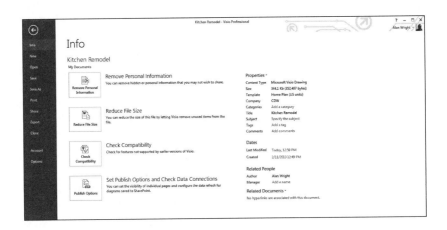

FIGURE 2.13

The Info tab of the Backstage area provides information about the current drawing.

If you select the File tab while working on a drawing, it opens to the Info tab. Here you see document properties related to the drawing you are working on, such as size and date information. When you first open Visio, you are brought to a different part of the Backstage area, allowing you to choose from recent drawings or start a new template.

In this book, you revisit this Backstage area often as you learn about the purpose and content of the different tabs.

The Status Bar

Shown in Figure 2.1, the status bar occupies the bottom horizontal strip of the Visio window. As indicated by the name, it provides status information regarding the drawing that is currently open, revealing the page you are on, language settings, and zoom settings. When a shape is selected, information related to the size of the shape is displayed on the status bar. You occasionally see status messages and progress bars displayed in the middle of the status bar related to file tasks like saving and printing. Use your mouse pointer to hover over items on the status bar to reveal additional information when in doubt.

Figure 2.14 points out a couple of buttons located in the status bar that are worth mentioning. To the left of the zoom controls is the Presentation Mode button. This displays your drawing at full screen and allows you to scroll through the pages much like you would in a PowerPoint presentation. Press Esc to return to the normal Visio window. The second button is the Switch Windows button. Select it to see currently open drawings and select a drawing to jump to it.

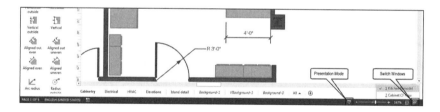

FIGURE 2.14

The status bar provides tools related to what is displayed in the Visio window.

A Look at the Drawing Window

You have looked above, below, and even behind it; now take a look at the heart of Visio; the drawing window. The drawing window includes all the space between the ribbon and the status bar. Besides the actual page area used for the drawing are a few elements that are usually present when you use the drawing window; these can be hidden if you prefer. Figure 2.15 shows the drawing window with some of these additional elements present, such as task panes.

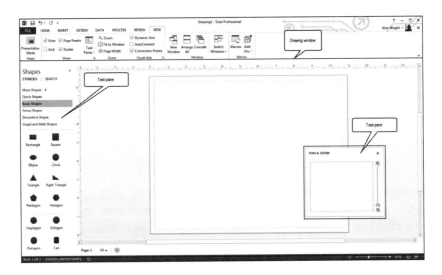

FIGURE 2.15

You work on your drawings in the drawing window.

Task Panes

There are a few task panes that you use when working in Visio. Task panes are basically small moveable windows. They can be docked to the side of a drawing window, like the Shape task pane shown in Figure 2.15, or they can float like the Pan & Zoom task pane in the same image. You use task panes often when working with Visio.

➜ To learn more about task panes, see page **53**.

Rulers and Grids

You can use rulers around the drawing window, and you can add grids to assist you in placing shapes. Figure 2.15 shows rulers along the top edge of the drawing window and to the left of the drawing area. Notice in this image that rulers and gridlines can be displayed or hidden by selecting their check boxes located on the View tab and in the Show tool group.

Manipulating Shapes

A foundation of any Visio drawing is the shape. A few chapters in this book are dedicated to shapes and how you can work effectively with them. It is important to understand some basic characteristics of shapes and how to interact with them using their control handles, sometimes called control points.

Imagine moving a big trunk or suitcase that has handles in the wrong place. Shapes have plenty of control handles that are designed to be used in diverse situations. You look at the basic types of handles here. You can click and drag a handle using the Pointer tool, which is the default pointer when working with Visio. Later in the book, as you see how to use these handles, you know how to find them.

1D Shape Handles

Shapes that are considered one dimensional (1D) include arrows, lines, and connectors. When you select a 1D shape, you see two control handles or points that allow you to position the endpoints themselves. You may see additional yellow control handles that allow you to change additional characteristics.

Figure 12.16 shows an arrow shape, and the two endpoints can be seen. A yellow control handle is located at the top corner of the arrowhead, and dragging this allows you to change the length of the arrowhead itself. The second yellow control handle allows you to widen or narrow the entire arrow shape. All the control handles work around a one-dimensional axis.

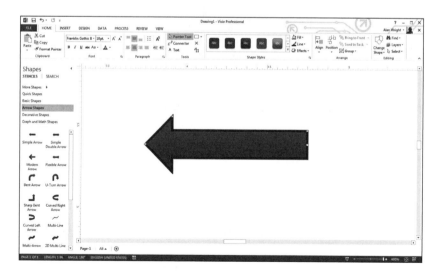

FIGURE 2.16

1D shapes have limited control handles used for resizing.

2D Shape Handles

Shapes that are considered two dimensional (2D) have more control handles, allowing resizing to be done in more than one direction. Think of 1D shapes as having length, while 2D shapes cover area. The box in Figure 2.17 shows a 2D shape with eight control handles around its perimeter and another control handle for rotating the shape.

Grab a control handle at a corner, and you can resize in two directions at once. Using midpoint handles you can change the size in one direction. Rotate handles are used to rotate shapes by clicking the circular control handle and then dragging to rotate the shape. You can control the sensitivity of the rotation by how near your cursor is to the shape.

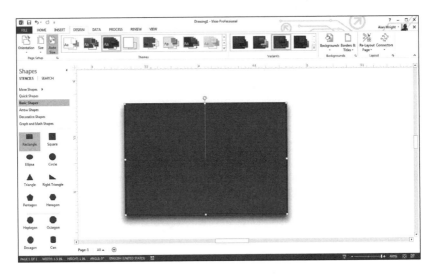

FIGURE 2.17

2D shapes provide more control handles, allowing you more options when resizing.

Vertex Handles

Control handles can serve more than one purpose, depending on the tool you select. As you've seen in previous examples, the Pointer tool affects basic resizing when you select and drag a control handle. Change the tool on the Home tab to a line shape tool, as shown in Figure 2.18, and then you can change how a control handle responds when dragging it. Vertex handles appear as small blue dots, and the cursor changes to a four-headed arrow when you hover over a vertex handle. A *vertex* refers to the point where two or more line segments meet.

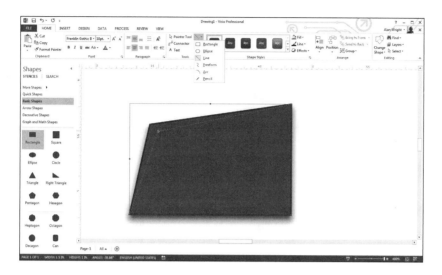

FIGURE 2.18

Change shape geometry using vertex handles.

Select a corner using the Line tool, and the vertex handle at the corner allows you to reposition just that corner, resulting in the shape in Figure 2.18. Select the Pencil tool; grab a midpoint between two vertex handles, and pull the side of a shape into an arc. Freeform and arc tools also turn control handles into vertex handles. Experiment with these tools to see how you can use vertex handles in your shapes. Remember that you can always undo actions when you don't like the results.

Eccentricity Handles

When working with arcs or curved lines, you may see control handles called *eccentricity handles*. These are used to adjust the severity of an arc and are used when curved connectors have been selected. Figure 2.19 shows a curved connector between two shapes. The two endpoints are easy to see, and extending from those endpoints are two dashed lines ending in eccentricity handles. Pulling and positioning these handles enable you to fine-tune the appearance of the curves seen in the line.

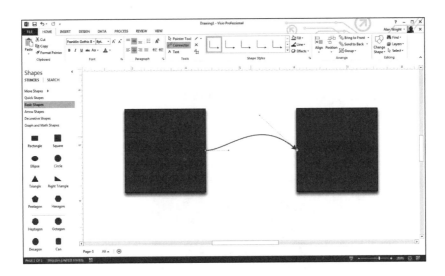

FIGURE 2.19

You can adjust curvy lines by using eccentricity control handles.

Get Around Using Your Keyboard

This is a section you should return to occasionally as you get comfortable working with Visio. Power users often rely on their keyboard to work faster by opening dialog boxes or activating commands without having to switch tabs or navigate menus with their mouse. As you continue through this book, you will see references to basic keyboard shortcuts that are especially worth knowing and using. Table 2.1 presents a list of the most commonly used keyboard shortcuts. As shown in Figure 2.20, you can often hover over a command on a tab with your mouse pointer to reveal a ToolTip that indicates what the keyboard shortcut might be.

Some may not seem as useful and are appreciated only with time. Keyboard shortcuts truly become effective when they become second nature and you can use them without thinking about it. Don't try to learn them all, and don't feel bad if it takes you time to remember some of these. Many individuals start by using sticky notes around their computer display to refer to, and this may help you, too. Try each shortcut out as you read through the table and pick a handful to master; then return later to see if others might be useful.

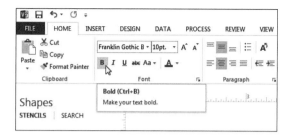

FIGURE 2.20

Hover your mouse pointer over a command to see if there is a keyboard shortcut. Bold text effect can be applied to text by pressing the keys Ctrl+B according to this ToolTip.

 NOTE Another handy way to see keyboard shortcuts within Visio is to press F10. You will see letters and numbers that appear next to tabs and commands. Pressing these letters or numbers will activate that tab or command. This only works while the letters or numbers are visible. Use F10 to turn this off and on as needed.

TABLE 2.1 Visio Keyboard Shortcuts

To Do This:	Do This:
Zoom in	Ctrl+Roll mouse wheel forward
Zoom out	Ctrl+Roll mouse wheel backward
Zoom in	Ctrl+Shift+Left click
Zoom out	Ctrl+Shift+Right click
Zoom in	Ctrl+Shift+Left click and drag to area
Select multiple shapes	Press Shift or Ctrl while clicking shapes
Select all shapes on a page	Ctrl+A
Bring a selected shape to front	Ctrl+Shift+F
Send a selected shape to back	Ctrl+Shift+B
Group selected shapes	Ctrl+G
Ungroup shapes in a group	Ctrl+Shift+U
Clear shape selection	Press Esc
Duplicate a selected shape	Ctrl+D
Duplicate a selected shape	Press Ctrl+drag
Move a shape	Arrow keys

Move a shape	Shift+Arrow keys
Repeat an action	F4
Change to the Pointer tool	Ctrl+1
Change to the Connector tool	Ctrl+3
Open the Format task pane	F3
Save your drawing	Ctrl+S
Save your drawing using Save As	F12
Print your Drawing	Ctrl+P
Select the Text tool	Ctrl+2
Open the text dialog box	F11
Copy selected shapes or text	Ctrl+C
Paste content that has been copied	Ctrl+V
Remove a selected item and place it in the Clipboard to paste	Ctrl+X

THE ABSOLUTE MINIMUM

Spend time looking at the ribbon tabs and their contents. A little time invested here helps you later as you associate tools with specific tabs.

If you think you are losing time by jumping back and forth between tabs, or if you want commands to be more readily available, consider creating a custom tab and adding tools you like to use all in one place.

Add a few commands that you use a lot to the Quick Access toolbar so that they are always available.

Right-click to open context menus. Do this often and especially when working with new shapes. Many tools and options can be seen only from the context menu.

Spend some time experimenting with control handles on shapes. Make sure you understand what you can and cannot do now; this helps you later as you make your own drawings.

Learn a few keyboard shortcuts. It's not about being a power user; it is about feeling comfortable and efficient as you work in Visio. Of course, your workmates might consider you to be a power user, which is kind of cool.

IN THIS CHAPTER

- How will templates save me time?
- What make templates different?
- How can Visio save my diagram?
- How will using multiple windows help me develop mad multitasking skills?

3

WORKING WITH BASIC DIAGRAMS

Visio is all about making great visuals, and you will spend a lot of time focused on the drawings themselves. This chapter provides a good point to step back and see all the other features of Visio that will help you later as you work on those drawings. Consider how choosing the right canvas and frame can make a great work of art look awesome.

Templates, file formats, pages, backgrounds, and your work area are all fundamental to having the right canvas and frame for the drawings you create. We look at templates and the drawing window in detail in this chapter. Chapter 4, "Taking Control of Your Diagrams," considers how pages and backgrounds further accentuate your work.

Making Diagrams

I enjoy building cabinets from scratch. Despite how satisfying the final product can be, finding the right wood and materials can be time consuming, and the project can also take much longer than expected (sorry, dear). For that reason I have on occasion been quite happy with purchasing a cabinet from IKEA and spending a fraction of the time assembling a very nice-looking cabinet.

Templates serve a similar purpose. No one questions your imagination and artistic abilities, and you certainly can create drawings from scratch in Visio if that is your preference. You will quickly appreciate the many advantages of using templates when you see how they save you time.

What Is a Template?

We've thrown this term around quite bit, but what is a template? Templates refer to the overall framework that determines appearance, purpose, and even the tools that are used to make your diagram. They include the sets of shapes and stencils present in the Shape panel; the size and scale of the page you work on; the paper size for printing; settings related to font, color, and many others that dictate the default behavior of shapes and connectors in your diagram. You might even see additional Ribbon tools unique to that template, as in the case of an Organization Chart template.

Find the Right Template

We used a Basic Flowchart template in Chapter 1, "Getting to Know Visio 2013," and you no doubt were tempted to check out some of the other templates in the Template Gallery (see Figure 3.1). Visio 2013 Standard includes many predefined templates, and Professional has even more. The included templates have a very modern look with shapes and content that have been selected to reflect the times we live in.

When you choose to start a new Visio diagram, you are presented with featured templates by default. You can refine the choices by using categories, which presents eight groups of templates as shown in Figure 3.2 (Business, Engineering, Flowchart, General, Maps and Floor Plans, Network, Schedule, and Software and Database).

In addition you can search for online templates. We'll come back to this feature later in this chapter.

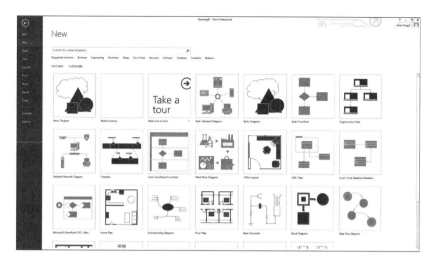

FIGURE 3.1

Right away, you may recognize a few interesting-looking choices in the Template Gallery.

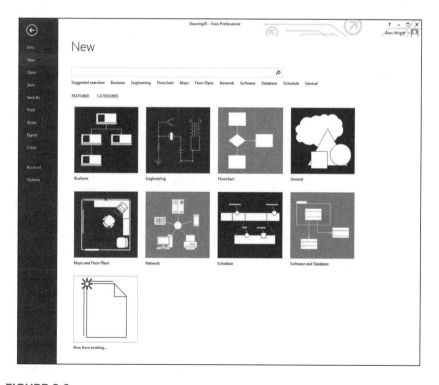

FIGURE 3.2

There are eight categories of templates.

Take a look at the purpose of these categories and what sets them apart from each other.

- Business templates include Organization Charts, Marketing, and Charts and Graphs. You find tools for analyzing processes such as Cause and Effect or Fault Tree. Many people have learned to use mind mapping or brainstorming diagrams.

- Engineering offers several templates, including Basic Electrical and Part and Assembly Drawing (see Figure 3.3).

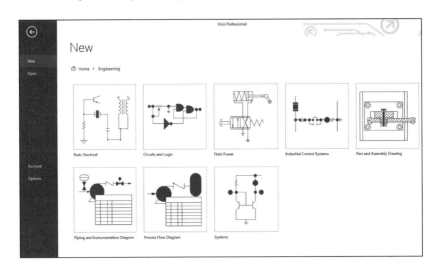

FIGURE 3.3

Looking at a category of templates provides an array of choices, as these engineering templates illustrate.

- Flowchart templates include the Basic Flowchart, BPMN Diagram, and Workflow Diagrams.

- General includes Basic Diagram and Block Diagrams. This is a good area to start with if the diagram only needs very basic shapes and stencils.

- Maps and Floor Plans include many types of templates. You can create 2D or 3D map graphics for advertising, floor plans and layouts, detailed HVAC, ceiling grids, and site plans.

- Network templates include ways to represent the physical network, rack diagrams, and more conceptual diagrams to visualize Active Directory or LDAP Directories.

- Schedule templates provide tools for calendars, Gantt charts, and timelines.

- Software and Database has many templates, such as Data Flow, Database Notation, Program Structure, and Web Site Map.

When you select a specific template , a small window appears (see Figure 3.4) with a few details related to the purpose of the template and its origin. You can choose to use Metric or U.S. units of measurement and then select Create. You can also scroll to the left or right, clicking arrows to browse other templates.

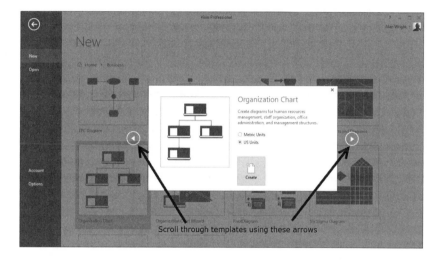

FIGURE 3.4

Selecting a template provides you with an explanation of how you would use this template.

HOW TO VIEW TEMPLATES

Think of a template as an advanced starting point for your diagram. At times it is enough to have a flowchart template and a blank page. However, if you find that you often are creating similar content or variations on the same diagram, you might consider setting up and saving your own template.

In a personalized template you can determine the shapes and stencils available. You can also include personalized elements, such as company logos. To further customize the starting point of your diagrams, you can even include a page with prepopulated content.

➜ To learn how to create your own templates in Visio, see page **252**.

➜ To learn how to create your own templates in Visio, see page **252**.

Working Without a Template

You can start with a blank drawing if you decide not to use the templates for the sake of a quick diagram. You simply choose Blank Drawing from the selection of templates featured when you first open Visio.

If you have been working in Visio and want to create a new drawing, follow these steps:

1. Select the File tab to open the Backstage area.

2. Select New from the vertical menu to the left. You see the list of featured templates to the right.

3. Select Blank Drawing and Create on the pop-up window that appears. Blank drawings open with no shapes, stencils, or any other configuration settings (see Figure 3.5). You can still work right away, selecting shapes and such from the Home tab and the Tools menu.

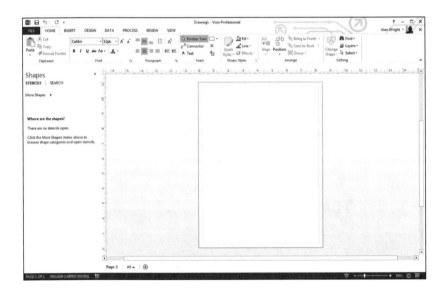

FIGURE 3.5

Starting a drawing from scratch using a blank drawing.

Clone Your Drawing

When you have invested blood, sweat, and tears into a diagram, you might not want someone else to tamper with it. Imagine that you need to make an updated version of an organization chart after a promotion has occurred in your company. Maybe you want to present a couple of similar variations of a diagram in a proposal with your customer. Rather than grabbing the original and modifying it, it might be wiser to clone the original and modify the copy. That way, you always have an intact original to refer back to.

Use a Recent Drawing

If you need to tweak a diagram or present variations of the same diagram, a nice feature is the capability to easily create a copy of an existing drawing from the Recent Drawings list in Visio.

1. Open Visio and look for the list labeled Recent off to the left.

2. Right-click a file and select Open a copy as shown in Figure 3.6. (The link at the bottom of Recent files labeled Open Other Drawings will take you to the Recent Drawing list discussed in the next set of steps.)

3. Notice a copy has opened with a name like Drawing1. Any alterations to this drawing will have no effect on the original; they are completely separate.

4. To save this copy, Select File and Save As to assign a unique name and location.

If the drawing is not listed in the Recent Drawing list, open it first so you have the option to right-click as described.

There is another way to get to this list of recent drawings:

1. Select the File tab and then select Open.

2. As shown in Figure 3.7, helpful thumbnails display when you view the list in this way.

3. Right-click a drawing and select Open a copy.

If you anticipate using a drawing as a base for future copies or just want to keep it handy, you can also pin the drawing to the Recent Drawing list. As you hover your mouse over the document in the Recent list, you see a pushpin to the right. As shown in Figure 3.6, when you click the pin you see the document pinned to the top of this list until you unpin it.

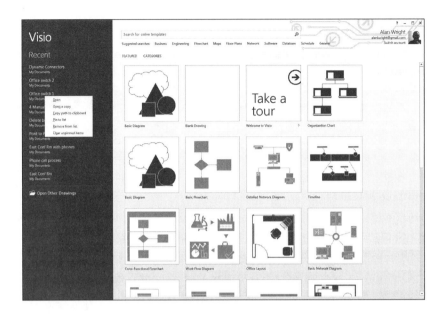

FIGURE 3.6

Use Open a Copy to protect your original diagram from accidents.

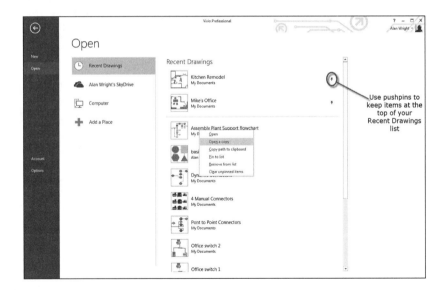

FIGURE 3.7

The Recent Drawings list can also display thumbnails of your diagrams.

Find Online Templates and Samples

As mentioned earlier, when you look at the Template Gallery you see at the top of the page a field that allows you to search for templates from office.com. In addition, you can search other websites and then download templates and samples to use as a starting point for your own diagrams. Try to download from trusted sources to avoid unexpected surprises.

➜ To find recommendations for online templates and samples, see page **311**.

Save Your Diagram

Save your work. It's easy to say, but it's not something we always remember to do. The mere thought might bring back memories of frustration and the Luke Skywalkian cry of "Nooo!" that escaped your lips when an application froze or power was lost once long ago. Visio provides a few ways to save you from those feelings of remorse.

Save As

Save As is an important place to start soon after you create a new drawing. When you select the Save icon in the Quick Access toolbar for the first time, it automatically takes you to the Save As screen (see Figure 3.8). You can also click the File tab and choose Save As on the left, or you can use Ctrl+S on the keyboard.

FIGURE 3.8

You have a few places to choose from when saving your work.

A new feature in Visio 2013 is the inclusion of SkyDrive as a location to save your work. This cloud-based location is associated with your Live ID. When saved to this SkyDrive, you can access the content from any computer with Internet access, and you can even share files from your SkyDrive.

➡ To learn more about sharing your drawings using SkyDrive, see page **230**.

THE NEW VISIO FORMAT .VSDX

Visio 2003, 2007, and 2010 all used a common .vsd format. So why change things now? Don't worry; this is not a ploy to force people to upgrade. Every new release of Visio has used a proprietary .vsd format that has evolved from version to version. So it should not surprise us that Visio 2013 has a new format. So what are the advantages of this new format?.

The new .vsdx format uses XML content and essentially saves your file in a zipped compression that results in much smaller file sizes. This is also consistent with other Office applications that now use XML for their default formats, thus Word has .docx and Excel uses .xlsx. This is great when sharing files, and it also conserves storage space. Another perk is that XML is considered safer and more resistant to data corruption and viruses.

With this new file format, new features can be used when working in a SharePoint environment, such as coauthoring a diagram. For developers, .vsdx provides new ways to work with Visio drawings, for example, programs can be designed to read and extract data from drawings, and content in drawings can be updated to reflect a new logo without opening the files.

When you use Save As, you can choose the file format that you want to use. As you can see in Figure 3.9, there are many formats to choose from. The default is named Visio Drawing; it is a new format and uses the .vsdx file extension. The Visio 2003–2010 Drawing format choice may be practical when sharing drawings with others who use older versions of Visio.

➡ To learn more about other formats, see page **235**.

FIGURE 3.9

From Visio, you have many choices when choosing how to save your diagrams.

AutoSave

AutoSave does what the name implies; it automatically saves your work—if it is configured, that is. Whereas your concern about saving a test diagram may not be the same as saving an organization chart you have worked on for the past three days, it is a good idea to know AutoSave is enabled and which settings are being used (see Figure 3.10).

1. Click the Home tab to access the Backstage area.

2. Click Options at the bottom of the vertical menu on the left.

3. Select Save under Visio Options and verify your settings.

4. Click OK to save changes.

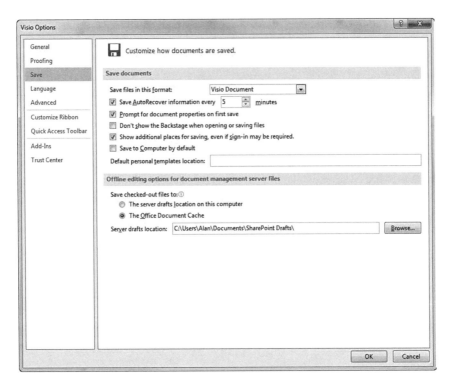

FIGURE 3.10

You have several options when using AutoSave.

In Figure 3.10, you see the setting options for Save. Here you can change the default format using the Save Files in This Format drop-down menu. Save AutoRecover Information Every X Minutes allows you to enable and change the default of 10 minutes to a shorter period of time. It is not enabled by default. To minimize the amount of work that can be lost due to a power outage or because a computer suddenly stopped working, some people change this to 5 minutes or even less. If the file itself is extremely large or complex you might notice a slight hit on performance. If that happens then increase the interval. You may prefer to enable or disable other settings here if you desire to further fine-tune your save experience.

TIP If you find that the AutoSave settings do not work consistently, they may have been applied only to whichever drawing was open at the time you made adjustments. Close all drawings and follow the previous steps to open the Save options. Confirm the settings you want enabled and then click OK. Now when you open new or old drawings they should have these Save settings.

Working with Drawing Windows

As you become more proficient with Visio, you might want more than one drawing open at a time. Visio allows you to easily navigate among open drawings. The way Visio handles multiple open drawings deserves a quick overview.

The Visio application is itself a window and can be moved, resized, and minimized, like any Microsoft application. This application window includes the tabbed ribbon interface. The main Visio application window can contain any open Visio files, the same as modern web browsers allow for multiple tabbed web pages in one window. You might notice what appear to be several stacked windows on the Windows task bar; they are likely all contained in one Visio application window. For this reason the ribbon and tabs across the top do not appear to alter when changing from one diagram or drawing window to another.

NOTE You may occasionally have a diagram that has a unique tab that is needed only by that diagram, as in the case of an office layout that uses a Plan tab. If you switch between a flow-chart diagram and an office layout diagram, the Plan tab appears or disappears, depending on the drawing window that is active.

Drawing windows refer to the work area below the ribbon interface where you create your diagrams and drawings. Drawing windows can be minimized, maximized, and arranged below the tabbed ribbon bar.

CAUTION If you decide to close a drawing window, make sure you choose the correct X to do this. When your drawing window is maximized, you see the standard application window controls in the upper-right corner of the Visio window for Help, Minimize, Maximize, and Close. Below that you see a second X, which is the one to use to close the drawing window.

Task Panes

Besides the Drawing window, you have likely noticed task panes by now. These may reveal more detailed information or provide additional options to work with your diagram. There are four common task panes in Visio:

- Shapes
- Shape Data
- Pan and Zoom
- Size and Position

In the Show section of the View tab you can enable or disable task panes by clicking the Task Panes drop-down button and selecting to toggle it on or off. In Figure 3.11 you can see four task panes listed. Shapes and Pan & Zoom are toggled on and can be seen below in the drawing window.

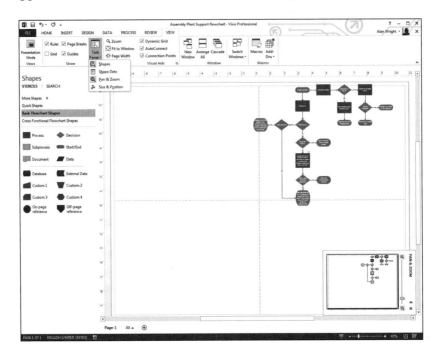

FIGURE 3.11

Task panes can be turned on or off from the View tab.

The Shapes task pane we used previously and by default is turned on anytime we open a new drawing window. It is docked on the left side of the window by default.

TIP You can undock the Shape pane and let it float elsewhere. Hover your pointer over the word *Shapes* in the header area of the pane. When you see the cursor change, click and drag the pane to a different location. Alternatively, you can minimize its size by clicking the small arrow to the left of the word *Shapes*, as shown in Figure 3.12. The pane shrinks to the left and reveals a single column of shapes. Click the arrow again to expand.

You may see other task panes occasionally, and some are unique to certain templates. They all can be moved, docked to the edge of a drawing window, resized, and anchored to the edges of a drawing window. Anchoring the pane allows you to automatically hide (Auto Hide) them so they fly open only when you hover over them.

Switching Between Windows

If you open the View tab, you notice a section labeled Window. This refers to the drawing windows you may have open. You see four buttons here:

- New Window

- Arrange All

- Cascade

- Switch Windows

To quickly jump between windows, you may be able to use Ctrl+Tab on the keyboard. Another option is to click Arrange All to split the available screen space among the open drawings. This provides a way to see a portion of all open drawings, as shown in Figure 3.12. You might use this to compare drawings side by side.

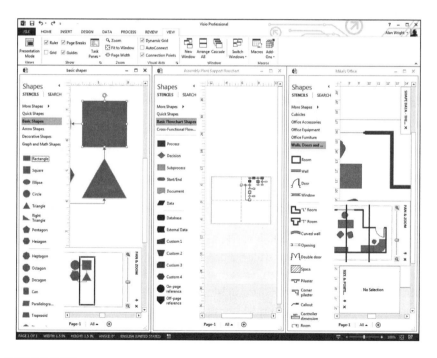

FIGURE 3.12

You can see all open drawing windows at once using Arrange All.

You can also select the Cascade button to see the open windows arrayed by their Title bar (see Figure 3.13). This can be useful when you have many open drawings and you need to quickly find a specific one. When you select the drawing you want, you can maximize the drawing window by double clicking the Title bar or by using the traditional Windows maximize button located in the upper-right corner of the window. This also removes the cascade effect.

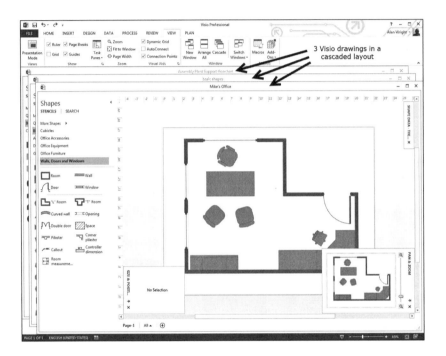

FIGURE 3.13

You can use Cascade view to get a handle on what is open.

Use the New Window button to open a second view of the current drawing. You are not making a copy; you have an additional drawing window to the same drawing. Changes made in the first window are seen in the second, and vice versa. This can be useful when working with a large diagram; one window can focus on one area, and the second can position over another area. Now you can jump between drawing windows rather than move back and forth on the diagram. Notice how this is used in Figure 3.14; both Kitchen Remodel:1 and Kitchen Remodel:2 are different views of the same drawing arranged side by side.

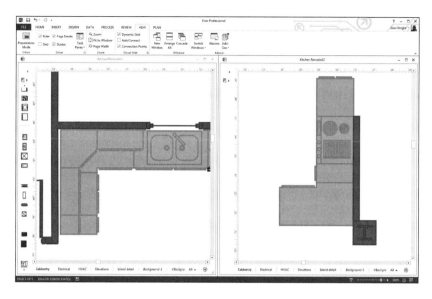

FIGURE 3.14

The New Window feature enables you to see the same drawing from different perspectives.

Working with Full Screen Windows

Full screen or Presentation mode enables you to look at your Visio drawings like a PowerPoint slideshow (see Figure 3.15). To enter Presentation mode, click the projector screen on the bottom status bar just to the left of the zoom slider, or press F5. To escape, hit F5 again, Esc, or right-click and Close.

You are not able to modify the drawing while in full screen, but you can evaluate how the finished product will look. You can navigate through multiple pages by right-clicking and using the Go To menu or by using your arrow keys.

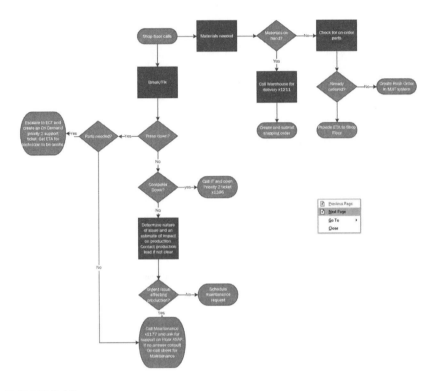

FIGURE 3.15

Full screen provides an unobstructed view of your drawing page.

THE ABSOLUTE MINIMUM

You have seen the value of templates when you start a diagram. It is a good idea to poke around a bit the first time you use a template. Make sure you are comfortable with the way elements in this template connect to one another. Read the description for the template to see if it really fits the style of diagram you need to create.

Protect your work by using copies of diagrams when appropriate and save your work often. If you haven't used the AutoSave feature, take the time to enable and configure it to minimize lost work.

It is important to understand how and when to use the Arrange All and New Window features to help you be as efficient as possible. Visio is designed to help you easily navigate between drawings and avoid frustration. Experiment with some of these display features now and you will feel more confident as you quickly create impressive diagrams that amaze your co-workers.

4

IN THIS CHAPTER

- How can Pages keep my large project organized?
- Why would I provide a little Background in my drawing?
- How can I use Themes to give my diagrams pizazz?
- How can I reveal my inner artist using color?

TAKING CONTROL OF YOUR DIAGRAMS

In Chapter 3, "Working with Basic Diagrams," we discussed making great visuals by using templates. We'll continue that discussion as we consider ways to keep your drawings organized and avoid cookie-cutter looking diagrams. Visio is one of the best pieces of software ever made in terms of instant gratification. You can make impressive and colorful diagrams in a matter of minutes.

When we say "colorful," we do not mean throwing color at our diagram until something looks good. Themes and backgrounds can quickly jazz up a diagram, in part because the color combinations are well thought out and locked into tasteful color sets, which is a good thing for us artist-wannabes. Having said that, themes and backgrounds contain enough flexibility that you will not feel limited when it comes time to express yourself.

Working with Pages

As you begin to create awesome diagrams that grow in size, you may quickly feel thwarted by the limits of your workspace. The drawing page itself has many properties that are set by the template you used to open the drawing. Although you may often work with a single page, Visio allows you to spread a diagram over several pages, making things easier to organize and track in a single place rather than having multiple separate diagrams floating around while you try to keep track of them.

Adding Pages

Suppose you are using Visio to create the working plans for the remodel of a kitchen. You may have a drawing with the layout of the cabinets, countertops, and appliances. Instead of starting a new drawing for detailed drawings, you can add pages to the layout and use a different scale on those pages to present more detailed diagrams.

To add a page, click the plus symbol (**+**) to the right of your current page tab below the drawing. (See Figure 4.1.)

FIGURE 4.1

As your drawing gets more complex, add pages using the pages tools at the bottom of the drawing.

The new blank page has the same page properties as the previous page with the same stencils and shapes. You get the same results if you use the Insert tab, New Page, and Blank Page from the upper ribbon.

 TIP You can easily duplicate an entire page. To do so, right-click the lower page tab and click Duplicate. A new page is created with the same content as the source page. Changes made to the duplicate page have no effect on the source page.

Inserting Pages

You can customize the page settings when you add a new page. To do this, follow these steps:

1. Right-click the Page before the point of insertion.

2. Select Insert. A Page Setup window appears.

3. Modify the properties of the new page. For now it may be enough to provide a name for this new page. Click OK to apply.

You are presented with the Page Setup dialog box (see Figure 4.2). There are 5 important tabs here:

- Print Setup provides settings specific to printing the page.
- Page Size allows you to change settings related to the drawing window. This is separate from print settings.
- Drawing Scale provides settings to establish or modify a scale for the drawing.
- Page Properties indicate whether this is a normal foreground page or a background page, the page name, and units of measurement used.
- Layout and Routing allow us to tweak basic settings used for laying out the shapes relative to one another and how connectors behave on the page.

These same adjustments can be made to an existing page if you right-click the page and select Page Setup. The different features of the Page Setup dialog box are discussed throughout this book.

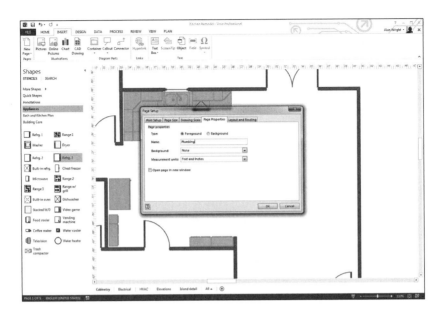

FIGURE 4.2

Many page properties can be fine-tuned when using Page Setup.

Using Background Pages

You may rightly be wondering what background pages are and why you need them. They are intended to save you time by establishing common elements for a multipage drawing in one place. You can set up background graphics, reference text and borders, and then easily apply them to any or all pages in your drawing. The content of the background is protected and cannot be accidently altered as you work on the individual pages of your diagram.

Creating Background Pages

To create a background page, follow these steps:

1. Select File and New. Select the Basic Diagram template. You now have a default page named Page-1.

2. Open the Design tab; from the Backgrounds section on the ribbon, click the Backgrounds button and then select a background image.

3. Click the Borders & Titles button located next to the Background button and choose a combination.

4. From the Design tab, choose a theme from the Theme gallery and apply a

theme variation from the Variant gallery. Notice how this modifies both the background graphic and the border title set (see Figure 4.3).

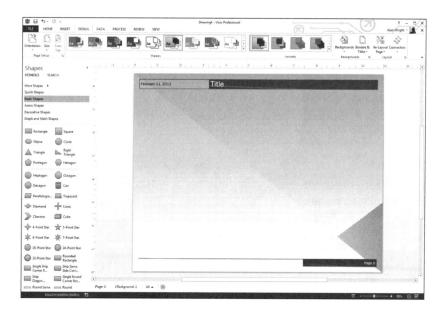

FIGURE 4.3

Add background graphics and effects to your drawings using background pages.

5. Open Page-1 and drag a couple of shapes to the left side of the page. Notice that you can move and resize the shapes.

6. Compare Page-1 with VBackground-1. The shapes do not appear on the VBackground-1, only the background image and Title set.

7. While you have Page-1 open, add a new page by clicking the New Page (**+**) button below your work area.

8. A new page opens with the background elements but no shapes.

9. Open the VBackground-1 page, and add two shapes to the right side of the page.

10. Return to Page-2 and notice that two shapes now appear on the right. You cannot select or move them.

11. Return to Page-1; you see two shapes to the left and two to the right. Notice you can manipulate only the shapes to the left that were added to Page-1.

12. Right-click the page tab for Page-2 and then select Page Setup. Change the background to None. Click OK.

13. Notice that you now have a blank page with no background effects at all.

14. On Page-2 select the Design tab and choose a different background. Notice that a new VBackground-2 background page was created.

As you can see, background pages allow you to easily maintain a uniform look and add as much or as little to a page before you even start working on the drawing. If you decide later that the theme you chose for the background is too distracting, just modify the background page; the change applies instantly to all the pages using that background. Background pages can be removed from print jobs with a simple click.

➡ To learn how to remove Background pages from print jobs, see page **217**.

If the border you chose displays a page number, those numbers update automatically as pages are added and moved. The title your border displays is whatever title you create on the VBackground page. To modify the title, simply select and edit the text.

➡ To learn more about the use of borders and titles in your Background pages, see page **157**.

Rename Pages

As you may have noticed while adding and inserting pages, the default naming is generic and uninformative. Many Visio users rename their pages.

To change a page name, follow these steps:

1. Right-click a page tab.

2. From the right-click menu select Rename. The cuurent name will appear highlighted.

3. Type a new name in and press Enter.

You could also open the Page Setup page we looked at previously and rename the page from the Page Properties tab. The easiest way to change a page name is to double-click the name on the Page tab which selects the text. You can now type the new name. Easy peasy.

Reorganizing Pages

During the creative process you may find that pages are not where you want them to be in the final presentation. Don't be alarmed. In Visio you can select a page tab and drag and drop to its proper location. This is the same way you move spreadsheets around in Excel, or browser tabs in your web browser. The exception would be your background pages, which are locked into place at the far right of your page tabs and are not meant to be moved.

Another way to reorganize your pages is to right-click a page tab and select Reorder Pages. The window shown in Figure 4.4 will open. You can select pages and use the Move Up and Move Down buttons. As a bonus, when using the default page names, you can enable them to rename themselves by selecting the Update Page Names check box.

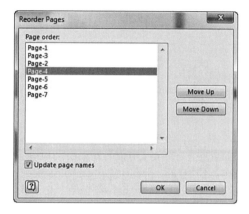

FIGURE 4.4

Pages can be reordered using the Reorder Pages dialog box.

Customizing Pages

Visio pages may start life with a size and orientation configured into a template, but this setting can be changed to accommodate your needs.

Orientation

You likely know how page orientation works, such as portrait (tall) or landscape (wide). If you are creating a widescreen presentation, naturally you are better served with a landscape-oriented page. A drawing that has a longer vertical axis should use portrait orientation. Both settings can be modified on the Design tab (see Figure 4.5). The first section of this ribbon tab offers you Page Setup tools, and you can quickly toggle orientation here.

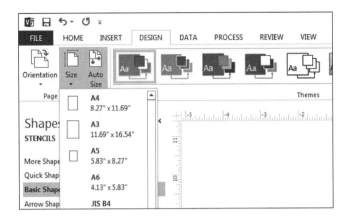

FIGURE 4.5

Basic page setup changes can quickly be made from the Design tab.

Set the Page Size

Also located to the far left of the Design ribbon in the Page Setup section, is the Size tool (see Figure 4.5). This drop-down enables you to quickly select the page size you want. The last entry on this list—More Page Sizes—opens the Page Setup dialog box mentioned earlier in this chapter. The Page Size tab of this dialog box allows you to select additional predefined paper sizes (see Figure 4.6) or manually set the size you want to use without being limited to a standard paper size.

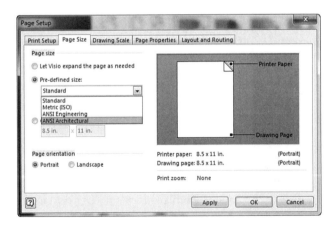

FIGURE 4.6

You can make the drawing canvas any size you want.

Notice in Figure 4.6 that Drawing Page and Printer Paper are also shown. These two separate settings may not always be the same. The Page Size tab allows you to configure the size of your canvas in the drawing window, whereas the Print

Setup tab is limited to the paper size and orientation when printing. The Preview image on both tabs is a nice feature to confirm that the Print Setup and Page Size tabs complement each other. Chapter 11, "Printing Visio Diagrams," discusses printing process and settings in more detail.

CAUTION   When resizing a diagram that may be printed, be aware of the page breaks that indicate the paper size. If a shape or text lands on a page break, this may create quality issues when the diagram is printed and assembled. Printing and dealing with these challenges is discussed in Chapter 11.

The Auto Size Feature

Another tool on the Design tab (see Figure 4.5) is the Auto Size tool. The tool will add page space automatically to include any shapes added, which can be a nice feature since you do not need to pause work to manually increase the page size as a drawing grows. But it can be a problem if you have the habit of dropping shapes off to the side of a page to position later because the drawing page just grows to include them and shrinks when they are moved—quite distracting!

When you create a flow chart, some diagrams can easily outgrow their page as new processes are added. The flow chart in Figure 4.7 has spilled over the edges of the page. One click to Auto Size can create a bigger canvas to accommodate the sprawling flowchart, as seen in Figure 4.8.

The Auto Size button toggles this feature on or off. Rather than a one-time execution, it continues to adjust the size of your drawing page as you work until you toggle it off.

CAUTION   Auto Size resizes the page anytime an object is dropped into the work area. This includes shapes you meant to leave off the drawing and arrange later. If this is a technique you use when working with diagrams, you may prefer to keep Auto Size disabled and adjust your page size manually.

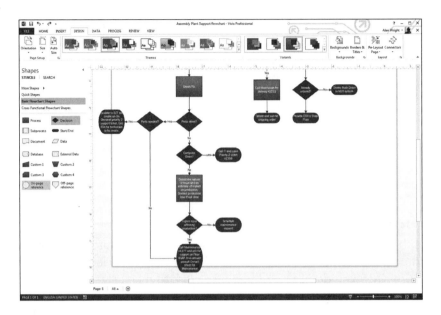

FIGURE 4.7

When a diagram spills off the page....

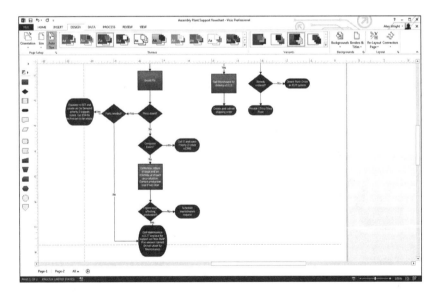

FIGURE 4.8

Auto Size can quickly expand the page size of your drawing windows.

TIP   Some prefer to leave Auto Size disabled and change their page size on-the-fly. If the page size needs to be a bit bigger, either horizontally or vertically, bring the pointer over the edge of the page and hold the Ctrl key down on your keyboard. Your pointer should change and allow you to click and drag the page to the desired position.

Scaling Your Page

Unless you worked with Design products at some point in the past, the idea of *scale* may be a little foggy. Often, scale refers to the difference or ratio between the life-sized dimensions and those represented by a drawing or model. For example, a Matchbox car is 1/64 the size of a real car. That would be expressed as 1:64 scale. All parts of the model or drawing have to respect this scale to maintain accuracy; otherwise, it can quickly lose value as a representation of the real item. Scale always refers to a constant ratio that helps the viewer calculate the proper proportions.

You don't need to worry about calculating the correct scale for your drawing because Visio takes care of this for you. Notice the Drawing Scale tab and settings in Figure 4.9. It tells you that every half inch on this page is equal to 12 inches using U.S. measurements. You also can see that the 11×8.5 piece of paper represents 22×17 feet. The furniture on the drawing was rendered to this scale automatically when it was dropped onto the page.

From the drop-down items for predefined scale, you can choose from other standards, including engineering and metric. Also, there are options to use no scale (1:1) or a custom scale that suites your needs.

Changing these scale settings immediately resizes all components in the drawing to conform to the new scale. The drawing maintains its accuracy and usefulness.

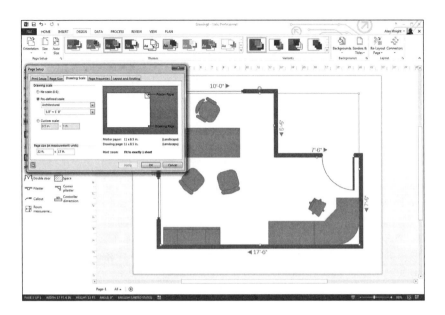

FIGURE 4.9

You can make changes to the scale of the drawing using the Page Setup dialog box.

Working with Themes

One of the upgrades that makes Visio 2013 especially attractive is the effort that went into updating the Themes and Variants features, which can make ordinary diagrams pop. Themes refer to the combination of colors, effects, and formats that govern the overall appearance of your diagram. And variants refer to variations on the theme currently selected, perhaps just different color combinations while retaining most other settings of the theme. Themes will have 4 pre-defined variants to choose from.

Themes are more than just pretty colors, though; they can influence the effect a diagram has on your audience. In Figure 4.10, notice the categories used: Professional, Trendy, Modern, and so on. These categories help you make intelligent choices to better suit your audience and your message. A rather simplistic diagram that might otherwise appear to have been quickly thrown together can instantly appear polished and well thought out when you apply a tasteful theme.

The Visio developers did an outstanding job of assembling an assortment of themes and variations. It's easy to express your individual tastes and match established color schemes used by your business.

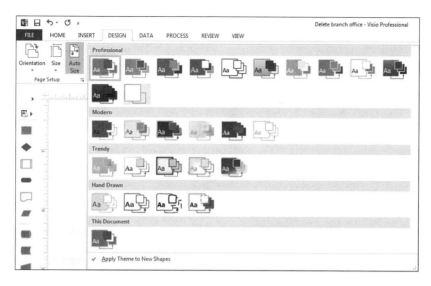

FIGURE 4.10

There are many new themes that you can explore in Visio 2013.

The Theme Gallery

Select the Design tab and you see a section called Themes. To expand the list of Themes, click the unlabeled More button that appears to the right in the Theme section; it's a minus sign with an arrow pointing down (see Figure 4.10). You can hover over a theme and immediately preview the effects on your drawing. Select the theme to see all the shapes in the Shapes panel displayed with that theme, which is a nice touch. Be sure to browse through the list and check out the themes. Radiance has a cool shadow effect, for example.

Each theme has four variants that enable you to alter the tone or colors a bit. The effect can be subtle or bold. The variants are indicated to the right of the themes on the Design tab. Again, the hover preview works for them as well (see Figure 4.11).

While you are looking at the Variant gallery on the Design tab, click the More button nested under the up/down arrows to the right of the variants. Shown in Figure 4.12, this opens up a few menus that allow you to further customize the major components of the themes. The menu items labeled Colors, Effects, and Connectors are all pretty straightforward.

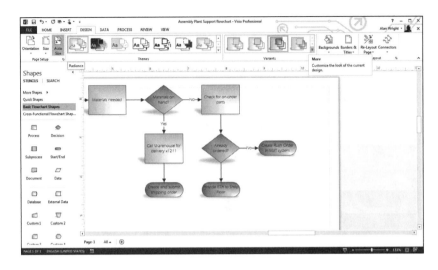

FIGURE 4.11

Variants provide a way to fine-tune a selected theme.

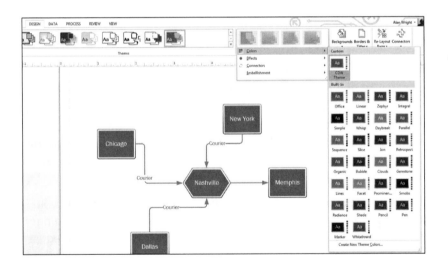

FIGURE 4.12

You can alter just the theme colors if you are happy with everything else.

If you like the way everything appears but wish you could use the colors from a different theme, you can choose just the color scheme from a different theme. To do so, follow these steps:

1. From the Variant gallery on the Design tab, select the More button.

2. Select Colors from the menu.

3. Choose a color set from one of the themes listed (see Figure 4.12). Notice that only the colors are changed, no other modifications to shapes or connectors are applied from the theme.

If you do not see a theme color combination you like, or if you want to create a theme combination to fit the colors you have established in a business logo and artwork, you can choose to create your own custom theme.

1. From the Design tab, click the More button in the Variants section.

2. Click Colors and then choose Create New Theme Colors from the fly-out menu.

3. In the New Theme Colors dialog box (see Figure 4.13), choose from six accent colors and dark, light, and background colors for your theme.

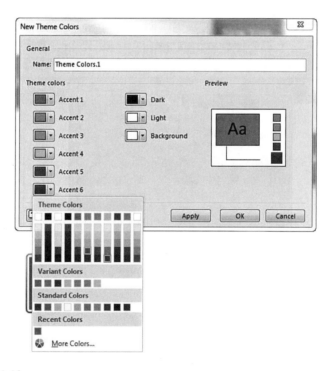

FIGURE 4.13

You can create your own theme color set using new theme colors.

4. Give this color set a name in the Name text box and then click OK.

5. Now when you open the Design tab, and select More from the Variants gallery, then Colors from the menu, you see your new creation in the Custom section above the Built-In themes (refer to Figure 4.12).

EMBELLISHMENT

Embellishment is a new feature to Visio users. This is an effect that can be seen when working with containers and shapes that have been designed to respond to this setting. (To see an example of shapes that work with embellishment, check out the new shapes in the Org Chart template.) This setting adjusts the degree of influence that certain settings have on the overall appearance of your container. For example, a background for the container or a header design may change its shape or the size used, creating either a bolder or a more toned-down visual effect, and corners may be sharper or rounder.

To adjust it, open the Design tab, expand the Variants section using the More button, and choose Embellishment to open the fly-out menu. The default setting is automatic, but you can select High, Medium, or Low, which equates to a range from elaborate to subtle.

The intensity of the embellishment setting is applied to the drawing page, but affects *only* elements on the page that have been designed to work with this new setting, so don't worry if changing the setting seems to have no effect.

➜ For more information on the use of embellishment, see page **147**.

You can also choose to change the theme color for a selected shape using styles. Shape Styles can be seen on the Home tab, or you can right-click the shape and select Styles, which provides a plethora of theme styles or variant styles that still complement the theme you are working with (see Figure 4.14).

Changing Themes on-the-Fly

As you may have noticed, Visio makes it easy to preview themes and to select and apply them. The theme you choose can apply to the page you are currently working with, or you can apply the theme to all your pages by right-clicking the theme and selecting either Apply to Current Page or Apply to All Pages (see Figure 4.15).

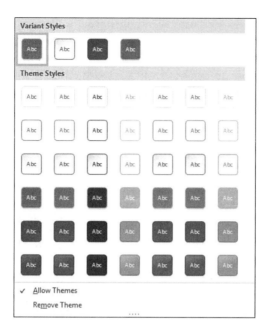

FIGURE 4.14

Styles allow you to choose from theme colors and variations without changing the entire drawing.

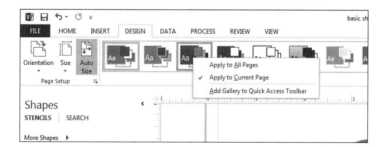

FIGURE 4.15

You can choose to apply a theme to all your pages at once, or only the current page.

Working with Color

Although themes provide you with a plethora of color choices, you may also need to use specific colors in your drawings from time to time. The easiest way to do this is from the Home tab. After selecting a shape or connector, you can assign colors using the Shape Styles section of the ribbon to make changes using

Fill and Line. Notice in Figure 4.16 that there are three types of colors: Theme, Variant, and Standard. If you assign a theme or variant color, it is altered by any later change to the theme or variant used on this page, as discussed earlier in this chapter. To lock in a color and avoid surprises, choose a standard color or choose More Colors and select a color from the Color window that opens. You will be able to select any color using the Standard and Custom tabs by choosing from palettes or even RGB and HSL color models.

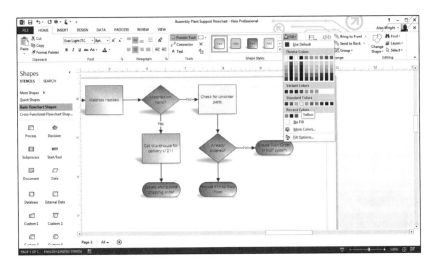

FIGURE 4.16

You can manually assign colors to shapes and lines in your diagram.

You can also change colors by right-clicking the shape or connector and selecting Format Shape. This opens a task pane that gives similar choices, but with even more granular control. For example, you can use a slider to change the Transparency setting or use gradients and patterns, as shown in Figure 4.17.

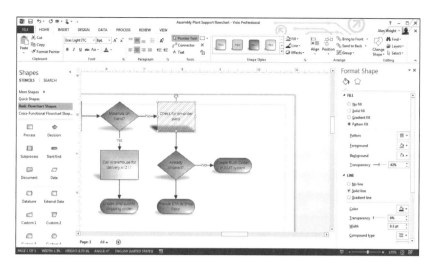

FIGURE 4.17

The Format Shape task pane provides more options for customizing color choices.

THE ABSOLUTE MINIMUM

Use pages to add structure to your larger Visio drawings. By adding pages you keep all the components of a diagram together in one file, but still have separate pages for sections or different complementary information.

Be aware of how to manually resize a page when your diagram has grown too large to be contained. Use Auto Size sparingly until you are comfortable with the results. Also be aware of how resized drawing pages are printed, and if possible avoid placing shapes on a page break to avoid issues with rejoining pieces of a printed diagram.

Use background pages to maintain a uniform look, and frame the drawing with a title, background graphic, and borders.

Themes provide you with many predefined options to tweak the appearance of your diagram. Take the time to experiment a bit with combinations and variants until you have a handful of go-to combinations.

For companies that have established a color palette for presentations and advertising, take the time to set up a custom color set that you can apply as a theme to diagrams. This gives your work an extra polished look and marks your diagrams as a product of the company by their appearance.

WORKING WITH SHAPES

Interaction with shapes is so crucial to creating diagrams in Visio that there are a few chapters focused on the ins and outs of shapes. This chapter focuses on the process of finding the right shapes for your diagram and how to keep your trusty go-to shapes handy.

Shapes are associated with stencils, so this chapter spends a little time considering stencils and how to make them work for you.

Find the Right Shape

When you open any drawing window in Visio, you see the Shapes pane. This is your principle means of accessing and finding shapes for your drawings. The Shapes pane has two major modes: Stencils and Search. Stencil mode presents you with readily available shapes grouped into stencils so that you can get right to work. And Search gives you the ability to locate shapes that may be in different stencils.

➜ To learn more about working with the Shapes pane, see page **53**.

Figure 5.1 shows shapes preloaded based on the template used to start the drawing. These are the shapes you get after opening a Block Diagram template.

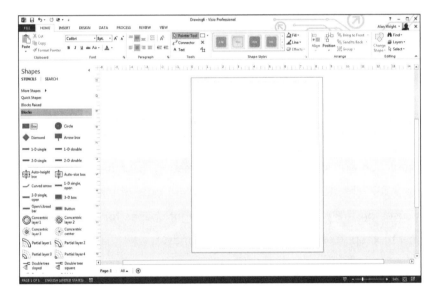

FIGURE 5.1

When you open a new drawing from a template, you see shapes in the Shapes pane.

Selecting Available Shapes

As you saw in Chapter 1, "Getting to Know Visio 2013," dragging shapes into your drawing is very easy. Take a look at how to do this again by creating a simple drawing that shows a few network servers connected in a small office.

1. Go to the File tab, New. Change from Featured to Categories and choose Network. Select Basic Network Diagram–3D.

2. Select Create to open the template. You are presented with a collection of shapes right away in a stencil labeled Network and Peripherals–3D.

3. Find the Router shape and then drag it over to the middle of the drawing window and drop it.

4. With the Router selected, hover over the router until you see four faint arrows. Hover over an arrow and select the Server shape.

5. Add a couple more servers using this technique until you have something like the layout shown in Figure 5.2.

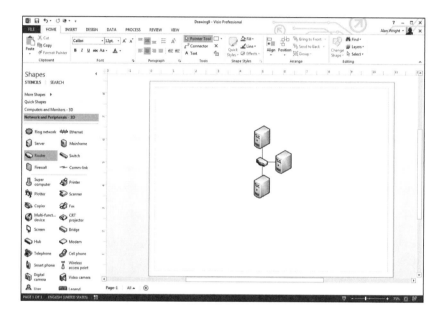

FIGURE 5.2

You can populate your drawings with shapes from the Shape pane.

Although this is by no means a completed diagram, it reviews a fundamental way to interact with shapes that have similar characteristics. You continue to build on this diagram, so save it now with the name VisioServers. You will refer to this file throughout the chapter.

Frequently Used Shapes

The shapes you most likely use appear in an unlabeled grouping called Quick Shapes at the top of each stencil, they are separated from the entire group of shapes by a faint horizontal line which can be seen in Figure 5.2. Groups of Quick

Shapes are also brought together into their own stencil in the Shapes pane. Take a look at what the Quick Shapes stencil contains with the Basic Network Diagram–3D you just used.

Choose the Quick Shapes stencil and see that two groups of shapes are displayed: Computers and Monitors–3D and Network and Peripherals–3D. As shown in Figure 5.3, these correspond to the Stencil tabs displayed in the Shapes pane that was opened by your template. The contents of this Quick Shapes stencil will vary depending on the stencils we have open at the moment.

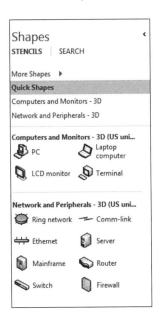

FIGURE 5.3

Quick Shapes provide a way to see many frequently used shapes at once.

Quick Shapes are considered to be the most frequently used shapes for a particular stencil by the developer that created the stencil. This is an arbitrary grouping that does not change even if you use other shapes more often in the stencil. You can manually modify this group, however, and make it work for you.

Open the Computers and Monitors stencil tab, and you see four Quick Shapes above a faint horizontal line and six *other* shapes below the horizontal line. Imagine that in your office you use a lot of iMac computers but not any terminals. In the following steps we will use the VisioServers diagram you created in the previous section. To modify the group of Quick Shapes for a stencil, follow these steps:

1. In the Shapes pane select the Computers and Monitors – 3D stencil.

2. Drag and drop the New iMac shape above the line into the Quick Shapes group.

3. Drag and drop the terminal shape to the other shapes area below the horizontal divider.

4. Hover over the router shape and notice that the arrow produces a different set of shapes now—computer and monitor shapes. Because you added it to the Quick Shapes group, the New iMac shape is now one of the shapes offered (see Figure 5.4).

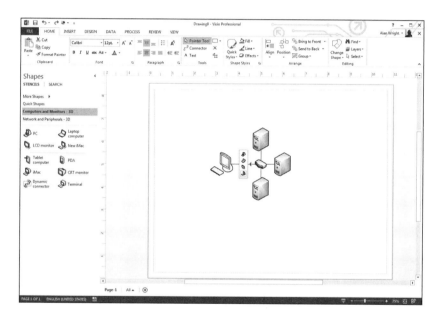

FIGURE 5.4

You can manually modify the list of frequently used Quick Shapes.

5. Select Quick Shapes. Notice the contents have been updated here also, and New iMac is now included.

> **TIP** You can also right-click a shape and choose Add to Quick Shapes or Remove from Quick Shapes.

NOTE Your list of Quick Shapes can be smaller or larger than four shapes; in many stencils, the list is larger. To make sure a particular shape is part of a Quick Shapes list that appears when using hover to add shapes as described in these steps, you may need to limit the group to just four shapes. Also make sure that stencils are arranged to reflect your usage hierarchy because the hover Quick Shapes list pulls from the top stencil in the Shapes pane.

You can grab and move individual stencil tabs. Notice in Figure 5.5 that the Computers and Monitors–3D stencil has been pulled out of the Shapes pane and is now a separate task pane. It is anchored and pinned so it auto hides when not in use. To restore this stencil tab to your Shapes pane, grab it and drag it back to the Shapes pane.

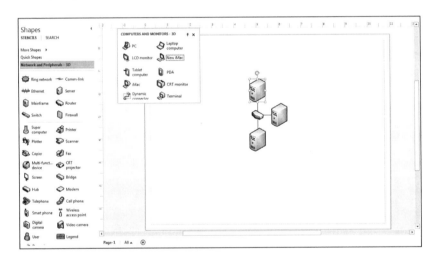

FIGURE 5.5

You can work with stencils in separate panes.

More options for stencils are revealed by right-clicking, as shown in Figure 5.6.

- You can close a stencil at any time by selecting Close.

- View is related to how shapes are displayed in the stencil.

- Reset Stencil removes any changes made to the stencil.

- Float Window removes the stencil from the main Shapes pane, just as you did using drag and drop earlier.

- Order allows you to change the position of the stencil in your list of tabs, moving up or down.

FIGURE 5.6

Stencils have a right-click menu that provides additional display options.

As previously mentioned, a template includes certain stencils that are considered appropriate to that template. You may need shapes that are included in a different stencil, and the More Shapes tab allows you to browse through those other stencils. Take time to browse through the different categories as well as the many stencils available to you (see Figure 5.7). Select a stencil to add it to the open stencils listed in your Shapes pane.

Changing Shapes

Many Visio users like the capability to painlessly swap a shape that was placed into a diagram for a different shape. Perhaps they made a diagram with simple shapes and now want to place more appropriate shapes. Don't delete and then drag a new shape; use Change Shape.

1. Open the diagram from your earlier exercise saved with the name VisioServer.

2. Select a server shape.

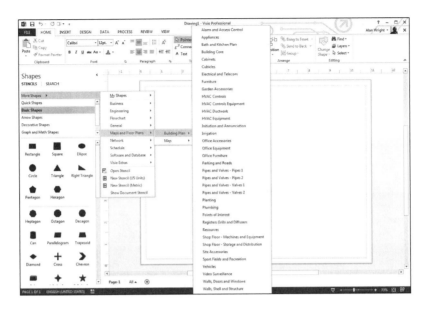

FIGURE 5.7

You can browse for stencils that contain additional shapes for your drawings.

3. Select the Home tab, and in the Editing section, select Change Shape (see Figure 5.8).

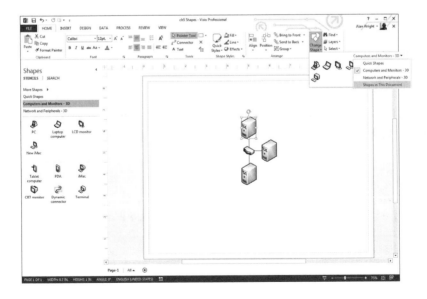

FIGURE 5.8

You can swap a shape using the Change Shape tool.

4. Notice that a selection of shapes are available for substitution. Click the drop-down menu to navigate to more shapes.

5. Select a shape, and it replaces the selected shape with your new selection.

Shapes that are selected and swapped using this tool keep connections and save time compared to manually reconnecting and aligning your shapes and connectors. Besides selecting Change Shape from the Ribbon menu, you can also right-click a shape and select Change Shape from the context menu. It has the same overlapping shapes icon and appears just to the left of Styles.

 NOTE When you use Change Shape in Visio 2013, a lot happens behind the scenes. Although it may appear that the old shape is deleted and a new one is inserted, important properties of the old shape are transferred to the new one by default. This includes formatting, text, and local shape data. Hyperlinks, layer property, and alignment properties are also transferred to the new shape. Additionally, some shapes are considered special and can be replaced only by like shapes. Callouts are an example of this.

Saving Favorites

You can create your own collection of favorite shapes that behave as a stencil. These are saved by default in the Favorites stencil. This stencil is located in the My Shapes category, which can be seen in Figure 5.7 at the top of the list of More Shapes from the Shapes pane. To open the Favorites stencil you would select it like any other stencil, and it will appear in the list of open stencils in the Shapes pane.

To add a shape to your favorites, right-click a shape and then select Add to My Shapes, Favorites, as shown in Figure 5.9.

If you open your Favorites stencil, you have the option of selecting your Quick Shapes.

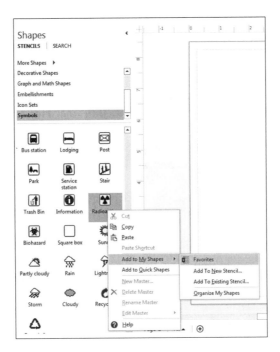

FIGURE 5.9

You can add shapes to your Favorites stencil.

Understanding Stencils

We talk about stencils in this chapter, and you no doubt grasp the idea that stencils are predefined groups of shapes that have been assembled for particular templates. By default they are located in the Shapes pane and appear as vertical tabs under the heading STENCILS (see Figure 5.10). Much more takes place behind the scenes when you work with stencils, and this section briefly explains the mechanics and provides some tips for using stencils.

What Is a Master?

The shapes that you find in a stencil are considered masters. When you open a stencil and drag a shape from the stencil to a drawing, you use a master shape, and Visio understands that you want an instance or copy of that shape placed where you have indicated.

You might compare the master to a cookie cutter. Shapes you create inherit the properties of the master shape and remain linked to the master shape that spawned them. One benefit of this behavior is that the master shape can be edited or modified after a diagram is created, and all linked shape instances will reflect this change.

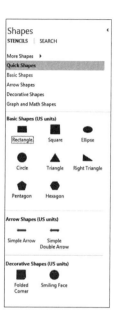

FIGURE 5.10

Open stencils are listed in the Shapes pane.

It is possible to copy and edit existing masters as well as create your own master shapes from scratch. Finally, you can download custom stencil sets of master shapes from many sources. In Chapter 16, "Additional Visio Resources" we'll offer suggestions about looking for stencils on the internet and other Visio tools.

Creating Personalized Stencils

Creating your own stencil can be practical for a variety of reasons. Large companies often create and provide their own stencils that include custom shapes that are used in graphics, web content, or advertising. You may find it convenient to put some of your favorite shapes and company logos all in one place as well.

To create your own custom stencil, follow these steps. Remember that *master* shapes are the ones in a stencil.

1. Right-click a master shape; then select Add to My Shapes and Add To New Stencil (see Figure 5.11).

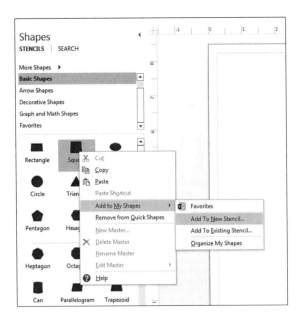

FIGURE 5.11

In Visio you can quickly create your own custom stencils.

2. Choose a filename for your stencil. Notice the default location and the file type in Figure 5.12. Click Save.

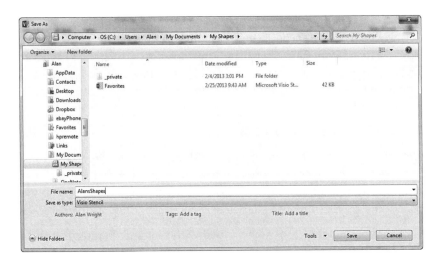

FIGURE 5.12

It is practical to save stencils in the default My Shapes folder.

3. Right-click another master shape. Select Add to My Shapes, and then select your new stencil named in step 2. Notice in Figure 5.13 how the name appears above Favorites.

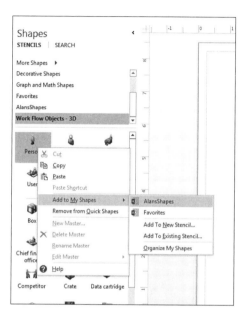

FIGURE 5.13

Stencils saved to My Shapes appear when you use the right-click menu.

4. In the Shapes pane select More Shapes, My Shapes, and then select your newly named stencil. It now appears among the open tabbed stencils.

You can continue to add more shapes to your custom stencil following step 3.

Edit Stencil Sets

You know how easy it is to add shapes to your favorite stencils and how to create your own custom stencils. Although you are unable to directly edit the stencils that were provided with Visio, you can edit your own custom stencils to add, remove, or update shapes.

Take a look at a couple of common editing tasks:

1. Make sure your stencil created in the previous exercise is open in the Shapes pane.

2. Right-click a master shape in your stencil and notice that Delete Master is grayed out.

3. Right-click the Stencil tab and select Edit Stencil. Notice that an asterisk appears on the tab. (Right-click again, and Edit Stencil appears as enabled in the menu. You can leave the editing mode by selecting again, and the asterisk is removed.)

4. Right-click a shape, and notice you now have the Delete Master option (see Figure 5.14).

FIGURE 5.14

Enable editing for your stencil to remove master shapes.

5. From the Home tab, use the Shape tool to create a custom shape, as shown in Figure 5.15.

6. Use the Pointer tool to select your new shape, and drag and drop the shape into your stencil.

7. Notice that your shape disappeared from the drawing and now appears as a master shape in your stencil. It has a generic name, like *Master.1*. Also, the asterisk is replaced by a Save icon on the Stencil tab. This lets you know that there are unsaved changes to your stencil (see Figure 5.16).

8. Right-click your new master shape and select Rename Master. Type a name.

9. Click the Save icon on the Stencil tab. You can right-click the Stencil tab and disable the Edit mode to lock in the contents of your stencil.

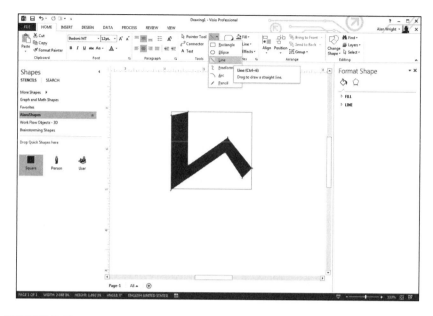

FIGURE 5.15

Create a custom shape to use as a master shape.

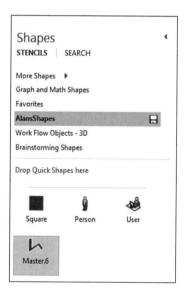

FIGURE 5.16

You can create your own master shapes from scratch and then add them to your stencils.

10. Drag the new shape you created onto the drawing and place it as you normally would. This newly created shape behaves as a master shape.

If you have not enabled Edit mode, you see the warning message shown in Figure 5.17 when you drag shapes to your stencil. This is to remind you that the stencil is protected from accidental changes. Click Yes; the shape is added, and you can save and exit Edit mode.

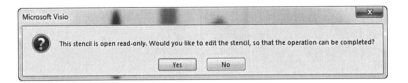

FIGURE 5.17

Visio will warn you if an action will alter a stencil, thus preventing accidental changes to your stencils. Click Yes to continue which will enable Edit mode.

Searching for Shapes

In addition to the Stencils category in the Shapes pane, there is Search tool as well. As you would expect, this is a tool to help you locate shapes that are tucked away inside all those stencils. Suppose you are looking for a shape to add to a drawing but you do not know which stencil it is in, or even if you have a shape that would match your needs.

This is where the Search feature comes in handy. Try several searches to see how to work with the results. As an example, look for a standard traffic stop sign to insert in the flowchart in Figure 5.18 to emphasize the need to pause and follow the next step closely.

1. Open a new basic flowchart. In the Shapes pane, select Stencils.

2. Type in the word **stop** and then press Enter. Notice all the results from such a general search—many stencils and shapes. Scroll down until you see Transportation Shapes with the stop sign shape.

3. Type **stop sign** into the search field and again press Enter to initiate the search. Notice the search results in Figure 5.19.

4. The shape can be placed in your drawing, and with a little positioning you have the traffic sign in the drawing, as shown in Figure 5.19. (Notice that with the sign selected, your Quick Shapes menu pulls from the matching shapes in that stencil.)

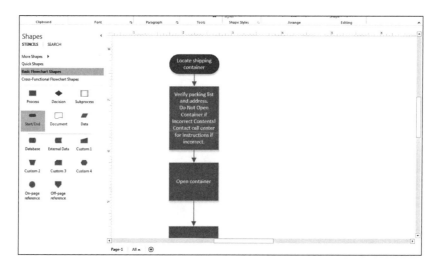

FIGURE 5.18

You can use Search to find additional shapes.

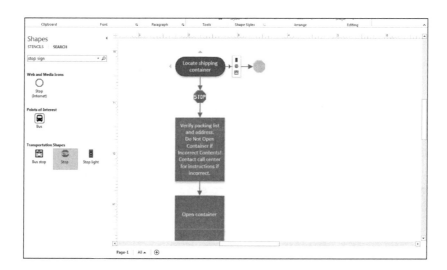

FIGURE 5.19

Use additional words to narrow your search results.

5. Right-click in the results area below the Search field and select Save As. Type the name **Stop Signs** and click Save. In the Stencils category you now have a stencil named Stop Signs with your search results (see Figure 5.20).

FIGURE 5.20

You can save search results to create stencils for future use.

 NOTE   Stencils that are downloaded from third parties and saved to My Shapes show up in search results if the shapes have metadata that matches your search. You can also find shapes you created by searching for them by name.

By using Search, you sometimes find great shapes that are in stencils you did not think to look in. Widen or narrow your search criteria until you have manageable results. If your search does not seem to show what you are looking for, look for the More Results link. Expanding this may reveal additional shapes.

THE ABSOLUTE MINIMUM

Customize the Quick Shapes group in stencils, adding or removing shapes from this group. This keeps your favorite shapes at front and center and it will make it easier to add shapes in the drawing window with a mouse using the hover technique to add Quick Shapes.

Although the Shape pane displays the shapes from one selected stencil, you may detach other stencils and float them so that additional shape sets are displayed.

Remember that masters are the shapes saved to a stencil. Any shapes you place in your diagram are instances or copies of that particular master. Changes to that master at a later time modify shapes in your drawing that inherit properties from the master.

In addition to saving favorite shapes, create your own stencils. Give your custom stencil sets names related to drawings you are likely to work on.

Use the Change Shapes feature to minimize work when you need to replace or swap a shape and avoid rearranging a diagram and breaking connections.

When creating your own shapes, give them names that help you find them when searching.

MANAGE SHAPES

Chapter 5, "Working with Shapes," considered the ways you can select the shapes you want to use in your drawings. It also examined how you create your own collections of shapes and arrange them into stencil sets. In this chapter you start working with shapes placed into the drawing window. You look at fundamental tools like Groups and examine other tools and settings that allow you to keep things neatly arranged in your diagram.

Left to themselves, shapes can become unruly and difficult to position. They do not always have uniform shapes, and sometimes shapes overlap on a complex diagram. Although it would be nice to blame everything on shapes, Visio users contribute to the chaos—they work fast, deadlines must be met, and they can toss shapes into their drawing like nobody's business. Visio's creators want users to succeed in creating organized, structured, and polished looking diagrams. This chapter looks at the tools that help make this happen.

Using Groups to Organize Shapes

Groups have long been a feature in Visio, and they continue to be useful when you're working with shapes. You might initially relate this concept with how you group pictures or files in other applications as a way of interacting with two or more shapes and allowing you to move or modify the properties of the group all at once. Although that is a valid way of grouping shapes in Visio, grouping shapes in Visio has even more robust uses.

If you look through some of the templates in Visio, you may notice a few shapes that were created from grouped shapes. For example, check out Figure 6.1 where a Cube workstation shape was dropped onto a drawing. Hovering over the shape in the Shapes pane reveals the option to subselect individual shapes; in fact, you see a chair is selected in the drawing.

 NOTE Many shapes are simply grouped shapes that were combined to create common master shapes. By design, you do not have the option to subselect the individual shapes. An example is the PC shape mentioned in the following exercise. If you ungroup one of these shapes, you can then subselect the shapes. This is not something you would likely ever need to do for practical reasons, but it helps illustrate the nature and power of grouping.

Although grouping can be done with abandon, ungrouping should come with the severest of warnings when dealing with existing shapes. When shapes are grouped, a new shape is created, and the existing shapes are made subordinate to the new shape. There is no problem ungrouping at this point, but most shape designers add properties to this new shape and references from the subordinate shapes to this new shape. Ungrouping at this point deletes the new information and breaks the references. The correct way is to subselect and then edit the subordinate shapes. However, this is getting into an area beyond the scope of this book.

When to Use Groups

Groups should be used whenever you need to work with a combination of shapes as a unit, as was done in the case of the cubicle in Figure 6.1. Groups can save you time when applying common colors or other properties, and they are practical when you need to move or rotate multiple shapes. Groups can be formed as a temporary collection until certain changes are performed, and then a group can be ungrouped.

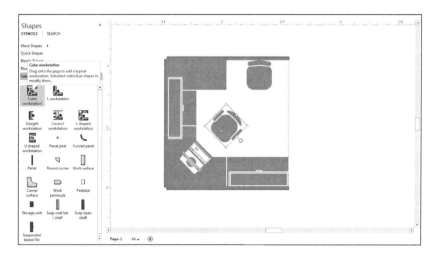

FIGURE 6.1

Shapes can be created from grouped shapes.

ORGANIZING SHAPES WITH LAYERS AND CONTAINERS

Although groups may be the first thing you think of when you consider organization, Chapter 8, "Making Advanced Diagrams," discusses some other tools that may better serve your needs when you organize shapes and other elements in your diagrams.

Layers give you better control in some situations, allowing you to hide or print elements assigned to a layer. To learn more about layers, see page **163**.

Containers are a more advanced type of shape. They have the capability to adjust dynamically to their contents, and it is easier to modify or even remove shapes from a container rather than a group. To learn more about containers see page **144**.

You can create a group using a current typical desk as a model.

1. Open a new Office Layout template.

2. From the Office Furniture stencil, select a desk and drag it to the drawing window. Select and drag a chair, and place it in front of the desk.

3. From the Office Equipment stencil, select a PC and place it on your desk.

4. Locate a nice plant from the Office Accessories stencil and place it by your desk. Go ahead and add a trash can as well.

5. As shown in Figure 6.2, use your mouse to click and drag to select all these shapes. After selecting the shapes, you will see a temporary group with each individual shape boldly highlighted because they are still individual shapes.

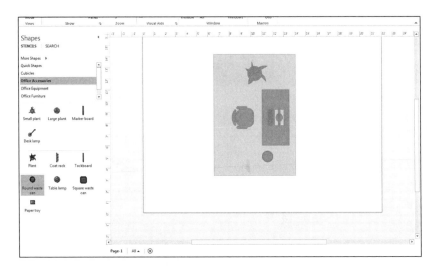

FIGURE 6.2

You can select multiple shapes to create groups using a click and drag.

6. Select the Home tab, and in the Arrange section select Group and then select Group again from the drop-down menu. The bold highlight goes away, and you are left with one selection area. Press Esc or click outside of the area and then click a shape in the desk area. The entire group is selected again.

7. Drag the group and notice that when all shapes move, they maintain their orientation.

8. Select the Rotate handle for the group and drag it clockwise. The entire group rotates (see Figure 6.3).

9. Select the group, and click again to subselect your plant shape. Notice the group has a dashed outline, and the plant shape provides handles to move, resize, and rotate apart from the other group shapes.

10. Grab the selected plant shape and drag to a location outside of the outlined group. Click somewhere outside of the selected area to remove the selection fields.

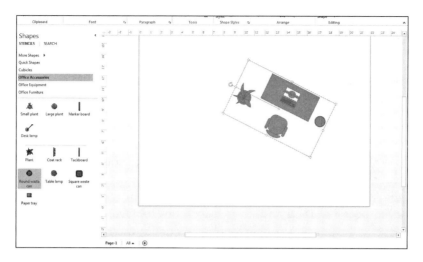

FIGURE 6.3

Grouped shapes can be moved, resized, and rotated as a unit.

11. Select the desk group and drag to a new location. Notice in Figure 6.4 that
the plant shape is still part of the group, even though it is located outside of
the group box.

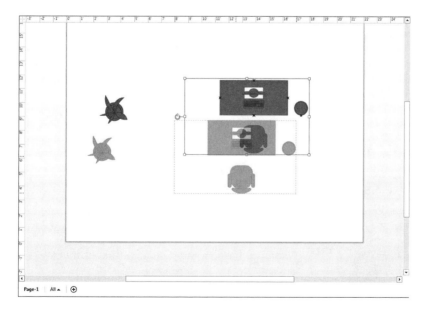

FIGURE 6.4

*This plant shape is still tethered to its group. Until it is removed from the group, it is subject
to changes made to the group.*

12. Select the plant shape. From the Home tab, select Group, and then select Remove from Group. The plant has been removed, but the rest of the desk group is unchanged.

13. Select the desk group and right-click. Select Group and then select Ungroup from the right-click menu. The shapes are now ungrouped shapes as they were in Step 5.

Groups are versatile, and as you experiment you see how intuitive it is to add and remove shapes. You may want to create a specific group and use it in the future. A grouped set of shapes can be added to a custom stencil. In Figure 6.5 you can see the Master.17 grouped shape was added to the stencil named AlansShapes. It is even possible using advanced techniques to have a grouped shape with all the needed shapes and connectors be designed to ungroup automatically when dropped into the drawing window.

FIGURE 6.5

You can create your own master shapes based on grouped shapes.

  TIP   When you have selected multiple shapes that you want to group, press CTRL+G. To ungroup press CTRL+Shift+U.

When It Is Better to Avoid Groups

Whereas groups allow you to perform movement-oriented tasks on multiple shapes and form complex master shapes, there are times when groups are not a good choice. If you use groups to organize shapes, consider the more advanced alternatives to organizing shapes discussed in the sidebar "Organizing Shapes with Layers and Containers" earlier in this chapter.

In large diagrams, groups that span areas of a drawing may cause confusion when overlapping shapes that are not part of that group. Some complex shapes have shape data, which may be difficult to access when the shape is grouped. Awareness of how to subselect shapes and work with them may be a factor if you plan to collaborate on a drawing.

Editing Groups

When you work with a selected group shape, you have an additional tool for fine-tuning and editing. Right-click and select Group; then select Open Group to open the group window. As you see in Figure 6.6, this group window zooms in on the group contents. In this view you can subselect and tweak your group contents and even add content to the group. To save the changes, click the Close button.

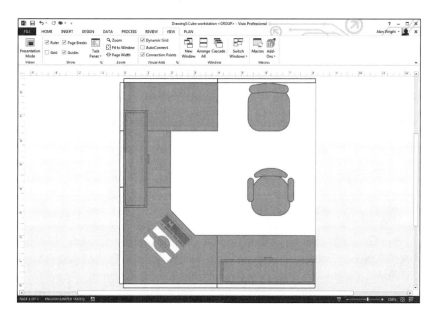

FIGURE 6.6

You can edit groups in a group window.

Arranging Shapes

The importance of arrangement can be critical in some diagrams, such as a hierarchal Org chart. Visio provides many tools to help you adjust the way shapes and connectors are laid out in your drawings, and with the Live Preview feature, it takes a lot of the guesswork out of using these tools. Most of the tools are located on the Home tab, but there are a couple useful tools that affect layout on the Design and View tabs.

Figure 6.7 has shapes just strewn about. As the tools in this section are described you will see a few ways that order can be brought to this mess.

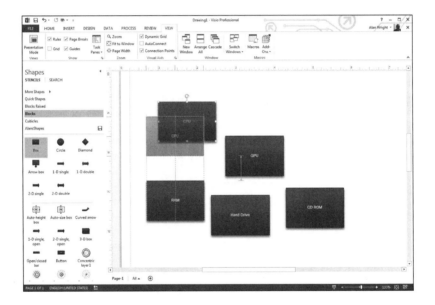

FIGURE 6.7

The Dynamic Grid tool helps provide uniform spacing when you move and add shapes.

Using the Dynamic Grid

Dynamic Grid is a useful tool that you will likely leave enabled. This tool provides reference layout information that helps control placement of your shapes on-the-fly. Visual cues appear when you move shapes, as shown in Figure 6.7. Notice how the CPU shape is aligned with the RAM shape below it. Also, the spacing matches a standard spacing for these two shapes.

This Dynamic Grid tool is enabled on the View tab, in the Visual Aids section. Notice the check box is enabled in Figure 6.7. Without this feature you would be guessing at how closely these shapes lined up.

Change Spacing

Spacing is really a dynamic setting that is often determined by the initial placement of shapes. If you place two shapes on a drawing, Visio tries to use that spacing as a gauge for the next shape you drop. If you have shapes arranged in a cluster and then locate another cluster elsewhere in the drawing, Visio treats these as separate dynamic grids. The goal of the Dynamic Grid tool is to maintain a uniform appearance.

How to Align Shapes on the Grid

As shown in Figure 6.7, similar shapes can be arranged using distance and center line references. When the shapes are dissimilar, Visio still works to provide points of reference. Figure 6.8 shows a center line; by shifting the pentagon to the left or right, the edges will be lined up. A spacing indicator appears, based on the horizontal spacing I established with the rectangles.

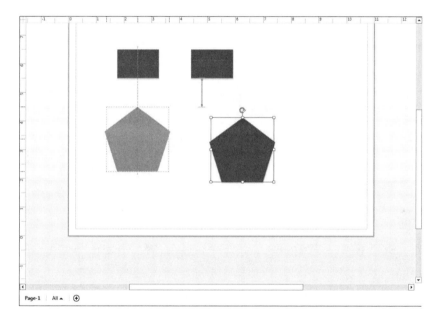

FIGURE 6.8

Visio provides visual cues to help place shapes with some sense of arrangement using the Dynamic Grid tool.

Straighten Up Shapes with Auto Align

The Home tab has a tool section labeled Arrange. The first main drop-downs provide powerful tools to quickly adjust your page. Selecting Align and Auto Align attempts to straighten the paths for connectors by aligning shapes on an entire page if nothing is selected. The tools under Align are more useful when working with selected shapes; in fact, most are grayed out until you select one or more shapes.

Align provides the following options for aligning the selected shapes:

- **Auto Align** moves selected shapes so that the shapes are all arranged at right angles with no concern for spacing. This allows connectors to have straight paths. The focus is on lining up the center axis of the selected shapes. The presence of connectors influences how much Auto Align moves the shapes. Notice in Figure 6.9 how orientation is similar to Figure 6.7; however, the five selected shapes are now aligned with one another.

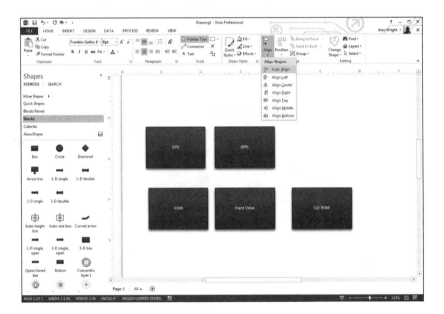

FIGURE 6.9

Auto Align moves selected shapes to properly align them.

- **Align Left** slides all shapes horizontally until they have the same left-side alignment as the first shape selected.

- **Align Center** moves shapes horizontally until the vertical axis is matched to the first selected shape (see Figure 6.10).

- **Align Right** moves selected shapes horizontally to match the right plane of the first selected shape.

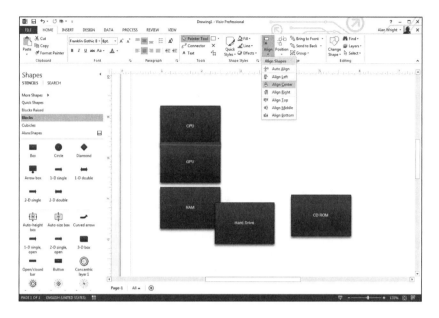

FIGURE 6.10

Align provides many ways to align selected shapes. Here, three selected shapes from Figure 6.7 are aligned using Align Center.

- Align Top moves selected shapes vertically to match the top alignment of the first selected shape.

- Align Middle moves selected shapes vertically to match the center or middle alignment of the first selected shape.

- Align Bottom moves selected shapes vertically to match the bottom alignment of the first selected shape.

NOTE   Align creates overlaps if the focus is solely to align selected shapes vertically or horizontally. Also when working with multiple shapes, Align focuses on the first selected shape. This is recognized by a slightly bolder outline than the rest of the shapes. Hold the Shift or Ctrl key while you select shapes to control the order of selection.

Using Position to Arrange the Diagram

The second drop-down button in the Arrange section of the Home tab is labeled Position. This is home to many tools that focus on spacing between shapes.

- Auto Space moves selected shapes until the minimum spacing requirements are met between the selected shapes. It can be a little unpredictable when you work with selected shapes; sometimes Auto Space moves the entire group. With nothing selected, it adjusts the spacing between all items on the page to provide a minimum spacing.

- Auto Align & Space combines the Auto Align and Auto Space. Shapes are neatly aligned, and the spacing between shapes is uniform. Although live preview doesn't show which shapes are selected, Figure 6.11 has only GPU, RAM, and Hard Drive selected, and they are the only shapes aligned and spaced on the page. Notice the Tell Me More Link that opens additional information for these tools in a Visio Help window.

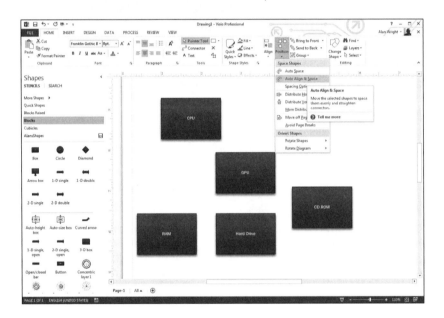

FIGURE 6.11

Auto Align & Space provides both spacing and alignment in your diagram.

- Spacing Options opens a dialog box labeled Spacing Options where you can set the spacing (see Figure 6.12). The default in the U.S. is .5 inches, whereas Metric is 7.5mm.

FIGURE 6.12

You can override the default spacing used for positioning shapes.

Distributing Shapes

There are a few commands related to Distribute under the Position button on the Home tab. You may not immediately see how these tools can assist you with your diagram; however, recall the horizontal and vertical reference lines used for alignment in your shapes. Those guidelines are the focus of these tools.

- Distribute Horizontally moves your shapes so that the center lines are equidistantly spread out on the page.

- Distribute Vertically does the same using the middle line as a reference.

- More Distribute Options opens a window labeled Distribute Shapes (see Figure 6.13). This allows you to spread shapes out using left, right, top, and bottom reference points, as well as to spread the spacing horizontally or vertically.

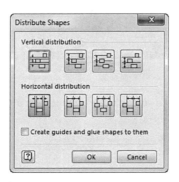

FIGURE 6.13

Distribute Shapes provides additional ways to spread shapes evenly across your drawings.

One practical way the Distribute tools are used is to establish reference points for diagrams. For example, think of the vertical and horizontal numbers and letters common on many maps. Distribute and Align tools can make quick work of setting up these kinds of professional reference points on a plan or diagram.

Rotating Shapes

Also under the Position button on the Home tab are several Orient Shapes tools related to rotation. As shown in Figure 6.14, the Rotate Shapes tool allows you to rotate the selected shapes or flip the selected shapes from left to right or top to bottom. (Compare to the orientation shown in Figure 6.7 before rotation.) The results are similar to the basic Rotate tools you use when working with photos.

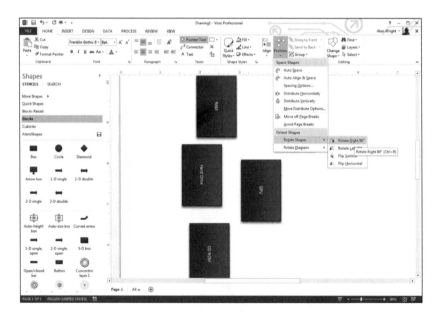

FIGURE 6.14

Rotate Shapes allows you to rotate shape orientation and swap shape orientation.

CAUTION   If you use Flip Vertical, the shapes appear upside down, whereas the text maintains the orientation. There may be unintended consequences of flipping a shape with this tool. For example, gradients display upside down compared to unselected shapes.

Rotate Diagram tools allow you to rotate the orientation or position of the shapes with one another. Compare Figure 6.15 with 6.14 to see the difference between the shape orientation and rotating the diagram orientation. (Compare to the orientation shown in Figure 6.7 before rotation.)

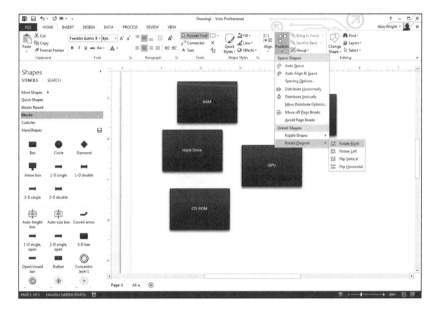

FIGURE 6.15

Rotate Diagram tools have a different effect from Rotate Shape tools.

When using the tools listed under Orient Shapes, you might encounter overlapping shapes. The preview is invaluable in determining whether the tool accomplishes the desired change.

Many of the tools under Align and Position are especially designed to work with connected shapes; therefore, they may have a stronger visual effect when shapes are connected.

Old-School Grid, Ruler, and Guides

Maybe you have worked with graph paper in the past. There was a time when all designers relied on lined graph paper and hand-drawn drafting equipment when doing design work (I still have my T-square!). Visio was designed back when those techniques were still fresh in the minds of users and are included to this day. Although Dynamic Grid allows you to have the benefits of these tools without the need to have visual references on the drawing window, Grid is still a nice option for some situations. (Sorry, Visio licenses do not cover riding a Light Cycle around on a grid, although that would be an awesome selling feature!) The Ruler and

Guides tools are generally enabled by default. Nevertheless, you can easily show or hide these visual cues from the View tab by checking their boxes, as shown in Figure 6.16. Enabling the grid in your drawing window does not cause the grid to be printed; that is a separate setting.

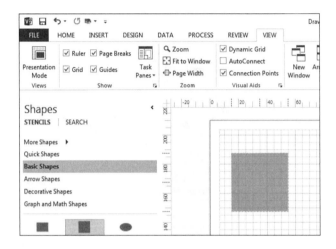

FIGURE 6.16

Visual tools like the Grid can be shown or hidden from the View tab. Guidelines show where the shape is in relation to the ruler.

When zooming in and out of a drawing, the grid adjusts to maintain the same size reference squares. To prevent this and to make other adjustments to the ruler, open the View tab and then open the Ruler and Grid dialog box. This is the small launcher button under Task Panes in the Show section of the View tab. Notice in Figure 6.17 that you can lock in values for the grid size, and even increments used by the ruler.

Under Visual Aids on the View tab, you can launch the Snap & Grid dialog box to enable or disable how shapes react to the grid. The General tab displayed in Figure 6.18 has options for both shapes and connectors. The Advanced tab allows you to adjust the strength of these tools. Be cautious about making drastic changes here because the effects could become quite frustrating later by enabling or over strengthening a setting.

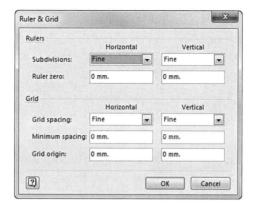

FIGURE 6.17

The Ruler & Grid dialog box allows you to tweak display settings for the grid and ruler.

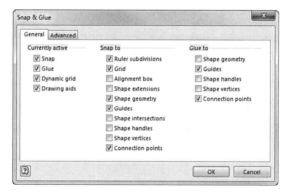

FIGURE 6.18

The Snap & Glue dialog box provides options to enable or disable the Snap to Grid or Ruler subdivisions.

When Overlaps Occur

As much as you may try to avoid overlaps, they can occur as your diagram evolves and becomes more complex or as processes or components are added. In some cases the overlap is intended, but the shape may hide rather than slip behind another shape. There are a few techniques for dealing with this. Although 2D drawing refers to X and Y coordinates, overlapping shapes make this a 3D problem and you now use the Z coordinate or 'z-order' as it's commonly referred to in Visio circles.

Z-Order

Z-order refers to the positioning from front to back. New shapes are placed on top of older shapes by default. In the Home tab look at the Arrange section again. There are two drop-down options you can use to quickly change the z-order of a shape (see Figure 6.19).

- Bring to Front puts the selected shape in front of all overlapping objects (use Shift+Ctrl+F).

- Bring Forward puts the selected shape one position forward in a stack of overlapping objects.

- Send Backward moves the selected shape one position down in a stack.

- Send to Back places the selected shape behind all other overlapped objects (use Shift+Ctrl+B).

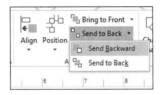

FIGURE 6.19

It is easy to change the z-order of your shapes with the Bring to Front and Send to Back menus.

Using Layout to Organize Shapes

Layout is a very powerful tool in Visio that is used to improve and correct certain types of drawings such as flowcharts. When quickly putting steps or processes together, you may have steps or processes accurately represented, but not efficiently visualized. Back in Chapter 3, "Working with Basic Diagrams," a flowchart is shown in Figure 3.15. Notice that same flowchart with a hierarchal layout applied in Figure 6.20. When you click the Re-Layout Page drop-down and then choose the best layout, the entire flowchart is redrawn in what may be a more efficient manner.

TIP   **Re-Layout Page** is especially useful after edits or additions have occurred that impact the appearance of your charts. Rather than trying to manually rearrange the steps or content, see if the Layout tool can fix the chart.

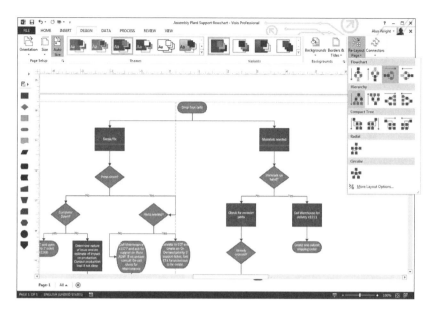

FIGURE 6.20

Re-Layout Page allows you to modify the appearance of your diagram.

Notice that the button labeled **Re-Layout Page** from Layout section of the **Design** tab provides choices for Flowcharts, Hierarchy, Compact Tree, Radial, and Circular charts. **More Layout Options** opens the Page Setup dialog box; click the **Layout and Routing** tab where you can further adjust the overall layout of the page.

THE ABSOLUTE MINIMUM

Use groups to edit and modify multiple shapes at a time and create units out of multiple shapes. For certain situations, though, it is important to understand the benefits offered by containers and layers considered in Chapter 8.

Dynamic Grid is a great tool to rely on; however, when you need to rearrange shapes and diagrams, it is good to understand the way the Align and Position tools allow you to make quick adjustments. Use Align to fix issues related to the vertical and horizontal alignment of your shapes and to straighten out connector paths. Use Position to fix spacing between shapes.

Distribute tools are useful for creating reference points for your diagrams and plans.

Correct z-order issues using the Send to Back and Bring to Front tools.

Take time to look at the Re-Layout Page tool on the Design tab. This provides a means to quickly polish or adjust for edits to certain types of charts. The ability to preview layout variations in your chart may provide unexpected results that you would not have chosen initially. It can save you a lot of time after updating or altering a chart.

PART II

CUSTOMIZING

IN THIS CHAPTER

- How do I connect all those great ideas?
- Can I glue safely without getting any on me?
- How will connectors and glue add meaning to my diagram?
- How do I work with connector paths and line jumps?
- How do I add my own points using the Connection Point tool?

7

CONNECTING SHAPES

A big part of Visio's power is showing how objects such as shapes interact with each other. The capability to accurately represent this relationship is crucial to an effective diagram.

You could imply relationships by the way you arrange your shapes, but Visio diagrams should be clear and easily understood without forcing viewers to guess what they are seeing. In fact, some diagrams by their very nature require the use of lines and arrows to sort out the steps that need to be followed to see a process through to its conclusion. This chapter takes a look at how connectors are used in Visio diagrams.

What Are Connectors?

Connectors are the lines and arrows that connect one shape to another. Similar to the string that threads a pearl necklace, connectors ensure that steps, thoughts, or processes are followed in the correct order.

Connectors are technically considered one-dimensional shapes. As such, they have properties that influence the relationship between your shapes. They can be simple lines slapped into a diagram, as shown in the basic org chart in Figure 7.1; however, you occasionally need to jazz up your diagrams by using connectors in a more elegant manner.

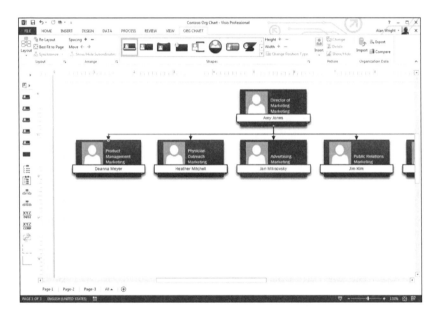

FIGURE 7.1

The connector lines connecting the components in this org chart make it easy to see who reports to whom.

How to Connect Shapes

Connectors are fairly docile and easily tamed. To understand how they work, take a look at how to connect a few steps in a basic flowchart that has been created for a new secretary. In this example, you rely on the AutoConnect feature that is often the default method used to connect shapes.

1. Start a new basic flowchart.

2. Drag a start/end shape onto the drawing and type **Greet Caller** into the shape.

3. Hover your pointer over the Greet Caller start shape and look for four faint arrows that point away from this shape.

4. Hover over the lower arrow. When a choice of shapes appears, select the rectangular Process shape (see Figure 7.2).

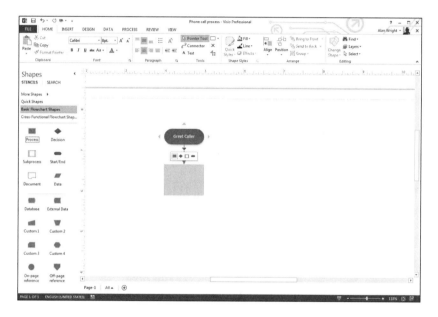

FIGURE 7.2

Shapes can generate context menus to allow you to select an autoconnected shape.

5. Check out the new process shape in place and connected by a connector that has an arrow indicating the direction of the flow in this process. Select the shape and then type **How may I assist you today?**

6. Repeat Steps 3-5 to create a series of autoconnected shapes until your flowchart resembles the one shown in Figure 7.3. Add a diamond shaped decision shape along with an end to the process in the case of a wrong number.

7. Select and drag your second step in the flowchart and move it to a different part of the drawing page. Notice that the connected lines stretch and adjust to the new location (see Figure 7.4).

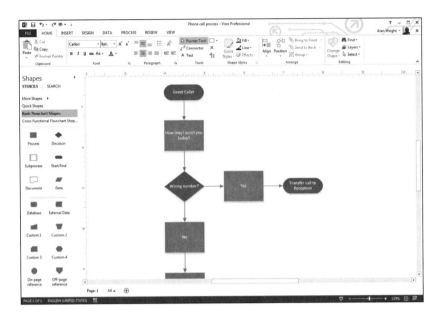

FIGURE 7.3

A quick flowchart with some connector lines slapped in takes just a few seconds to create.

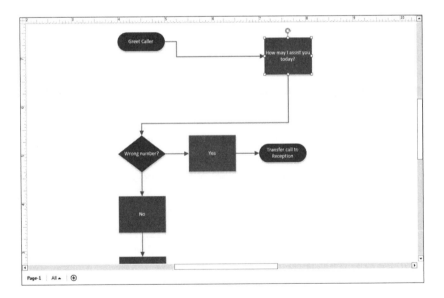

FIGURE 7.4

Your flowchart can be quickly rearranged without having to reconnect everything.

As you can see, connecting shapes is very easy using AutoConnect. The ability to move shapes and keep the connection saves you lots of time. Later, this chapter covers the glue that allows shapes to stay connected to the connector lines.

Using the Connector Tool

Despite how easy it is to use the AutoConnect feature, there may be times when you prefer or need to manually create these connections.

For one thing, it can be faster when you know what connections need to be created, and you do not want to wait for the hover-generated options to appear. Also, when a shape has another shape autoconnected, you do not have another AutoConnect option offered on that same side.

There are other times when Visio does not offer AutoConnect options. This is generally the case when working with templates that seldom use lines and arrows to connect shapes, such as the Office Layout template and the Timeline template. A layout of your conference room is not likely to need any relationships illustrated between the table and the credenza on the wall; however, suppose you need to show the cables that connect a phone on the credenza to another telephony device on the conference table, as shown in Figure 7.5.

1. With your drawing window open, switch from the Pointer tool to the Connector tool (alternatively, you can also press Ctrl+3). Select the first shape; hold down the left button on your mouse and drag a connector line to the second shape to establish a connection (see Figure 7.5).

2. Repeat until all connections have been established.

3. You may modify the properties of the connectors. In Figure 7.6 the lines are changed to a bold color to stand out, and instead of arrows they have bullet-ended lines. Also notice that one is formatted as a curved connector whereas the other is a right-angled connector.

The Connector tool can also resize and move connector lines that have been placed in a drawing. As you mouse over your drawing, notice the cursor change from the default cursor to crosshairs (move) and two-sided arrows (adjust). The Pointer tool also can handle these tasks if the connector has been selected, thus saving you from unnecessarily switching tools.

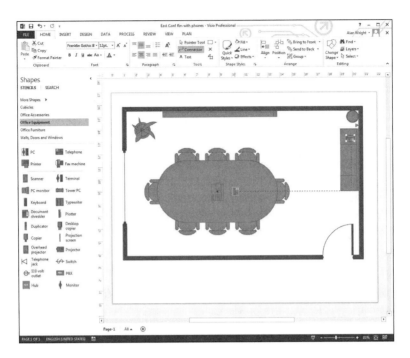

FIGURE 7.5

You can always create manual connections between shapes using the Connector tool.

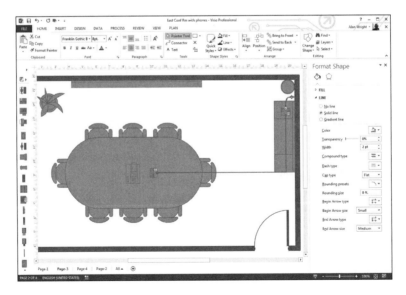

FIGURE 7.6

The Connector tool allows you to quickly create connections that can then be customized to suit your needs.

Understanding Connectors

As mentioned earlier, connectors are technically one-dimensional shapes. Similar to regular shapes, they have properties that can be changed to suit your needs. For example:

- You can change the color and line weight of your connector.

- You can modify the line ends.

- You can modify the shape and position of a connector using its control handles.

- You can add text that is placed on the connector. It can be moved off the connector, but it follows the connector if the connector is moved because it is a property of the connector.

- You can copy, cut, paste, and duplicate connectors.

- You can change the style associated with a connector.

Connecting Shapes Versus Points

We have connected shapes and even moved shapes around to see how the connector behaved. The magical ability that enables the connector to follow the shape is referred to as glue.

This glue comes in two flavors. Next, you learn how and when you most often use both of them.

Using Point-to-Point Glue

Point-to-point glue, as the name implies, sticks to a specific point on a shape while Dynamic glue just connects shapes using whichever point is convenient. Point-to-point glue forms a static and permanent bond to the selected point. Most shapes have predefined points that you can choose that appear as dots around the shape when the Connector tool nears the shape. After you position the cursor over the dot, a colored box highlights the point, and you can click to apply the glue.

If the dots are not visible, it is possible that the shape does not have predefined points. Also, you may want to check to be sure that they are not disabled. Check the View tab, Visual Aids, and make sure the box is selected for Connection Points.

Point-to-point glue gives you greater control over how two shapes are linked together. You may need to exercise that capability to avoid confusing or inappropriate points from being connected in your diagram. Dynamic glue tends to combine multiple connectors to the same point when it feels the need. This may work against your diagram's intention.

The downside of point-to-point glue is that this type of glue might make things appear more jumbled if shapes get moved around later. Consider the connector lines linking points A and B in Figure 7.7. The same points are used between points C and D, and E and F. By forcing these two points to always be used, the drawing has some issues after rearranging and could even complicate the print job as one of the connectors is forced off the page area.

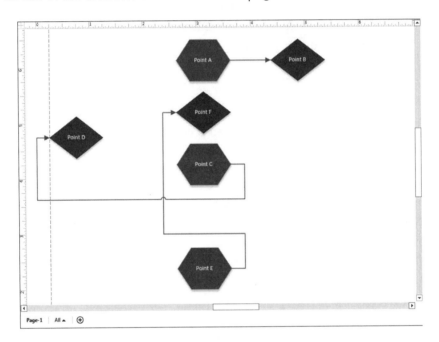

FIGURE 7.7

Point-to-point glue could make your drawing appear unnecessarily complicated.

Using Dynamic Glue

The purpose of dynamic glue is to maintain the relationship between the two shapes; thus, it uses whichever point seems to be better suited. Dynamic glue uses the shortest routing between two shapes that is possible unless shapes are too close together. For that reason it can result in neater and better organized diagrams.

AutoConnect creates dynamic glue bonds automatically. To create a dynamic glue connection manually with the Connector tool, you can choose to select the shape instead of a specific point.

TIP You can mix your glue styles when necessary. One end of the connector can be glued to a shape with dynamic glue, and the other can be glued to a specific point.

All the shapes in Figure 7.8 are connected with dynamic glue. Dynamic glue has used different points to make the connection as easy to recognize as possible under the circumstances avoiding crowding and crossed lines. Compared to the point-to–point glue used in Figure 7.7, dynamic glue has provided a simpler and cleaner diagram.

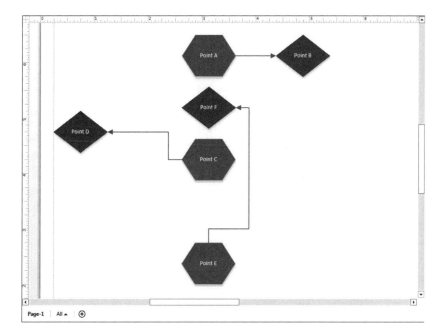

FIGURE 7.8

Dynamic glue uses any point on a shape and avoids making a mess.

Now that you see how to use both types of glue, you might want to mix both types to suit your needs. Visio provides visual cues that appear when you have selected an end of a connector and are about to attach it to a shape. Hover for a second before releasing the mouse button and you see a confirmation of the type of glue that is about to be used. You will see the text Glue to Connection Point, and the point itself is highlighted, or it highlights the shape and the text Glue to Shape appears.

What Happens to Connections...

As a designer, you probably have felt that nagging sensation that you could break an elaborate spreadsheet or maybe lose work by accidently clicking something you shouldn't have. Consider some situations that you might get into and see how connectors will behave...

...When I Drag a Shape?

You have seen examples of rearranging a drawing while discussing glue in Figures 7.7 and 7.8. Your connector lines stretch and reroute based on obstacles and the type of glue used. You won't break your drawing, and you can always move your shape again and the connector knows to follow. If you decide you do not like the way a connector has routed dynamically, you can select the offending end of the connector and drag it to a different point on your shape. It is now statically glued. No worries.

...When I Split a Connector?

Have you ever forgotten a step and then had to go back later to add it into a process? It happens. In Visio you can easily insert a shape onto an existing connector. As you select a shape and drag it over the connector, both ends of the connector are highlighted, letting you know the connector is ready to accept the new shape (see Figure 7.9). You simply let go, and the shape nests itself. You are actually splitting the connector because now it becomes two separate connectors (see Figure 7.10). Again, nothing is broken here.

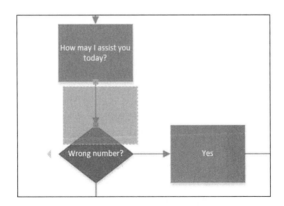

FIGURE 7.9

You can insert a shape into a connector path.

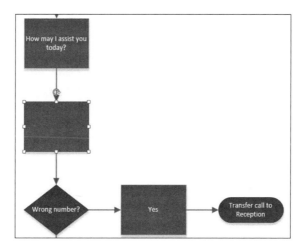

FIGURE 7.10

Connectors expand or even shift portions of a diagram to accommodate a new shape.

You should be aware of how the split affects your diagram. When there is enough space, the connector absorbs the new shape, and you have two shorter connectors as a result. The glue is dynamic for the new shape.

If the space is less than adequate, as was the case in Figure 7.9, you see the entire diagram shift to create the minimum space required to accept the new shape. It is incredible to see a very complicated diagram morph and shift to accommodate the addition, and as a result of this addition you may want to tweak some spacing or positioning.

Although a few templates do not have this capability enabled, for most practical scenarios wherein you might need to split connectors, the feature is ready to go.

…When I Delete a Shape?

You might be nervous about deleting a shape from your diagram when it is connected to other shapes. In Visio the effects are fairly predictable. If the shape is at the beginning or end of a process, the shape and connector are both eliminated. The exception to this behavior is in the case that the connector has text associated with it. In that case, only the shape is deleted. The connector is left hanging because Visio assumes this connector is important because you took the time to add text.

What happens to a shape that is in the middle of a process? Again, the connector is able to bridge the gap, and the flow would find itself connected to the next shape (see Figure 7.11). A word of caution, though; the connector would be unable to repair the gap if text were assigned to connectors on both sides of the shape. In that case you need to manually repair the gap afterward, or remove the text before deleting the shape.

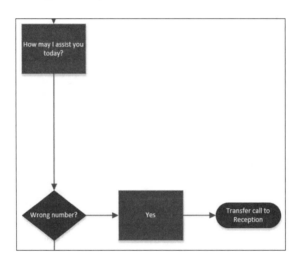

FIGURE 7.11

Deleting a shape from a flowchart does not cause major damage. In this case, the shape added to Figure 7.10 has been deleted, and the gap was absorbed by the connector.

 TIP When you have adjusted diagrams and added or removed shapes, you may find things in a bit of disarray. Rather than trying to manually repair all the chaos these changes have caused, use the Auto Align, Position, and Layout tools discussed in Chapter 6, "Manage Shapes," for managing and arranging shapes.

Modifying Connectors

Depending on the template you use, the connectors have a default appearance and style that is appropriate to that type of template. A flowchart has connectors that help make the order of steps clear, and they tend to have rigid lines and right angles that emphasize that these are established, clear-cut policies. A diagram used for mind mapping is not rigid; instead, it uses connectors that flow and that connect shapes. Direction of flow is not indicated. You can likely think of other variations based on what you have seen.

Does this mean that you are forced to use the connectors included in the template? Of course not. Visio connectors can be modified in many ways, and you can do this on a single connector or on an entire page or document at once. Themes, discussed in Chapter 4, "Taking Control of Your Diagrams," provide an easy way to change elements of a diagram, including the style of the connectors used.

Formatting

To manually alter the format of your connector lines on a page, you could drag and select an area that includes the connectors you want to modify and edit the line properties. In the following steps, you change the arrows used in Figure 7.11.

1. On your keyboard press Ctrl+A to select all items on the page. Right-click one of the selected shapes, and select Format Shape. Expand the Line section of tools under the paint bucket in the Format Shape pane.

2. As shown in Figure 7.12, modify the End Arrow type and choose a style. Notice how all selected connector lines immediately change to reflect this new choice.

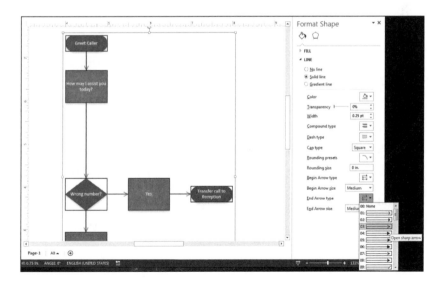

FIGURE 7.12

Use the Format Shape pane to change line formatting.

You can make additional formatting edits, such as line weight and color, transparency, and compound lines. As shown in Figure 7.13, you can also right-click a connector and select Styles and Lines to see many of the same format options.

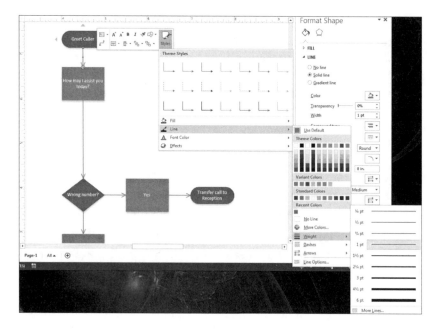

FIGURE 7.13

The context menu allows you to make quick format changes to connector lines.

Routing Styles

The routing style itself can be a straight line, right angled, or curved. You can right-click a connector to see these three available routing styles.

In the following steps, you modify these properties for a page.

1. Right-click the Page tab below your drawing and choose Page Setup.

2. Select the Layout and Routing tab (see Figure 7.14).

3. Change the style using options in the drop-down menu.

Using Line Jumps

Line jumps refer to the behavior of your connectors when you have intersecting lines or overlap of your connectors on the diagram. The visual detail provided by the line jump makes it easy to follow the route of your connectors. In Figure 7.15, notice that the group of shapes to the right shows a path from Point G to Point H, and you can see where the line hops over a connector in the path. In the group of shapes to the left, no hop is visible, and this clouds the path a bit. Is this drawing indicating that from Point A you can go straight to Point B, or go to Point D? This emphasizes the role line jumps play.

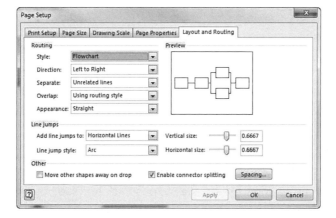

FIGURE 7.14

The Page Setup dialog box allows you to quickly change the routing style for the whole page.

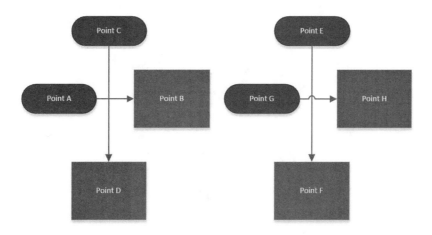

FIGURE 7.15

Here you can see the way line jumps make routing clear in your drawings.

From the Page Setup dialog box and then on the Layout and Routing tab, you can see a section devoted to line jumps. You can control when to use them, their size, and the style used on that page.

Styles include

- Arc
- Gap
- Square
- 2 Sides–7 Sides

Finally you can remove a line jump altogether from the page by selecting None from the Add Line Jumps To drop-down menu.

Manual Override

Until now, you have allowed connectors to be stretched and pulled on different routes by the way you position the shapes and the glue you are using. To add more finesse, you can use the control handles on the connector itself.

Connectors show end points, midpoints, and sometimes corner points. When you're working with curved connectors, notice points that allow you to bend shapes. To experiment with these handles, place at least three shapes on a page. Use a connector to connect the two furthest shapes, and practice adjusting the routing by selecting the connector and pulling the handles (see Figure 7.16).

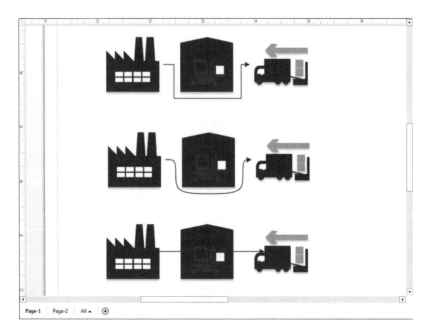

FIGURE 7.16

Handles provide easy ways to tweak the routing on your connectors.

Now that you have experimented a bit with these basic adjustments, try holding down the Shift key when you click the handle. When you choose midpoints and corners on straight and right-angled connectors, a new and better-refined adjustment is possible. Notice on the midpoint of a straight connector that you now adjust a portion of the path instead of moving the entire connector.

Finally, if you hold down the Ctrl key when selecting mid and corner points, you see an angular adjustment. Called nonorthogonal angles, this adjustment should be used with caution because it can detract from a clean and refined diagram if used indiscriminately.

 TIP At any time you can undo all your changes to a connector. Right-click the connector and choose Reset Connector from the bottom of the context menu. Voila! Your connector has been restored to its original form.

Figure 7.17 shows a few of the contortions you can put your connectors through. Although you may not use these manual adjustments very often, it is good to be aware of their presence.

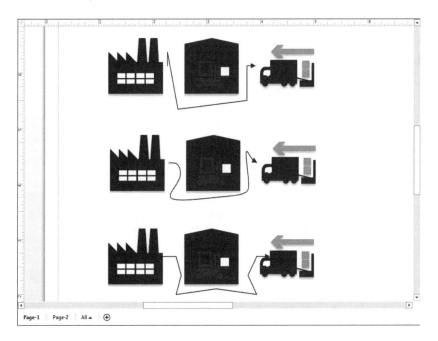

FIGURE 7.17

Manual adjustments to our connector permit a wide range of customized routing.

Working with Connector Points

Generally, you will likely be happy with your results using dynamic glue between shapes and connectors. Even so, you may find the need to occasionally add a connector to a shape at a very specific point. As you have seen, shapes often have a set of predefined points that meet most needs when you use point-to-point glue. You are not limited to those predefined points, however, and it may be useful to know how to add connection points to shapes.

Adding or Removing Connection Points

To understand how this can be done, imagine that you are sending instructions for the correct setup of a workstation to a satellite office. The network switch is being sent with a configuration that requires the printer, server, and computer to be plugged into the correct ports on the switch. The general diagram in Figure 7.18 might serve to show in a general way how things connect , but it would be nice to show the specific ports by adding some points to the shape of the switch and connecting your devices to those specific points.

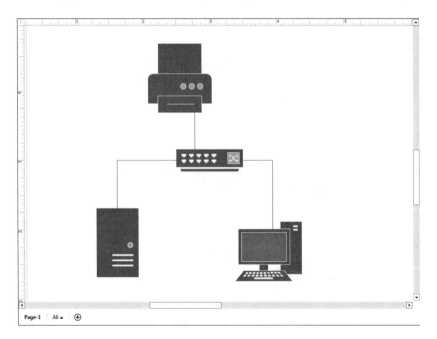

FIGURE 7.18

Occasionally you need your connections to be more specific than this generic set of instructions for a network switch setup.

1. Using the Basic Network Diagram template, open a new drawing.

2. Drag over a switch, a printer, and a server from the Network and Peripherals stencil. Add a computer from the Computers and Monitors stencil.

3. Arrange the switch in the middle and the other devices around the switch.

4. Check the View tab in Visio and make sure that Connection Points is selected under Visual Aids.

5. Zoom in on the switch, and select the shape until the ports are rather large and it is easy to precisely locate your points.

6. On the Home tab under Tools, select the Connection Point tool, which is represented by an X. Hover over the X to see a description of this tool (see Figure 7.19).

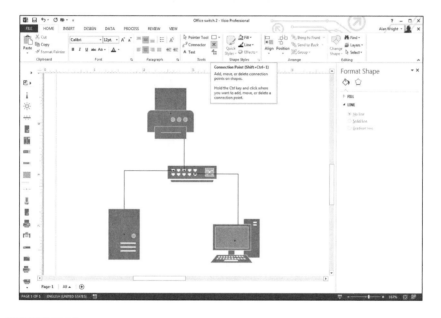

FIGURE 7.19

The Connection Point tool allows you to add custom points to your diagrams for point-to-point connectors.

7. Hold the Ctrl key and left-click a point in the switch shape to add a new point. This new point appears pink, indicating that it is selected. You can move or delete a selected point while using this tool. (This includes predefined points.)

8. Zoom back out and select the Connector tool. Connect the printer to the point you have just added. Repeat to select points for the server and computer shapes.

Adding and removing points to shapes is a little tricky and not something you are likely to use very often. Knowing how to use these tools can bring a bit more elegance to your diagrams and make you look like a Visio guru.

THE ABSOLUTE MINIMUM

When you are working with connectors, remember that deep down they are shapes, too. They can be formatted and have the capability to display text.

Understand when the AutoConnect feature helps you and when it is faster to manually create connectors using the Connector tool.

Make sure that you understand the difference between dynamic glue and point-to-point glue. These features offer added versatility when you design your diagrams.

Be familiar with the Page Setup dialog box and the options offered by the Layout and Routing tab.

Add extra connection points when the predefined options do not meet your needs.

IN THIS CHAPTER

- How do I keep shapes contained?
- How can I best use callouts and ScreenTips?
- Texting etiquette in Visio.
- If onions have layers, can diagrams have layers, too?

8

MAKING ADVANCED DIAGRAMS

As you look at advanced diagrams you will learn about a few tools that will help you add complexity to your drawings without getting lost in the process. In this chapter, you quickly embrace these tools as time-saving and valuable ways to present your ideas through Visio.

Although Visio is mainly a graphical presentation of your information, text is an important part of almost all diagrams. This chapter spends some time looking at text. Just like ogres and onions, Visio drawings have layers. You might recall Donkey explaining to Shrek that not everyone likes onions. You may find Visio Layers to be your new best friend, however.

Organizing Diagrams

We discussed using groups for organizing shapes back in Chapter 6, "Manage Shapes." This chapter looks at containers, which are a bit more of an advanced concept in Visio and have some unique features that give you further control over how your diagrams appear. Lists and callouts are also newer tools designed to provide additional structure to a diagram.

Containers

Containers were a new feature starting with Visio 2010; they provide you with a powerful way of grouping shapes in a visual container, but you have the flexibility to work with either the shape or the container. Containers can be used to represent a department, a geographical location, or even a concept that "contains" other resources or ideas.

Organize Your Shapes

To see how to add a container to a drawing page, let's create a new diagram to visually represent the network servers at two satellite offices.

1. Open a new drawing and select the Basic Network template.

2. Open the Insert tab and select a container from the Diagram Parts section of this tab. As you hover over Containers, notice that a preview displays on the page (see Figure 8.1).

3. With the container selected, start typing **Atlanta**. This is considered the header for the container.

4. Drag over two server shapes and drop them into the container labeled Atlanta.

5. Select and move the servers around within the container. Notice that you have no difficulty selecting individual shapes and that the container glows with a green outline to let you know that this is a container.

6. Drag one of the servers out of the container and drop it onto the drawing page. Again, no problems, and this was all it took to remove it from the container.

7. Select the server again that you just removed and drag and drop it back into the container labeled Atlanta. It is now part of the container again.

8. Select the container itself. You must click part of the visible container rather than empty space within the container, which helps you avoid unwanted selecting of the container when working within it.

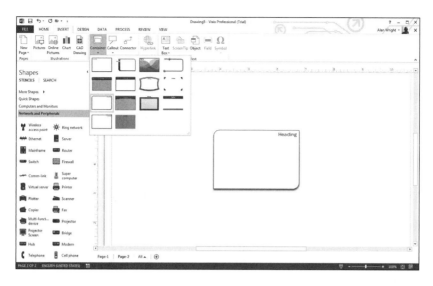

FIGURE 8.1

As you place a container in the drawing window you can choose from several styles as shown here.

9. Drag the container around the drawing page. As you can see in Figure 8.2, a ghost image moves around the screen until you drop the container; this becomes its new location. Notice all contents traveled together as a group.

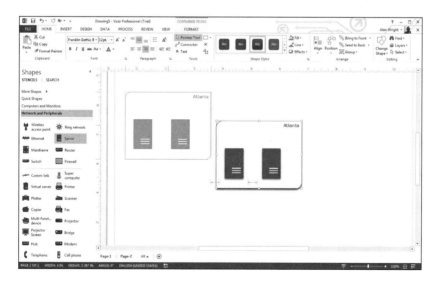

FIGURE 8.2

A container can be moved without spilling its contents.

10. Select the Atlanta container again, hold down the Ctrl key this time, and drag the container to another part of the page. When you drop the container this time, notice a clone has been created (see Figure 8.3).

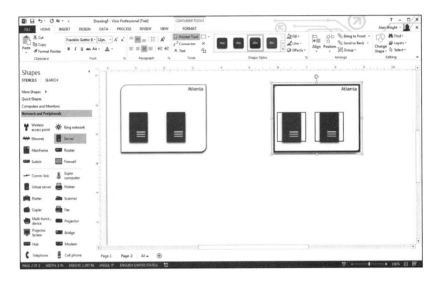

FIGURE 8.3

A copy can quickly be created of a container.

11. Name the new container **Detroit**.

12. Select the contextual tab labeled Container Tools Format and then right-click the container labeled Atlanta. Select Container in the menu, and compare the menu contents to the tools listed in the Container Tools Format tab (see Figure 8.4).

13. Select Atlanta and press the Delete key. Notice the entire container and its contents are gone.

14. Select Detroit and now choose Disband from the tab or from the right-click menu. Notice the contents remain, but the container disappears.

15. Select the two homeless servers and, from the Insert tab, select another container. Notice the new container forms around the selected shapes.

16. Select the new container and on the Container Tools, Format tab select Lock Container. Select a server from the container and drag to a location outside of the container and drop it. Notice the locked container expands to keep the shape within the container.

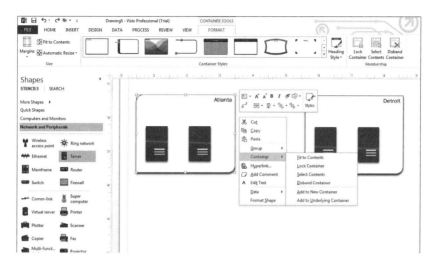

FIGURE 8.4

You have many of the same container tools on the tab and by using the right-click menu.

As you can see, containers provide a dynamic tool for managing your shapes. Containers can even be placed within other containers using the same characteristics to manage the structure that you just examined.

Modifying Containers

So far you have created, cloned, moved, and deleted containers. Now consider some further steps you can take to control and manage your containers.

In the Container Tools, Format tab there are still a few buttons to try out. The first section of this tab is labeled Size. The Margin button presents a drop-down menu that adjusts the container to fit to the contents, leaving the selected margin of distance between the contents and the container. It may also alter the header of the container, as in the case of the container style named Notch. (Each container style has a name that is revealed when you hover over these container styles with your mouse pointer.)

Figure 8.5 also shows the Fit to Contents, which makes the container as compact as the contents allow. This can be used in conjunction with the Margins button to tweak the desired space around the shapes within the container.

The Automatic Resize button opens the drop-down menu shown in Figure 8.5. You can set this at the container level, and the container can be locked into a size by selecting No Automatic Resize. Expand as Needed allows the container to grow as new shapes are added. Always Fit to Contents allows the container to expand and contract as you add or remove shapes.

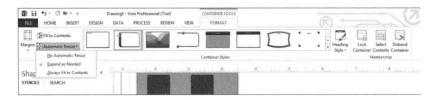

FIGURE 8.5

Containers can be automatically resized in a variety of ways.

On the Container Tools, Format tab you also have Heading Style, which presents some variations on the header position and orientation unique to that container.

Another way to modify containers is with Embellishment. This was briefly touched on earlier in the book when discussing themes in Chapter 4, "Taking Control of Your Diagrams" (see page **76**).

To modify the appearance of a container using the Embellishment tool, go back to the Atlanta and Detroit containers used previously. In Figure 8.6 notice that each container has a different container style assigned, and the Design tab is open. The Variants section has been expanded using More, and Embellishment is set to the default Automatic setting. You can preview the effects of overriding the Automatic setting by hovering your mouse pointer over another setting such as Low. You can see in Figure 8.7 how the container's visible presence has been altered in this preview to appear more subdued. If you like the appearance just select it to lock in this setting. Some containers do not respond visibly to the embellishment settings; others change radically.

Embellishment is a new feature for Visio 2013 and affects any shapes or containers that have been designed to use this setting. The Embellishment setting you choose is applied to the entire drawing page and cannot be applied to individual containers.

Lists

Lists are another type of container in Visio, which explains some similarities to the container characteristics you've already seen. They are used in certain situations where it is crucial to maintain the correct order and to arrange any added items in sequence. Because of their special nature, they cannot be chosen and dropped into a basic template like containers can.

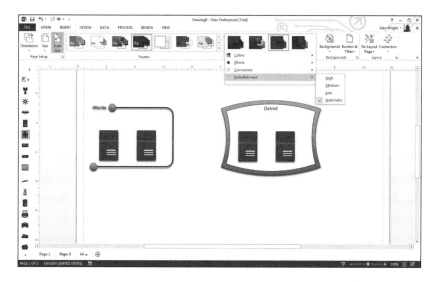

FIGURE 8.6

Embellishment is set to Automatic by default in Visio 2013.

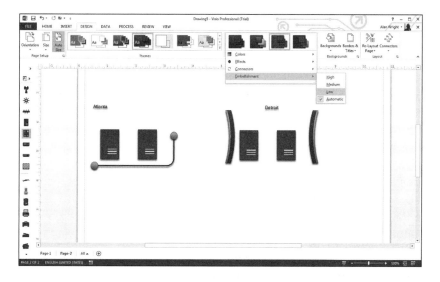

FIGURE 8.7

Changing the Embellishment setting alters the appearance of containers as shown here where Low is previewed on the containers from Figure 8.6.

Cross-function flowcharts are an example of this type of container. These flowcharts are often used to show the progression or sequencing of tasks, and they also identify the ownership of the tasks. Notice in Figure 8.8 how shapes are arranged neatly in the horizontal containers called Swimlanes. By hovering over the top or bottom of the left edge of a Swimlane, notice that a blue arrow tool appears and offers to Insert "Swimlane" Shape. An orange line indicates the location where the insert would occur. Also, the group of Swimlanes is surrounded by a glowing green line.

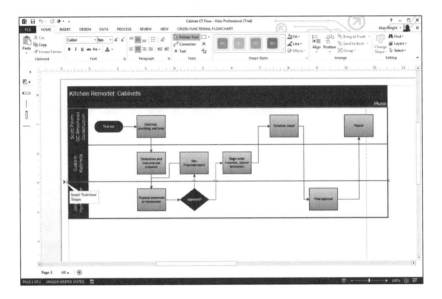

FIGURE 8.8

Lists are special containers used to keep their content arranged in sequence.

When a Swimlane is grabbed and moved, it is a simple one-step process. Just grab the header of the Swimlane and drag and drop. Notice in Figure 8.9 how the flowchart can still be understood; all the steps maintain their order despite the arrangement being busier looking.

You may never use the Lists feature, but if you do work with this type of flowchart, legend shapes for data graphics, or other unique templates that focus on sequential presentation, you will certainly benefit from their inclusion in Visio.

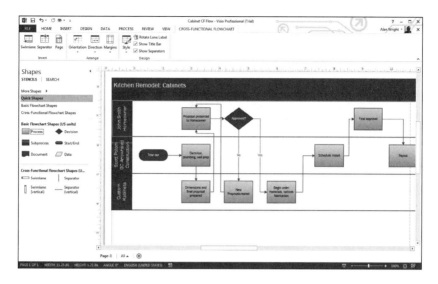

FIGURE 8.9

Lists allow you to rearrange shapes and connectors without losing the established order or sequence.

Callouts

Callouts are a great way to add textual information to your diagrams without distracting from the flow of the diagram. You might think of a comic book the first time you use them because they basically look like the way dialogue has been thrown back and forth in comic strips since before Charlie Brown missed the first football Lucy held for him. Their principal use is to draw attention to some detail in a diagram.

They have new properties since Visio 2010, and they certainly help in organizing and structuring your diagram. Used properly, they serve as yet another tool to take your diagrams to the next level of professionalism. Figure 8.10 shows many new types of callouts solely to illustrate their variety and appearance.

Technically, callouts have an associative relationship to a shape because the text balloon is associated with the target shape in a special relationship that is different from two connected shapes.

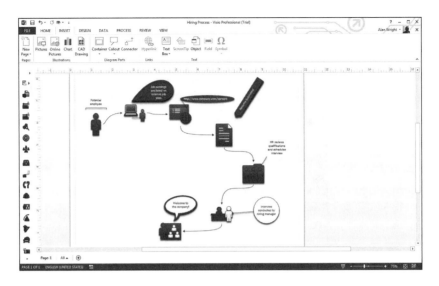

FIGURE 8.10

Callouts draw attention to details in your diagram.

Adding Callouts to Shapes

To add a callout to a shape, you must first select a shape.

1. Open the Insert tab.

2. In the section labeled Diagram Parts, select Callout and choose the one named Orb. Callout names are revealed with a hover.

3. Your shape is no longer selected, but notice the bright green line outlining the shape. In the selected callout, type some text (see Figure 8.11).

4. Press the Esc key on your keyboard, and now drag the callout shape to a different location. Notice that when dropped, the connecting line is redrawn to show which shape the callout is associated with.

5. Select the shape. Drag the shape to a new location. Notice that the callout travels with the shape and is an extension of the shape.

6. Select the shape and press Ctrl+D to create a duplicate of the shape. Notice that both the shape and the associated callout have been duplicated.

7. Select the callout on the new duplicate. In the center of the shape you see a small yellow control handle or association point. Select the point, and drag it to a blank area of the drawing. Notice that it is no longer connected (see Figure 8.12).

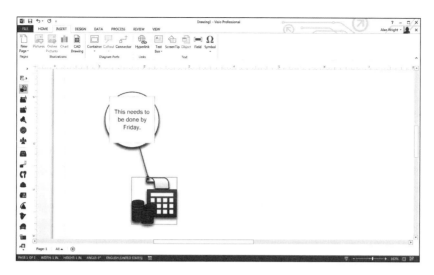

FIGURE 8.11

Callouts are linked to target shapes.

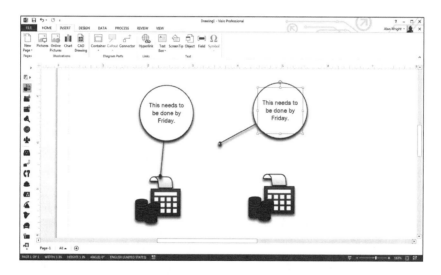

FIGURE 8.12

Callouts can be disconnected from target shapes.

8. Select the duplicate callout and then the yellow association point, and drag and drop into the first shape. Notice now that both callouts are connected, and moving the shape moves both callouts, as shown in Figure 8.13.

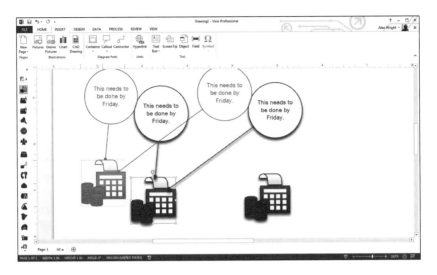

FIGURE 8.13

Target shapes can have multiple callouts attached. Here Visio shows how attached callouts move with a shape as it is repositioned in this image.

 CAUTION   Callouts stay on top of shapes or connectors they overlap. This means you need to position the callout to allow for this characteristic. Also, in the case of overlapping callouts, the newest formed callout is on top.

Callouts can be overused as a visual effect, so be careful how you use them. In Figure 8.10 you can see how inconsistent use makes the drawing look busy. Judicious use of callouts draws the eye to critical points of interest in diagrams and work flows, or highlight special features in advertising and maps.

CALLOUT SHAPES

Callouts have long been used for a variety of purposes. The callouts considered in this chapter are a special collection of predefined shapes that can be associatively connected to another shape and have unique behavior as a result. If you look for more callout shapes and do not need the connected relationship described in this chapter you can find many more callout shapes in the Callouts Stencil.

To find this particular stencil, go to the Shapes Panel. Expand the More Shapes fly-out menu and select Visio Extras. Select Callouts to see many more callout shapes that you can add to your diagrams. With the exception of three special callout shapes, these are plain old shapes with no special associative connections.

Custom callouts 1, 2, and 3 have highly customizable properties, and they can even be associated with a target shape.

ScreenTips

ScreenTips have been used in applications like Visio by developers for many years, and you have benefited from their presence many times. Usually they appear when you hover over an item on the screen; they provide additional information that evaporates when you move the cursor away. In Visio you can create your own ScreenTips.

They are an elegant way to have information available in a diagram without the clutter. Because they are hidden, your user has to be in the know or accidentally hover over the shape to trigger their appearance. Despite this potential limitation, you may find their inclusion in your diagrams to be a great training aid or a handy way of reminding yourself of important additional information or explanations.

Creating Useful ScreenTips

Follow these steps to create your own ScreenTip.

1. Open a new drawing using the Basic Diagram template.

2. Drag a couple shapes to the diagram.

3. Select a shape, and in the Insert tab select ScreenTip from the Text section (see Figure 8.14).

4. In the small Shape ScreenTip window, type in the text you want to use and click OK.

5. Click a blank part of the drawing window, and hover over your shape. Notice the ScreenTip appears, as shown in Figure 8.15.

 TIP ScreenTips are useful additions to a Visio diagram, but they are visible only if a person knows to look for them. They are not shown in printed diagrams. You might consider adding a visual cue to your diagram to alert others (and remind yourself) of their presence.

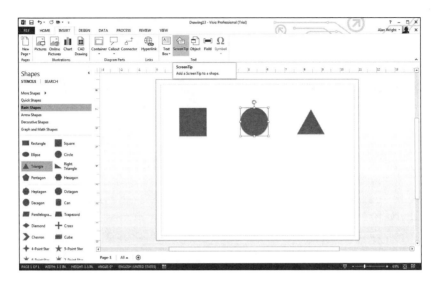

FIGURE 8.14

ScreenTips can be inserted into a shape.

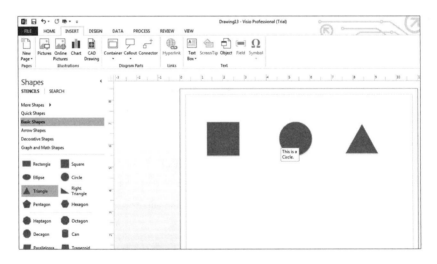

FIGURE 8.15

ScreenTips appear as you hover over an assigned shape.

Using Headers and Footers

In Chapter 4 we touched on the use of borders and titles on the background pages. It is good to spend a little more time on the usage of borders and titles in drawings.

Visio uses the background page to insert visible headers and footers into the drawings. In Figure 8.16 you can see this drawing is easily identified by the header and footer fields which provide a title, date, and page number.

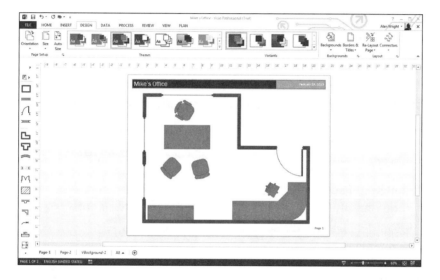

FIGURE 8.16

Drawings can be organized using headers and footers.

To add these features to a drawing, a few steps are required.

1. Create a new drawing using the Basic Flowchart template.

2. Drag a Start/End shape over to Page-1.

3. Add a couple Process shapes and a final Start/End shape.

4. Press Shift+F11 to insert a new page.

5. On Page-2 that was just created, open the Design tab and expand the Borders & Titles button. Select Blocks from the choices, as shown in Figure 8.17.

6. Notice that on Page-2 you are unable to double-click and modify the Title. Select the VBackground-1 page using its Page tab.

7. Double-click the word Title on the VBackground-1 page, and enter a name for the drawing.

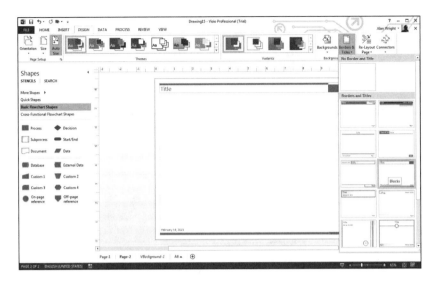

FIGURE 8.17

You add header and footer elements through the VBackground page.

8. Return to Page-2 and notice the title has been updated. Also notice that the footer has the date to the left and Page 2 off to the right.

9. Right-click the tab for Page-1 and select Page Setup to open the Page Setup dialog box.

10. On the Page Properties tab, change the Background to VBackground-1 and click OK, as shown in Figure 8.18.

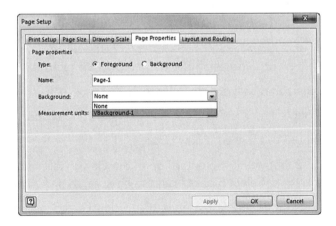

FIGURE 8.18

Use the Page Setup dialog box to assign a background.

11. Notice something similar to Figure 8.19. When using this in a presentation, the title is easily seen, and displayed page numbers provide easy reference for discussion.

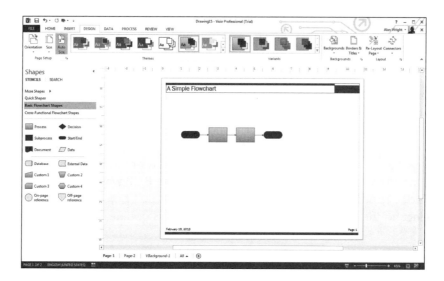

FIGURE 8.19

Pages can have background pages assigned to create headers and footers.

The creation of visual headers and footers using the background page in Visio is a bit rigid. Individual pages all have the same title as the assigned background page. However, you can create multiple background pages and assign the appropriate background page to a particular page in the drawing. To carry this concept even further, you can assign background pages to other background pages to further refine how common elements are brought to groups of pages.

→ To learn more about the use of background pages, see page **64**.

Another type of header and footer is available from the Print menu and is considered later in this book.

→ To learn more about printing header and footer fields, see page **211**.

Working with Text

You have already seen a few ways to use text with callouts and ScreenTips earlier in this chapter, and you have seen quite a few examples of adding text to shapes and connectors. Now look at a few more ways that you can incorporate text into your diagrams.

Creating Text Boxes

Visio includes horizontal and vertical Text Box tools right on the Insert tab in the Text section. You can quickly select one or the other and draw a box outline that is formatted for that orientation of text.

You can easily edit the text inside by double-clicking the text or right-clicking and choosing Edit Text, where even more tools for formatting are available. The text box itself is treated as a shape and can be resized, rotated, and connected to other shapes. Generally the box is invisible, leaving only the text visible and allowing you to strategically place text on the drawing page without any visible shape. An example of this can be seen in Figure 8.20 where the words "Text Fields" appear. You can also apply styles to the text box by right-clicking and selecting the desired style that applies color and outline to the surrounding box.

Using Text Fields

Text fields are a way to insert text into a diagram, such as date, author, page information, measurements, and other data types.

Follow these steps to learn how text fields can be inserted and used.

1. Open a new drawing using the Basic Diagram template.

2. Drag three shapes over and drop them onto the drawing window.

3. Select the first shape and go to the Insert tab, Text, and select Field.

4. Choose Date/Time from Category and Creation Date/Time from the Field name list. Click Data Format to see a variety of format choices in the Data Format window (see Figure 8.20).

5. For the second shape, choose Page Info and Name.

6. For the third shape, choose Document Info and Filename.

7. Press Ctrl+S to open the Save As File menu and type **Text Fields** for the name. Click Save.

8. Notice that the third shape updates the name of the drawing to show the name Text Fields.vsdx (see Figure 8.21).

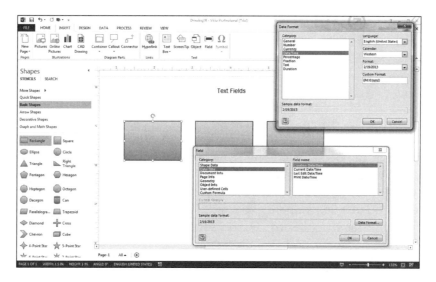

FIGURE 8.20

Field Text assignments can be formatted very selectively.

FIGURE 8.21

Field Text can pull text from key properties of your drawing file such as the file name, date, or page number.

TIP Text fields can even be inserted within regular text. For example, you can have a shape or a text box with normal text, such as "This was created on." You can insert a text field in this sentence after the word "on" and point to the current date in your category. This sentence automatically shows the current date each time the drawing is opened. This is one example that shows the power of text fields.

Text fields can be assigned on-the-fly to shapes in the diagram and even to text boxes. Another type of shape in Visio can be found in the Title Blocks stencil, as shown in Figure 8.22. These are essentially standardized text boxes that have predefined text fields where expected. They are often used when working with floor plans, for example. To find this set of shapes, open the Shapes Panel, More Shapes, Visio Extras, and Title Blocks.

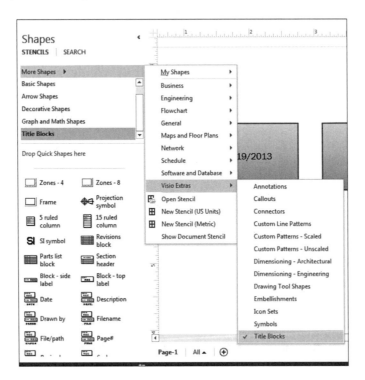

FIGURE 8.22

Title blocks are special shapes with predefined text fields.

Layers

Layers provide another way to manage and organize your diagrams. Most often this feature is used by farsighted creators of complex diagrams as a means to quickly see or select diagram components. Whereas you find that many layers are created automatically, layers can also be created based on any criteria you decide to use: shape, resource, date, color, and so on. They can exist in your diagram without being noticed and can be selectively printed or displayed at your whim.

 TIP Don't confuse layers in Visio with the way layers might be used in other applications. This is not a feature used for stacking and overlapping images, like transparencies on an overhead projector. They are designed to help you surgically organize and control groups of components without affecting the rest of your diagram.

Creating Layers

Compare Figure 8.23 and Figure 8.24. Two shapes are different, the same page is selected, and the only change is that the Visible setting has been toggled for the layers named Normal Hours and Weekend/afterhours.

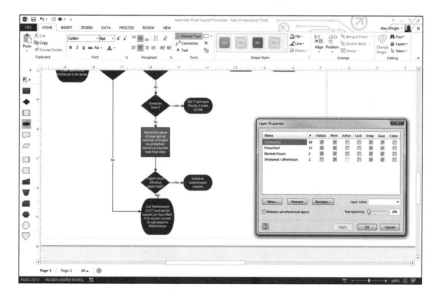

FIGURE 8.23

You can control the visibility of layers using the Layer Properties window.

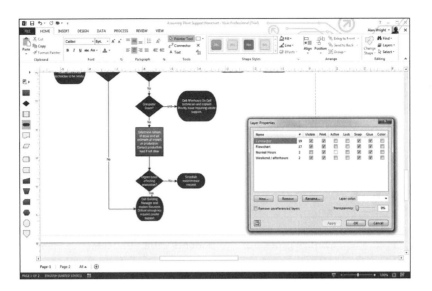

FIGURE 8.24

Layers provide a way to control multiple shapes assigned in one place. The Normal Hours layer has two assigned shapes that are not visible.

So how do you perform this magic?

1. A shape, connector, or multiple components must be selected.

2. Select the Home tab, then select Editing and expand the Layers menu. Select Assign to Layer.

3. In the Layer dialog box, select the layer or layers this item will be assigned to (see Figure 8.25).

FIGURE 8.25

The Layer dialog box allows you to assign a diagram component to one or more layers.

4. From the Home tab, select Editing, Layers, and then select Layer Properties.

5. As shown in Figure 8.24, you can modify many properties for a layer, such as visibility or whether it will be included in a printed format.

When to Add Layers

There are many practical reasons to employ layers. By assigning items to a layer you can lock them and prevent modifications or movements while working with content on another layer. The capability to select layers that print allows you to include sensitive or secondary information in a diagram, but not print that layer. Consider several other scenarios:

- Imagine you have a Site Plan diagram that shows the layout of a complex with multiple buildings that are under construction. You can assign structures to layers based on the projected completion dates, and by hiding layers or revealing them you have a handy way to provide snapshots of the project at different points in time.

- In a flowchart you can emphasize the impact of the removal or addition of a resource by your use of layers.

- A floor plan can show or hide furniture or electrical components.

These scenarios might help you imagine ways you would benefit from incorporating layers in your diagrams.

THE ABSOLUTE MINIMUM

The capability to make advanced diagrams enables you to set your Visio drawings apart and saves you time both now and later.

Structured diagram features like containers provide you with a flexible way to group shapes in your diagram. They allow you to easily adapt to changes and evolving conditions when used in your diagram. Use containers to group shapes that can be viewed as a unit, such as departments, geographic locations, and so forth.

Callouts have many benefits aside from the obvious visual aid of associating text with a shape in your diagram. Be discreet when using callouts in your diagrams because they tend to lose their effectiveness when overused.

ScreenTips are powerful tools for your diagrams that reveal there is much more to your drawing than meets the eye. If you use ScreenTips, consider establishing some visual cue that lets others know that there is hidden information here, such as a color, italicized font, or a special shape.

Take time to experiment with text fields and decide if they add to your diagrams. They provide an easy and dynamic way to display the scale, dates, page information, and other customizable data.

Layers are powerful tools for selectively working with selected elements in a drawing. Take time to experiment with layers and understand how they can be used to control the elements assigned. Locking a layer prevents those elements from being altered; hiding certain layers can reduce the clutter and may even provide a performance boost in extremely complex diagrams when moving around the drawing because less has to be rendered by your computer.

SHAPES: CUSTOMIZING

Several previous chapters touched on shapes, and this chapter builds on information about shapes considered in Chapter 5, "Working with Shapes," modifying groups from Chapter 6, "Manage Shapes," and customizing text considered in Chapter 8, "Making Advanced Diagrams." As you understand more about shapes and their capabilities, you are able to quickly produce more creative- and professional-looking diagrams using some of the tools considered here. In this chapter, you also look at tools for fine-tuning format, position, and size, which can take your abilities to another level.

Duplicating Shapes

Clones have a bad rap. They were used to establish the evil emperor in Star Wars, and in the new Battlestar Galactica they manipulated and confused us. (I still feel bad for Colonel Tigh.) In Visio, however, clones or copies of shapes are predictable, and you can make good use of them if you remember some basic pointers.

Creating duplicates or copies of shapes likely has become a habit. You used the Duplicate feature in Chapter 8 and you might recall that you can create a simple duplicate of a selected shape by pressing Ctrl+D. Now look at a few more tasks that you can accomplish with duplicates.

Making Several Copies

Suppose you need to create several copies of something. First, you need to create a honeycomb. Open a new drawing by selecting New, Basic Diagram.

1. Drag a hexagon to the drawing window.

2. Select the shape and press Ctrl while dragging to create a duplicate; then place the copy next to the original so that they share a side.

3. Press Ctrl+Y or F4 to add another duplicate shape. Notice how another shape is added in line with the first duplicate. Repeat a couple more times until your drawing window looks something like Figure 9.1.

4. Now drag and select the whole row of shapes. While this row is selected, hold Ctrl again while dragging the row to create a duplicate of the whole row. Position this group to create an attached row above the first row.

5. Press Ctrl+Y or F4 to repeat a few more times until you have something resembling Figure 9.2.

This certainly is faster than dragging several shapes over and worrying about the positioning each time. This technique can be used to create copies of tables, patterns, or copies of clusters of shapes.

With Visio Professional you can use several macros for similar effects. From the View tab open the Add-Ons menu from the Macro section and select Visio Extras. Look at the Move Shapes and Array Shapes options. Move Shapes allows you to duplicate selected shapes, whereas Array Shapes allows vertical and horizontal copies to be generated from a selected shape. In Figure 9.3 notice the layout created using the settings in the Array Shapes dialog box.

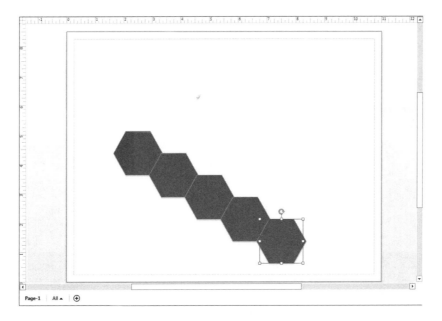

FIGURE 9.1

Create a series of shapes using the Duplicate feature.

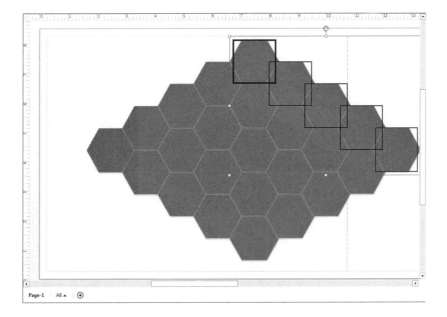

FIGURE 9.2

Create duplicates of groups of shapes quickly with Ctrl+drag and repeat.

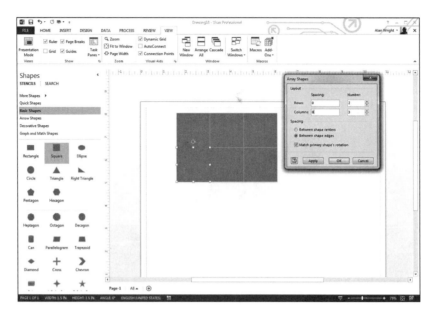

FIGURE 9.3

Predefined macros can also be used to duplicate and copy shapes.

Resizing Shapes

Resize handles are one of the first things you notice when selecting a shape or object in Visio. Most 2D shapes resize easily enough in Visio, but you may be frustrated by the tendency to maintain aspect ratio. If you want to override aspect ratio when resizing, try holding down the Shift key when you drag the control handle. A few shapes are meant to maintain an aspect ratio such as a square, and this override is not enabled in their case.

1D shapes such as lines can be resized by selecting an endpoint and dragging. If you hold down Shift while dragging, notice the direction is constrained to horizontal or vertical right angles.

Visio also provides a dedicated pane to working with size. From the View tab select Task Panes and enable the Size & Position pane. From here you can manually type in the size for a shape, as shown in Figure 9.4.

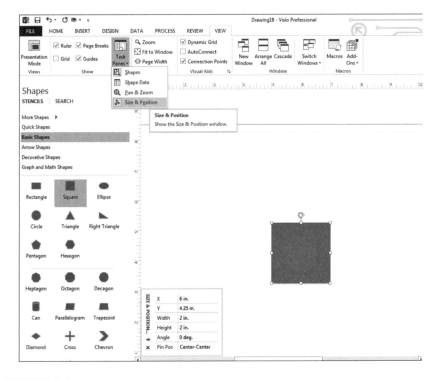

FIGURE 9.4

The Size & Position pane provides the option to type in size dimensions for a shape.

NOTE If you are having trouble with selecting a shape to resize it, check to see if the object is assigned to a layer that has locked content. From the Layer properties you can unlock the content and resize the shape. If a shape is placed on a background page, you need to resize the shape on the background page.

Rotating Shapes

There are a few ways to rotate a shape. Chapter 6 looked at the Rotate tools located on the Home tab, under Position in the Arrange tool group. Rotate Shapes allows you to rotate selected shapes using 90-degree increments and even flip vertically or horizontally.

Many people grab the rotate handle that is visible when selecting a shape, as shown in Figure 9.5, and drag to rotate the shape to the desired angle. This particular method leaves exact positioning to guess work; perhaps you have been frustrated when trying to rotate a shape to a particular angle. The further you are from the shape when using the rotate handle, the more granular the degree of rotation. Dragging the handle closer to the shape rotates by an increment of 5 or 10 degrees.

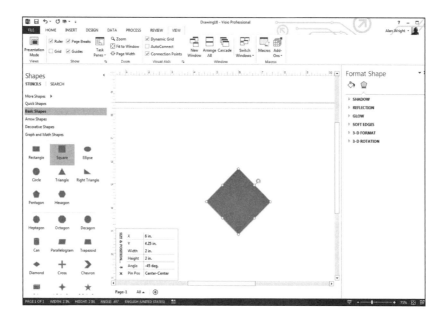

FIGURE 9.5

There are several ways to rotate a shape, including via the rotate handle and the Size & Position pane.

With the rotate handle, you can also move the center point used for rotation. Select the point and drag it to another place on the shape. This changes the center of rotation.

In Figure 9.5 the Size & Position pane is open to show how to use the rotate handle to get an exact 45-degree angle. You can also type **45** into the Angle field of that pane to achieve the same.

→ To learn more about Rotate Shapes tools, see page **114**.

How to Format a Shape

To change the appearance of shapes, you can use many predefined themes and variations built in to Visio. If you need to change the appearance of a shape without themes, or you do not see what you like, there are many ways to directly format shapes.

Modifying Common Format Attributes

From the Home tab you can change many attributes with options in the Shape Styles tool group shown in Figure 9.6. Another way to see those same tools is to select Styles from the context menu, also shown in Figure 9.6.

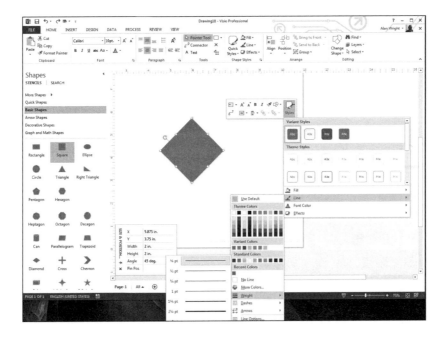

FIGURE 9.6

Many common formatting changes can be made from the Home tab or by using the context menu and selecting Styles.

These more common attributes include:

- Fill provides fill colors that include Theme Colors and Variant Colors, which change if the theme for the page is changed. Use Standard Colors or More Colors to ensure that colors stay.

- Line also provides the same types of color options as Fill, which are applied to the outline of shapes or to 1D lines and connectors. Additionally, you can change the line style, thickness (weight), and endpoints used (arrows, dots, or none).

- Effects provides many format options for things like shadows, bevels, reflection, glow, and so on.

Modifying Less Common Attributes

Visio 2013 makes it easier to work with many lesser-used attributes from the Format Shape pane. This can be opened from the Home tab and the pane launched from the Shape Styles tool group (see Figure 9.7). You can also right-click a shape and select Format Shape from the context menu.

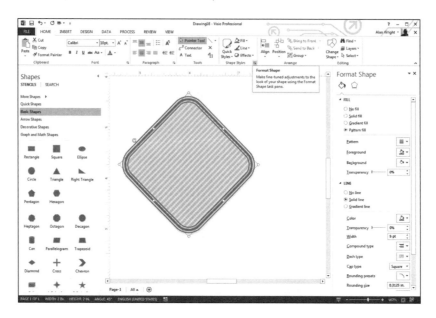

FIGURE 9.7

Format Shape provides many additional fill and line options.

There are two parts to the Format Shape pane. The first uses a fill paint bucket for a tab icon and contains expanded Fill and Line menus that include additional controls for gradient and pattern fills, transparency, and compound and gradient lines. The square in Figure 9.6 has been formatted in Figure 9.7 with compound lines, pattern fill, and rounded corners.

The second part of the Format Shape pane uses a pentagon for a tab icon. This contains the same Effects headings with many more control options. (Rather than Bevel, you find 3-D Format, which contains the Bevel controls.) Notice in Figure 9.8 that options like shadow color, transparency, and blur can be manipulated.

This same level of detailed formatting is found in the other Effects menus, which can be expanded or collapsed with a simple click.

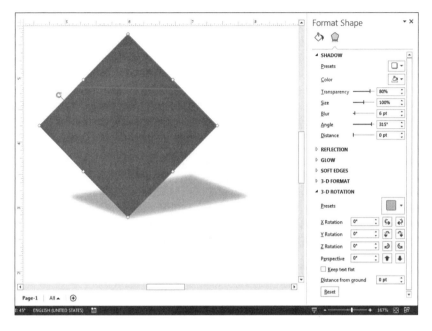

FIGURE 9.8

Format Shape has a granular set of controls for effects.

Using Format with Groups

There are a couple of ways to format multiple objects. You can select a group using various methods and format away, or you can use the Format Painter tool (see Figure 9.9). This is a handy tool that has long been a part of the Office suite.

By working with one object and getting your formatting down you can do complex formatting over a period of time without losing your focus on a group. After your group is the way you want it, select the formatted shape and click Format Painter once to apply formatting once, or double-click to keep the Format Painter enabled while you select multiple objects that can even span different pages. When you're finished, you can press Esc or click Format Painter again to disable the tool. (The keyboard shortcut is Shift+Ctrl+P. I like keyboard shortcuts, but I do not often use two-handed shortcuts.)

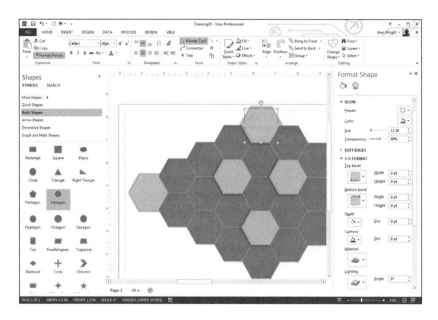

FIGURE 9.9

By double-clicking Format Painter you can apply formatting to multiple shapes.

Changing Text

When you work with shapes, text has two elements that can be formatted: the text itself and the space around the text. This section looks at some of the tools you need to understand when working with text in Visio.

Editing and Formatting Text

Anyone who has spent any time with Word, Excel, or just email in general is familiar with basic text editing. In Visio there is an expectation that you use text because shapes are, by default, text blocks, and they easily accommodate text; it is as simple as selecting a shape and typing text. There are many ways to edit and format your text after it has been entered into a shape.

Text Edit Mode

When you need to edit text for a particular shape, the easiest way is to double-click the shape containing the text. You are instantly placed into edit mode and can make your changes. To exit, press Esc or click outside of the shape.

If you need to change the text in a few different shapes, you can enable the Text tool as shown in Figure 9.10. From the Home tab, select Text from the Tools group. Any shape you select opens the text block to allow editing of the text rather than the normal handles for moving and resizing the shape. To exit you can press Esc a few times or click Text again to return to the Pointer tool.

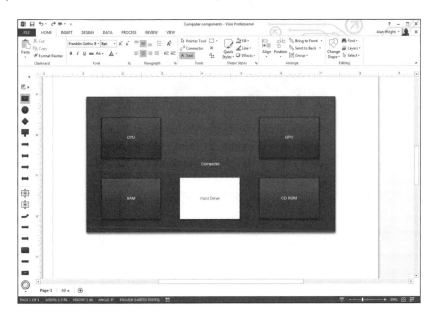

FIGURE 9.10

The Text tool puts you into edit mode for those times you need to do a lot of work with text.

Formatting Text

Working with text in Visio is different from other Office products in a few ways. For example, formatting text can be done by selecting the shape. Notice in Figure 9.11 that only the large block shape is selected. Working from the Home tab, you can change the text format using the Font tool group. To format portions of text, you need to enter Text Edit mode and select the portions of text to target your format changes.

To find a few more options, you can launch the Text dialog box by navigating to the Home tab and clicking the launch button from the Font tool group or by pressing the F11 key on your keyboard. Notice in Figure 9.12 that you can also change language and transparency for your text.

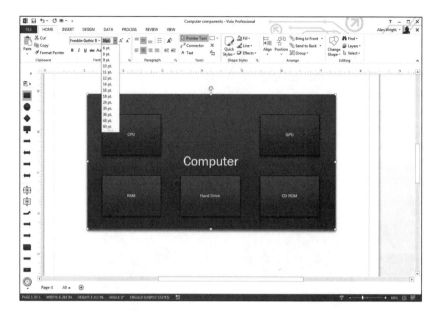

FIGURE 9.11

You can make most basic text format changes from the Home tab.

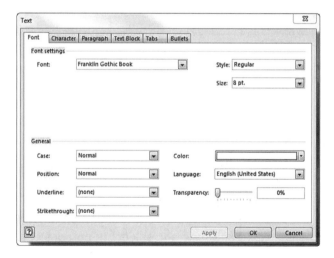

FIGURE 9.12

The Font tab of the Text dialog box provides further access to text formatting options.

Besides the Font tab, the Character tab of the Text dialog box lets you change scale and spacing for the text. The Tabs tab allows you to establish how tabs are used inside of a shape to create columns of text.

Resizing Text

To change the size of text, you can use the Font group from the Home tab, as shown in Figure 9.11. To the right of the font size you can choose to Increase or Decrease font size by one point using the two buttons with a larger and smaller A. These two buttons are also available in the context menu for shapes.

Aligning Text

In the Home tab you also see a set of Paragraph tools. These tools allow you to easily change the position of the text inside of a text block just as you might do in a cell from an Excel spreadsheet. Use the launch button to open the Text dialog box to the Paragraph tab for more fine-tuning options. Both options are shown in Figure 9.13 where the text alignment is set to right. The modified default bullet was done by selecting a different bullet format from the Bullets tab in this dialog box.

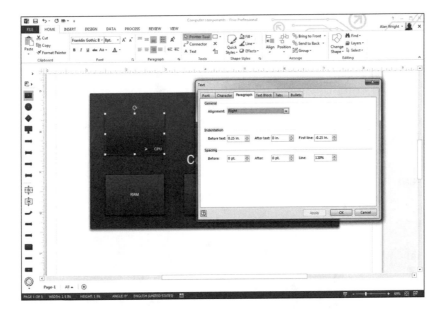

FIGURE 9.13

You can make several changes to the position of your text using Paragraph tools.

Modifying Text Blocks

Text blocks refer to the shape that actually holds your text. They can be created apart from shapes, but most often you deal with text blocks that start life when a shape is placed on a drawing. As mentioned earlier, shapes by default are prepared to accept text. You can think of a text block as a transparent skin that sits on shapes. When text has been entered, it can be treated like a separate shape, but it remains attached to the shape it started with.

In the Home tab, the Text Block tool has an icon that appears as a selected box with an arrow suggesting rotation. Select this and you have entered Text Block edit mode. You can create new text blocks or move, resize, and rotate existing ones while using this tool.

 NOTE Both the Text tool and the Text Block tool allow you to create new text blocks in your diagrams. Enable one and then click and drag to establish the size and location of your text block. You can press Esc to exit out of either tool and return to the default Pointer tool.

Moving Text Blocks

There are a few reasons you may want to move text around when working with shapes. If you have created a new text block for a diagram, it is not unusual to move it around as your diagram evolves. Changes to the orientation of text are desirable in some situations. Whereas resize and rotate handles behave the same for text blocks as for shapes, Visio offers a specific tool for rotating text. In Figure 9.14 you can see that the CPU has been rotated 90 degrees twice until it is upside down. In the Paragraph tool group you can use the Rotate Text tool to execute 90 degree clockwise turns of the text block.

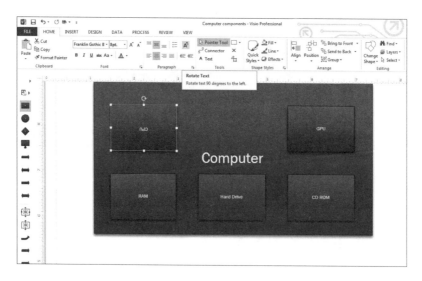

FIGURE 9.14

Rotate Text is a tool for rotating text blocks.

Don't forget that the text block continues to be subject to the shape it came from. Figure 9.15 shows how you can drag a text block to a different location away from the shape it was added to. Figure 9.16 shows that moving the shape also moves the text with the shape. This is to illustrate the relationship between a shape and the text block skin. Be cautious when moving text blocks away from shapes because this could cause problems later. The text block in Figure 9.15 would, of course, disappear if the original shape were deleted.

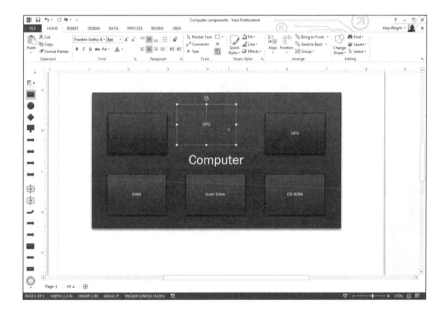

FIGURE 9.15

Text blocks can be moved using the Text Block tool.

Changing Backgrounds

Although the background of a text block is normally transparent, you can certainly add color. This might be helpful to make text easier to read or to provide a background to text blocks that were created as titles or labels.

There are a couple of ways to do this. One involves using the Fill tool for titles. Select Fill from the Shape Styles section of the Home tab, as shown in Figure 9.17, and choose your color. You may need to change the text color if you are adding a background color, so the Home tab is a handy place to be. You can also do this from the context menu by selecting Styles.

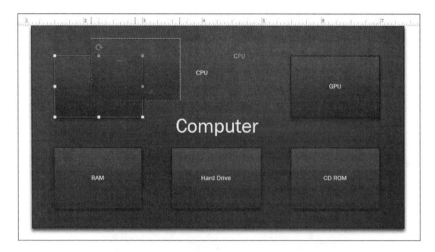

FIGURE 9.16

Text blocks continue to move with shapes because they continue to be a property of the shape.

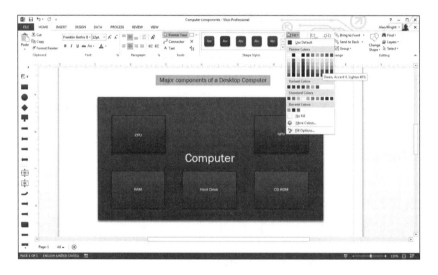

FIGURE 9.17

You can use Fill with a text block to create a background color.

When a text block is on a shape or connector, you can get better results by opening the Text dialog box and selecting the Text Box tab to fine-tune the background color (see Figure 9.18). The adjustable Margins determine the region that receives background color; by default it is just the area surrounding text. This is different from the way Fill fills the entire shape. Figure 9.19 shows the settings shown in Figure 9.18 applied to the CPU text box.

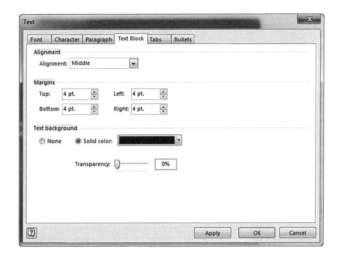

FIGURE 9.18

The Text Block tab allows you to surgically apply background color to your text.

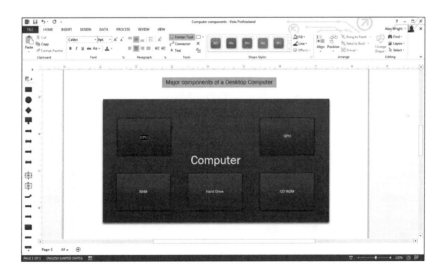

FIGURE 9.19

Fill can be added to the text itself to make text easier to see without filling the whole shape. Here just the word "CPU" has been filled with a black background.

THE ABSOLUTE MINIMUM

Use Ctrl+drag to quickly create and position duplicate shapes and groups.

Use the Size & Position pane to make precise changes to position, size, and rotation.

Use the Format Shape pane to change the Fill, Line, and Effect properties when you need to have full control over the results. Use the Home tab for more general changes to these properties.

Double-click the Format Painter tool to make multiple applications of a selected format.

Enable the Text tool to enter and stay in Edit Text mode when you have multiple text changes to make in a diagram.

Spend time looking over the Text dialog box. It has many tabbed features that enhance the way you use text in your diagrams.

SHAPES: MORE THAN MEETS THE EYE

SmartShapes are an important feature of Visio that can easily be taken for granted. This chapter spends a little time looking at what makes them so smart and how you can access all that extra shape potential.

Although you can read about how Visio has lots and lots of shapes, it is a picture that's worth a thousand words, right? Visio makes it easy to bring pictures and clip art into your drawings and even provides special tools for the job. You look at how integrated Excel tools allow you to insert and edit charts so that spreadsheet data can be visually presented in your Visio drawings.

Besides the common raster-based images you use every day, Visio enables you to work with vector-based graphics as complex as AutoCAD drawings. How can you work safely in Visio with these formats? That is also considered in this chapter.

Understanding Special SmartShape Features

Visio shapes have many properties that you have examined throughout this book. Because these properties allow for so much customization and functionality, they are often rightly called SmartShapes. Much of this flexibility is out of sight and you may rarely, if ever, need to change the shape data. A consideration of what makes a shape a SmartShape helps you understand the behavior exhibited by some shapes and opens you up to new possibilities.

What Is Shape Data?

The term *shape data* usually refers to information kept in shape date fields. To view this data you can right-click a shape to open the context menu and then select Properties, as shown in Figure 10.1. From the View tab you can also enable this Shape Data pane after selecting the Task Panes button.

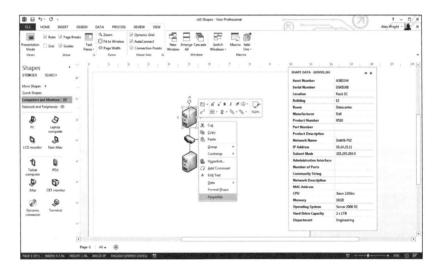

FIGURE 10.1

You can see shape data by selecting the properties of a shape.

As you can see in Figure 10.1, a lot of information is recorded and stored right in the shape.

Right-Click Menus

Another way to get an idea of how much data a SmartShape is carrying around is to look at the context menu. Notice in Figure 10.2 how the context menu reveals many special abilities for some shapes from different stencils. The top middle shape is a rather plain shape by comparison. When you see Properties listed in the context menu, it indicates that you can find additional information in the Shape Data pane, as shown in Figure 10.1.

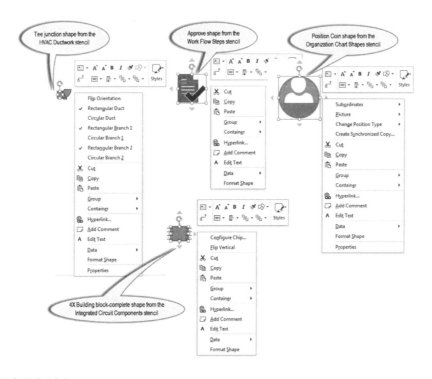

FIGURE 10.2

Context menus reveal special options that SmartShapes may have been created with.

Control Handles

Control handles are a standard feature for shapes when you are moving and resizing. You may see additional control handles from time to time that signal additional adjustments or purposes like glue points indicated for these handles. In Visio 2013 they appear as yellow control handles, and you find their purpose by hovering over them to reveal their tooltip, as shown in Figure 10.3.

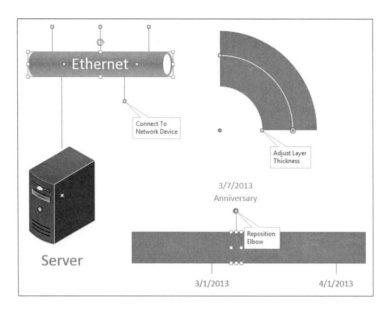

FIGURE 10.3

Hover over yellow control handles to learn what special control has been added to the SmartShape.

Hyperlinks

Shapes can provide a nice intuitive springboard to a website or network location by adding hyperlinks. Notice in Figure 10.4 that the shape labeled Invoices opens a network location. Selecting the Hyperlink option from the context menu allows you to name and point to a location. If a hyperlink is already established, you see Edit Hyperlinks and you can edit or add additional links. This is invisible on a SmartShape until you hover over the shape, as shown here.

Smart Tags

Not as common, and sometimes called action tags, smart tags are a SmartShape feature that you might come across eventually. A few developers add this feature to shapes, and they can provide additional actions or options from a clickable drop-down menu. Although it is similar to the context menus we rely on, one advantage is the presence of a visible indicator that actions are available here. Notice an example of a shape that has been created with Smart Tags from Chris Roth's Visio Guy website in Figure 10.5.

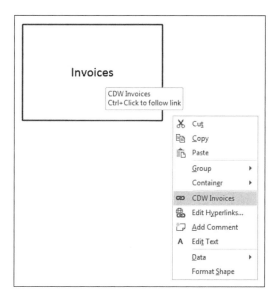

FIGURE 10.4

Hyperlinks can quickly be added to SmartShapes.

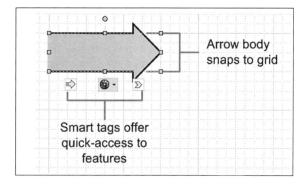

FIGURE 10.5

Smart tags can signal access to features not available in a context menu.

Import External Images

Because Visio communicates using visuals and graphics, it is natural to want the ability to work with graphics that originate outside of Visio. Not only does Visio allow for this, but quite a few built-in features simplify this for you.

Images can be copied and pasted into Visio. If you look at the Insert tab you see a group of tools labeled Illustrations, shown in Figure 10.6. You can browse to a file that is filtered for all pictures. Selecting the image file allows you to add it to the open drawing window, as was done here with the laptop-icon.png file.

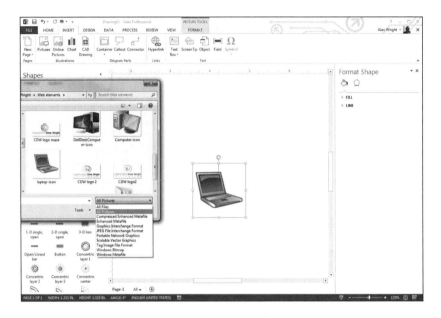

FIGURE 10.6

You can browse for image files and insert them into your Visio drawings.

What You Can Do with Images

After you paste and insert an image into Visio, you can work with it further using the Picture Tools Format tab that opens automatically. As shown in Figure 10.7, you can use Line tools to outline the shape, adjust the Z-order, and rotate and crop your image. The first tool group labeled Adjust allows you to adjust brightness, contrast, autobalance, and reduce the size of the picture using Compress Picture.

This Adjust tool group is better suited to photographs, and selecting these tools launches the Format Picture dialog box shown in Figure 10.8.

Besides the special picture tools, you can use the Format Shape pane to further modify the images because Visio already considers the image to be a shape. Notice in Figure 10.7 that a shadow was added, and a right-click reveals the familiar shape options that are available for this image. Because Visio considers the image to be a shape, you can resize using the eight control handles for size and movement. The Rotate handle works as expected.

FIGURE 10.7

Inserted images are automatically considered to be shapes and can be modified with Picture tools or standard shape tools.

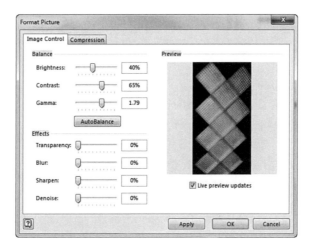

FIGURE 10.8

Visio provides a Format Picture dialog box to fine-tune the image quality.

Resizing Images

One downside to adding image files to your Visio drawing is that picture files can be quite large. With cameras and smartphones commonly taking 5MP to 16MP pictures, the size of the file is far larger than needed for a Visio diagram. Inserting a few of these uncompressed high-quality pictures can have very serious consequences if you use this type of drawing on a website—or even try to send it via email.

To avoid the hit on performance that accompanies large files, you can use the Compress Picture tool to quickly adjust the resolution. Shown in Figure 10.9, the slider provides a way to manually compress the picture size; the lower Change Resolution option buttons optimize the resolution of your picture for Web/Screen or Print quality.

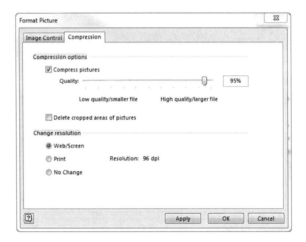

FIGURE 10.9

Compression allows you to optimize the image resolution for web/screen and print media.

 TIP If you notice your Visio drawing has a slower speed than expected when redrawing or loading, make sure that there are no uncompressed image files. Make it a habit to compress to optimize the resolution when you paste or insert image files.

 CAUTION Be careful when compressing images that will be resized and used at a larger size later. Too low of a resolution appears pixelated if you try to make it larger after optimizing. Also, optimizing for screen size (96dpi) is a lower resolution quality than print (200dpi). If you think the shape may be used at a larger size, consider optimizing at that larger size.

Working with Clip Art

Besides images we have stored locally or on a network, we can search for additional images and clip art from the Insert tab and the Online Pictures tool. This opens the Search interface shown in Figure 10.10. Notice you can search Office.com Clip Art and Bing Image Search. You may see additional options, such as browsing your SkyDrive, if you log in with a Live ID or search attached services like Flickr (see Figure 10.11).

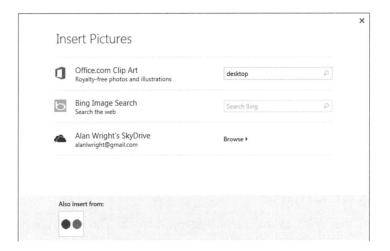

FIGURE 10.10

Searching for additional image content is easy using the Online Pictures tool.

Images found using this tool are inserted with the same Picture Tools Format tab, which enables you to fine-tune your selection. Images you use may be vector based or bitmapped and Visio will work with both. You should be aware of how each behaves when you resize an image. Just remember that bitmapped images can lose their sharpness quickly when they are resized while vector-based images handle size changes with no loss to their image quality.

 CAUTION By default you are provided with search results that keep you out of trouble with respect to licensing and usage rights for the images you find. Make sure that images you insert into your drawings are free for you to use. Some images can have strings attached related to the paying of royalties or limits on usage.

FIGURE 10.11

Search results can be inserted into your Visio drawing window.

Using Excel Charts

Visio has the ability to insert and edit Excel charts. The way Visio presents this depends on the version of Excel you installed because it actually pulls tools from Excel.

Select the Insert tab and Charts from the Illustrations tool group. As shown in Figure 10.12, Visio opens a session of Excel 2013 complete with the ribbon interface for Excel. (You may not even see a ribbon when using an older version of Office, although the tools are available as menus.) The chart is selected, and you have the Excel ribbon and Excel tools for editing the appearance and contents of the chart. If you look closely at Figure 10.12, notice that the only Visio commands available are a menu bar with File and Window options.

You launch into Edit mode by default when inserting a chart. While in Edit mode you can edit the spreadsheet and chart that accompany it. If you click outside of the chart, you go back to the familiar Visio ribbon interface, and the finished chart appears as a shape that is editable like any other picture shape (see Figure 10.13). If you need to edit the chart itself again, right-click and use the Chart Object menu to access the Edit, Open, and Convert options. The Open option opens the chart directly in Excel, and the Convert option allows you to change the format of the chart object from the choices shown in Figure 10.14.

FIGURE 10.12

You can insert Excel charts into your Visio drawings.

FIGURE 10.13

A completed chart has the properties of an inserted picture. To edit the chart, use the right-click menu that shows Chart Object tools.

FIGURE 10.14

You can convert a chart format from within Visio using the Convert dialog box.

CAUTION Visio opens Excel system processes to edit charts, which can be pretty intense for computer resources. You might even see a few seconds of unresponsiveness. This seems to be a byproduct of the way Visio takes over the Excel application. If you have open Excel windows, watch for alerts to pop up that were initiated by the chart inserted in Visio.

Importing Scalable Vector Graphics

Vector-based graphics are images that differ from pixel-based graphics (also known as raster graphics) because they render the image based on paths or lines to form shapes rather than a fixed assemblage of dots. If you have ever seen an embroidery machine that can sew a logo onto a hat or jacket, you have seen vector-based graphics converted into paths for a sewing needle.

Because they do not need to add or remove pixels when resizing, vector-based graphics present cleaner images when resized, and they are used for higher end graphics work because of this versatility.

SVG formatted images allow for great flexibility in your drawings. If prepared correctly, they are seen by Visio as grouped shapes with lines and shapes that can be worked with individually once ungrouped. This allows you to use colors and other effects in the case of SVG formatted maps. Some SVG formatted graphics may not allow for this degree of editing and they may appear as a single shape because they retain a sharp image. In either case they are superior choices when you will resize the image.

To insert an SVG formatted image, open the Insert tab and select Pictures. SVG files are seen with the default All Pictures file type; however, you can choose Scalable Vector Graphics to refine your search.

Importing AutoCAD Drawings

AutoCAD (which stands for Automated Computer-Aided Drafting) drawings are unique vector-based drawings created with special software used for architectural and engineering plans and diagrams. The most common format is DWG. They have a few similarities to some Visio templates, and this allows for a certain degree of interchange using the CAD DWG drawing format. You can view, annotate, and even add content to CAD drawings.

Importing CAD drawings is a straightforward process. Use a sample DWG file that you likely already have.

1. Open a new Floor Plan template.

2. Open the Insert tab and select CAD Drawing. Browse and select the sample CAD drawing file named BLDGPLAN.dwg installed by default in the path C:\ Program Files (x86)\Microsoft Office\Office15\Visio Content\1033. (This is the default 32-bit path Visio; you may need to look in the path C:\Program Files\ Microsoft Office\Office15\Visio Content\1033 if you have 64-bit Office applications. The 1033 directory provided here is for English; you will see a different number if you have a different language version. German would install to a 1031 directory for example.

3. In the CAD Drawing Properties dialog box, confirm the scale from the General tab as shown in Figure 10.15. In this case, you open a drawing plan so you can try Architectural for the Predefined scale. The scale itself you may adjust after opening the drawing. However, you will find that this CAD drawing fits your page well using a scale of 1/4" = 1'. Click OK to insert the CAD drawing. Presto! You have a floor plan complete with furniture.

4. Because you want to add furniture, remove the furniture that was included in the bldgplan.dwg file. Right-click the CAD drawing, and select CAD Drawing Object and Properties to reopen the CAD Drawing Properties dialog box. From the Layer tab select Layer 12 and click the Visible column to show No, as shown in Figure 10.16. Click OK to apply.

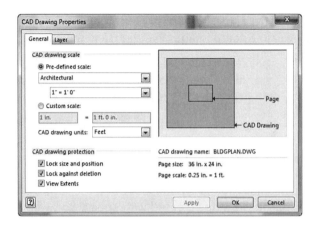

FIGURE 10.15

You are able to select scale settings when inserting a CAD .dwg drawing into Visio.

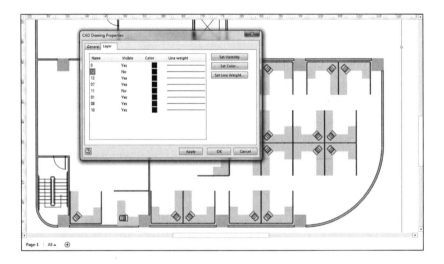

FIGURE 10.16

You can hide CAD drawing layer contents to replace with Visio shapes and content.

5. Compare the floor plan in Figure 10.16 to the one in Figure 10.17. Hiding the contents of a layer allows you to change content without permanently changing this file. This is important if you have further CAD work to do on the original file.

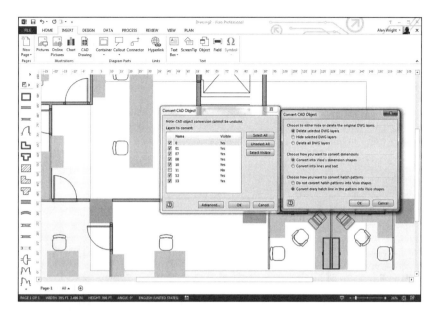

FIGURE 10.17

CAD drawings can be converted to Visio content.

Based on the choices you made in the CAD Drawing Properties dialog box, you may not be able to resize or move the CAD drawing object. If the default Size and Position settings are left as Locked, you see the drawing as a shape in your drawing window and the control handles are grayed out. To make changes, you can right-click and select CAD Drawing Object and Properties to reopen the CAD Drawing Properties dialog box.

From the right-click CAD Drawing Object menu, you can also select Convert to transform the content on selected layers of the DWG file into individual shapes. There may be times when you need to do this, but it is not as common as working with the DWG file format. The options shown in Figure 10.16 show the Convert CAD Object dialog box and the Advanced window options to perform this conversion.

CAUTION   Converting a DWG converts the lines and shapes in the AutoCAD drawing to lines and shapes in Visio. This is a one-way trip. The output does not have any special properties and may be difficult to work with as a consequence. For example, objects may appear as a desk or computer, but Visio does not know them to be furniture items.

Adding Content to AutoCAD Drawings

After you have a CAD drawing inserted into your drawing window, you can add content from your stencils. In Figure 10.18 notice how easy it is to add furniture to a floor plan. The shapes even interact with the elements in the drawing without having converted anything from the DWG format.

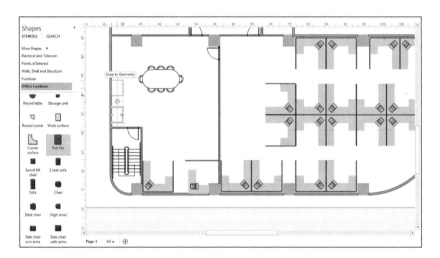

FIGURE 10.18

Add content easily to AutoCAD DWG drawings from Visio.

When you're finished, save the file using Save As, and use the type AutoCAD Drawing, which saves this as a DWG formatted file. You can send this file to a person who has AutoCAD, and the file will open without any need to convert the drawing.

THE ABSOLUTE MINIMUM

Take time to explore the interface options outlined in this chapter so that you recognize a SmartShape when you see one. There are many features that you can use to make your life easier, but they help only if you use them. Shape data can be added manually into a diagram so that it is readily available, and hyperlinks can be created.

Import images to add life to charts and diagrams, but don't allow your drawing to get bloated with oversized images. Optimize your images by using the Compress Picture tool.

When working with charts, remember that Excel is being used even if you appear to be working in Visio. If Visio becomes unresponsive, watch for Excel to be the reason.

Be aware of the advantages and limitations of inserting SVG images.

Use layers, if available, to manipulate DWG CAD drawings. Add content or comments and save your work using Save As with the CAD Drawing format to maintain the DWG file type when you're working with AutoCAD users.

PRINTING VISIO DIAGRAMS

Print is a little five-letter word. It really shouldn't be complicated. We have all felt the angst of intending to print one thing and getting something else entirely. Also, we live in a society that is becoming ever more aware of being ecologically friendly, which translates to using eco settings and less paper when we print. Nevertheless, printing diagrams may often be needed for handouts at meetings, advertising, hard copies for review, or plans for a worksite.

Visio diagrams range from simple and sleek to sprawling multipage complex diagrams that can be intimidating to look at, much less print. How do you select the parts you want to print and avoid taking out a forest? This chapter considers these questions as it analyzes the Print settings and options that Visio provides.

Just the Basics

Have you ever clicked the Print button, and after going through several pop-ups and choosing the correct files, you end up printing something totally different from what you expected? Many factors influence how printers interpret what users send to them. There may be issues or limitations at the printer (low paper or toner). The print server may have drivers that affect how the print job format looks by the time it gets to the printer. And on your computer there may be problems with the way the printer is configured or installed. That's why there are network administrators and help desks to keep all this set up and working.

This section focuses on the factors that you have control over when you print Visio content as you look at the basic settings within Visio and their purpose. After all, it is embarrassing when the print job failed because you made a mistake, right?

Print from the Backstage

As we have seen, Visio 2013 uses the Backstage to handle tasks related to Visio files and printing. This is accessed by selecting the colored File tab. From there, select Print from the vertical menu to the left. You can also get there by using the keyboard shortcut Ctrl+P when working with the drawing window.

Using the Print Settings Pane

As you can see in Figure 11.1, the Print Settings pane is a refined interface. It is divided into two sections—the Settings pane to the left that shows the current print selections, and the Print Preview pane.

The prominent Print button sends the job to the printer using the settings displayed. It does not get much easier than that. You can quickly choose a different printer from the Printer drop-down list. Notice that the status of printers is shown; this may help you immediately avoid problems by sending your job to a printer that is ready rather than to one offline.

Aside from the Ready status, you can use the information icon to see more detailed information regarding the connection or the IP address (see Figure 11.2).

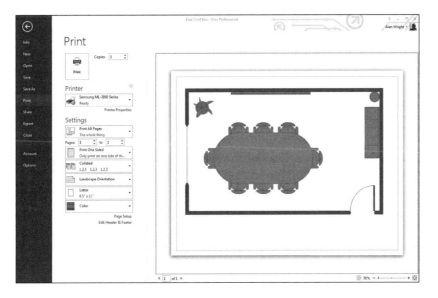

FIGURE 11.1

The Print Settings pane provides a user-friendly interface to your printer.

FIGURE 11.2

Hovering over the information icon provides more details.

Just below the Printer button is a link labeled Printer Properties. This brings up the properties of the printer that was installed in your operating system. You would get the same results opening the printer properties from Devices and Printers or the Control Panel in Windows. As you can see in Figure 11.3, these settings are unique to the printer installed. Although not all printers have the same options, you can expect to find certain basic settings here, such as color, quality, print selection, duplexing and paper settings.

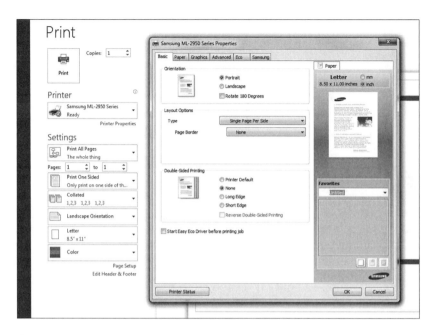

FIGURE 11.3

Click Printer Properties to see a dialog box that is specific to the printer installed.

Collation

In Figure 11.3, notice the button under Settings labeled Collated (see Figure 11.4). You use this only when printing more than one copy of a multipage document. This allows you to adjust the order the pages are printed out by the printer. Two options are presented, the first being Collated 1,2,3 1,2,3 1,2,3. This indicates that the pages print in order for the first copy and then another copy is printed in order, and so on. This saves time when you need several copies for handouts because they are already in order.

Uncollated means that all copies of page 1 are printed, then all of page 2, and so on. You may want this if another step is needed for a specific page before assembling the copies for distribution.

Orientation

In settings below the Collated options, notice a button that says either Landscape Orientation or Portrait Orientation. This is not the same as the page orientation that you can use when working on the drawing window. Orientation tells the printer how to reproduce the selected print job *onto paper*. In Figure 11.1 check out the preview of a page using Landscape Orientation on letter-size paper from a laser printer. Notice how this layout is changed after selecting Portrait Orientation in Figure 11.5.

FIGURE 11.4

You can easily select Collated or Uncollated printing.

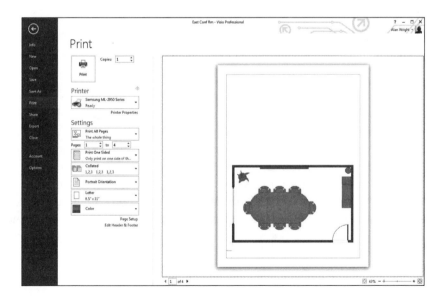

FIGURE 11.5

You can change the paper orientation on-the-fly when printing.

NOTE The Settings field may present extra drop-down menus depending on the capability of your printer. For example, if your printer has a duplexer, you might see options related to single- or double-sided printing.

Background Printing

Visio 2013 features default background printing. This refers to the way Visio handles the printing task in the background while you continue working without being forced to wait for the print job to complete.

In the status bar below the drawing window, you can see the status for sent print jobs until they are completed.

The Print Preview Pane

To the right you can't miss the Print Preview pane, which allows you to interact with the drawing without leaving the Print page. You can zoom in and out and pan across the drawing by clicking and dragging. To zoom in or out use the Zoom control, or use the scroll wheel on your mouse. To the right of the Zoom control is a Zoom to Page button you can use to jump to a view of the full page.

In Visio there is a Page Break preview that can be useful when locating shapes that extend past the page size. Figure 11.6 shows the same view you see in your drawing window. It doesn't look too bad, right?

Now check to see what the actual printed pages will look like. Remember that your drawing may occupy a single drawing page, but the print job for your drawing can be spread across several sheets of printer paper. To the left of the Zoom control is a small button that is grayed out for drawings that are contained in a single page size. The drawing in Figure 11.6 has at least four paper pages to print this drawing based on the dashed page breaks that are visible. Click this icon to Show/Hide Page Breaks. Figure 11.7 shows the result, and you can decide if you are happy with the way the print job will print or if some rearranging is called for. This useful feature removes any concerns you may have before sending files to the printer.

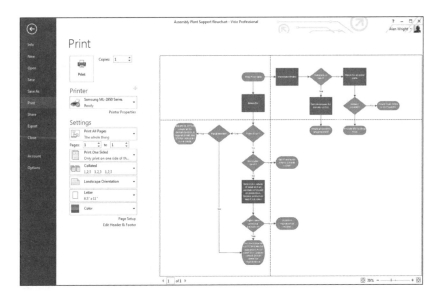

FIGURE 11.6

You can zoom in to check the way your diagram will look before printing in the Print Preview pane.

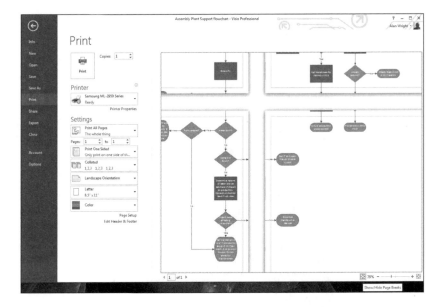

FIGURE 11.7

The Page Break preview feature allows you to see what the actual printed pages look like when printing overlapping pages.

Test Your Print Job

It can be handy to test print jobs when you have doubts. However, it is better to print to a file format rather than burn through the paper tray until you get your settings right. Besides, office administrators can be cranky when the toner gets low on the color laser printer. You may have the means to print to PDF already installed on your computer. PDF is a great option for this because it will not change any formatting and reproduces what would happen if the pages had been printed by a printer using the printer tool settings. Once the output has been generated, you just save the pages as a pdf formatted file. Because they look exactly as the printed pages would you can open the file to check the print job. If you are happy with the results you can send the same settings to a printer confident of the results. Another advantage is that .pdf files can readily be viewed by anyone, even if they do not have Visio installed, because PDF viewers are free applications and are commonly installed.

Another option is built in to Windows and Visio; you can choose Microsoft XPS Document Writer in your list of printers (see Figure 11.8). This creates an image that again corresponds to what is printed on paper. Windows has an XPS Viewer, which is normally included in the operating system. In Windows 7, for example, click Start and type XPS. The XPS Viewer is listed.

FIGURE 11.8

The XPS Document format provides a paperless way to test your print job.

Controlling the Space Around the Print Job

With laser and inkjet printers or plotters, generally there are limits to how close they can print to the edge of the paper. This physical limitation must be respected when setting up a print job. This area is usually referred to as a bleed, crop, or margin, depending on the context and application. In Visio this area is referred to as margins.

A separate feature on printed pages refers to the top and bottom areas of a document referred to as headers and footers. These have counterparts in the visual drawing window, but this chapter talks about *print* features.

Headers and Footers

You can print information at the header of your pages or at the footer. To configure this feature, open the link labeled Edit Header and Footer, which you'll find below Settings in the Print Settings pane. (Refer to Figure 11.7 to see this link.)

Notice the results in Figure 11.9 of various header and footer assignments to a drawing that has been printed. This additional information is visible only on a *printed* output of the Visio drawing and is not visible in the drawing window. The capability to add information when printing provides some nice ways to reference a printout when there are many printed pages and identify the date the drawing was printed, which can help avoid confusion if changes have been made or if the printout is used for review.

Refer to Figure 11.10 to see what can be added to the header and footer. The fields you can choose from are limited in scope and will use information specific to the print job. For example, page number and total printed pages will be related to which printed page and how many total printed pages are included.

These same nine information sources can be assigned to the Left, Center, or Right of either the header or footer sections. The drawing in Figure 11.9 used all but the Footer Center location. Click Choose Font, and you can adjust the font, font style, size, color, script, and use strikeout or underline effects.

 NOTE In Chapter 8, "Making Advanced Diagrams," you learned how to add visible title or header and footer information using background pages. Because you can customize the text fields and thereby better control what is displayed, you will find Borders & Titles to be a better solution when you want to display document information in your printed diagrams. For example, file path or last edit date cannot be displayed using the nine header and footer fields.

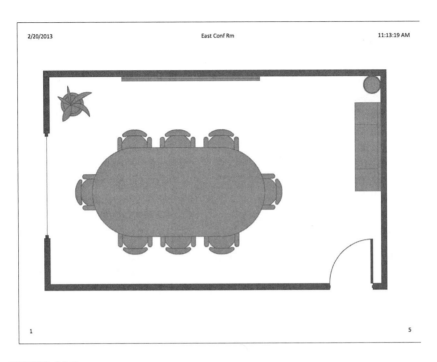

FIGURE 11.9

You can add information to your printed Visio pages.

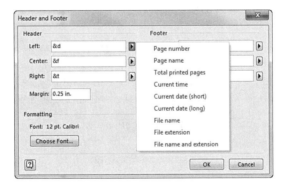

FIGURE 11.10

Page reference information can be targeted to specific points in the printed output.

→ To learn more about inserting visible header and footer fields to your drawings, see page **157**.

You can adjust the location of your header and footer information by adjusting the Margin setting, as shown in Figure 11.11. This also refers to the distance from the top or bottom of the printable area, but it is not the same as the print margins discussed next. Be careful with this adjustment because if you have shapes or background page data near the edge of the paper, this may create an undesirable overlap; check the results with the print preview pane.

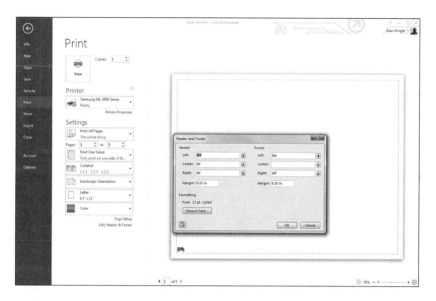

FIGURE 11.11

The Header and Footer dialog box allows you to adjust the distance of text from the edge of your printable area using the Margin settings.

Margins

Print margins refer to the space that you allow around the drawing up to the edge of the paper, and this is configured using the Page Setup dialog box. A few factors may influence your decision to change this. For example, using printed header and footer information discussed in the previous section may move you to adjust the upper and lower margins to provide better text positioning or the physical limitations of your printer may require increasing the margin space.

1. Open the Page Setup dialog box by pressing Shift+F5, or from the Print Settings pane using the link below Settings labeled Page Setup.

2. On the Print Setup tab, click the button labeled Setup to open the Print Setup dialog box.

3. In the Print Setup dialog box, you can adjust the margins for left, right, top, and bottom (see Figure 11.12.) Notice additional settings here, such as Center for smaller drawings.

4. Click OK to save changes to Print Setup and click OK again to close the Page Setup dialog box.

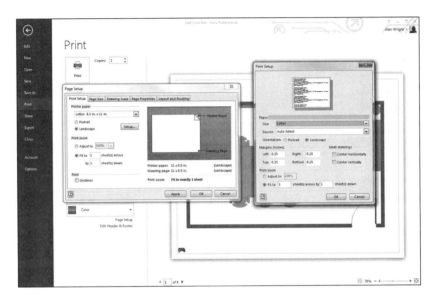

FIGURE 11.12

You can adjust the print margins from the Page Setup and Print Setup dialog boxes.

Selecting What You Will Print

Choosing what you print is easier than you might think. In other applications, such as Word, there is a tendency to print an entire document. When working with Visio it is common to limit your print job to particular pages or even parts of pages, especially with larger diagrams. Visio 2013 has refined the interface to put the tools right in front of you that allow you to make basic selections.

NOTE This chapter refers often to the Print Settings pane, which can be opened using the File tab and then selecting Print from the left vertical menu. Alternatively, you can press CTRL+P on the keyboard.

Look closely at the Print Settings pane and at the section labeled Settings. Settings presents you with a group of drop-down boxes to configure the print job.

Print All Pages is set by default. (Isn't it great how it sums it up with "The whole thing"?) Notice the other choices offered for the document in the drop-down in Figure 11.13.

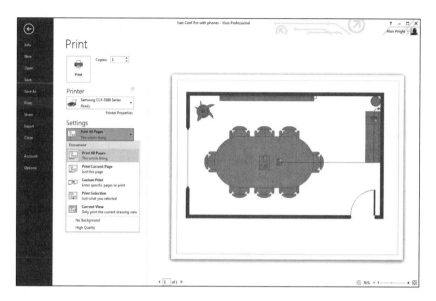

FIGURE 11.13

You can select how much or how little of your document is printed.

Remember that the *default* is Print All Pages, which prints all pages in your Visio file. The other options allow you to be more selective.

Printing Just a Portion of a Diagram

When working with large plans or complex flowcharts, you may be interested in printing only a small section for a meeting or for review. The following section shows how easily this can be done.

Using Current View

Current View does not refer to the view in the Print Preview pane, but rather to the view you establish in the drawing window.

1. In the drawing window, zoom into a drawing and pan until you see the area you would like to print.

2. Press Ctrl+P to jump to the Print menu. In the Print Settings pane under Settings, click Print All Pages to view other options.

3. Select Current View (see Figure 11.14). Notice the Preview pane adjusts to show the area that was visible in the drawing window.

4. Click Print, and you're done.

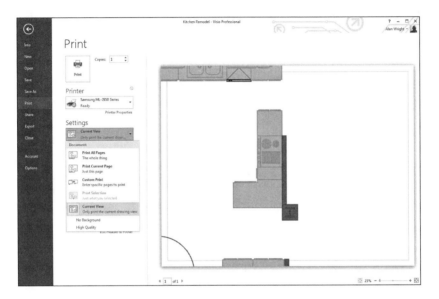

FIGURE 11.14

You can quickly choose a portion of a diagram for printing using Current View.

The print job is what is displayed in the Print Preview pane. There might be a slight difference between the Preview pane and the drawing window as Visio fills the paper; it may include more vertical or horizontal real estate.

Selecting Specific Pages in Visio

You can choose the specific pages to print in a couple ways. You can use the Print Preview pane to display a page and then select Print Current Page to print only the page displayed in the Print Preview pane.

One of the options shown in Figure 11.14, Custom Print, focuses the print job on a range of pages. You can alter the page number fields labeled Pages, and To and Custom Print are automatically selected.

Look at Figure 11.15. Under Settings, you see Pages: 2 to 4. In this document, which could have dozens of pages, you are focused on printing only pages 2 through 4. Notice the Print Preview pane shows 1 of 3 pages that you can scroll through. When you press Print, only those three pages are printed.

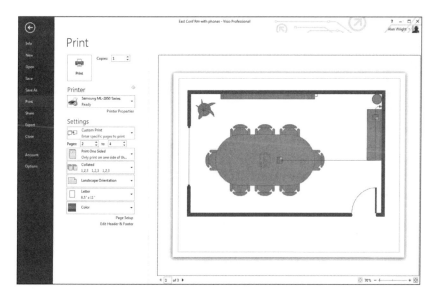

FIGURE 11.15

With Custom Print, you can select a range of pages to print.

Background Page Printing (or Not)

Background pages are special pages to which you can add graphics and visual text. If you decide you do not want the background content on the printed page, you can quickly strip this from the print job. In Figure 11.16 you see the effects of a background page with the title and page number. In the Document settings notice the words No Background toward the bottom of the list. Select this to remove the effects of all background pages in the drawing. The results are shown in Figure 11.17. Notice that No Background is checked, showing that the feature is enabled. Select it again to disable.

If you decide that you want to print a background page, make sure you have assigned this background to a foreground page first. When this page is printed it will include the background page content by default unless you have unchecked this option.

 NOTE Removing the background pages from the Print Setting pane affects only the print job and does not alter the pages in the drawing window. You may want to simplify for review or conserve ink or toner.

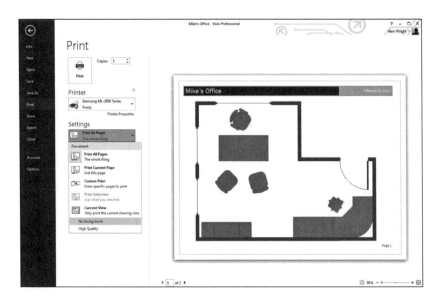

FIGURE 11.16

You can easily remove the visuals added by background pages before printing.

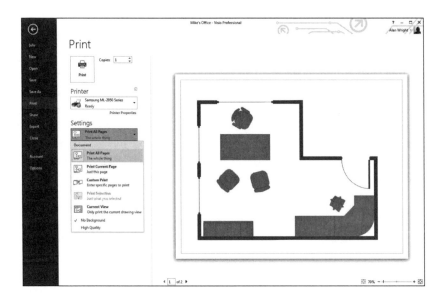

FIGURE 11.17

No Background can be turned on or off, and the results are immediately displayed in the Print Preview pane.

→   To learn more about background pages, see page **64**.

Notice High Quality is also listed here. This feature is explained toward the end of the chapter.

Selecting Shapes to Print

Another way to limit the items being printed is to manually select items first in the drawing window and choose Print Selection from the Print settings pane. The drawing shown in the print preview pane in Figure 11.18 is the same drawing shown back in Figure 11.1. The difference is that the walls, window, and the door have been selected by holding down Ctrl and clicking each item. The document is set to Print Selection in the Settings pane, which correctly adjusts the preview window to show you what will be printed.

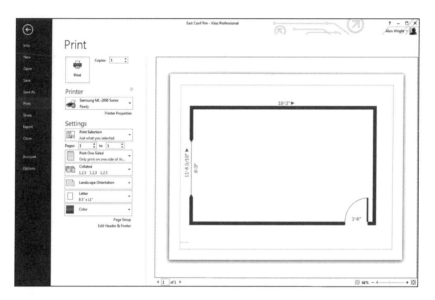

FIGURE 11.18

Using Print Selection, you can manually select items for printing.

You can also click and drag the pointer over an area and select a group of shapes and connectors if that is faster or easier.

Printing by Layer

Layers are discussed in Chapter 8. One of the benefits of working with layers is the capability to choose which layers print.

Notice how easy it is to select what is printed by using predefined layers. Figure 11.19 shows plans for a conference room upgrade with furniture and some communications equipment installed. You can print this image without all the furniture so that you can focus on the equipment that needs to be installed in this room.

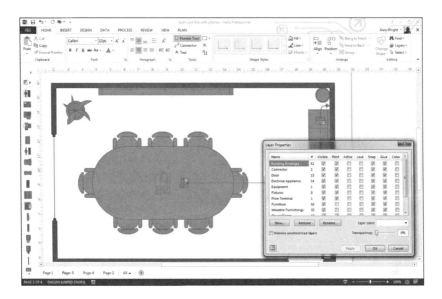

FIGURE 11.19

You can choose which layers print from the Layer Properties dialog box.

From the Home tab, click Layers and then Layer Properties to open the Layer Properties dialog box. The Furniture and Movable Furnishings are unchecked in the Print column. The results of this change can be seen immediately in the Print Preview pane shown in Figure 11.20.

Many layers are created automatically when you place shapes and connectors on your drawings, and it may be very simple to make selections like this one. Visio also allows you to create new layers as needed and assign content according to your criteria. In any case, printing or not printing a layer is a simple choice you can make.

➔ To learn more about creating and using layers, see page **163**.

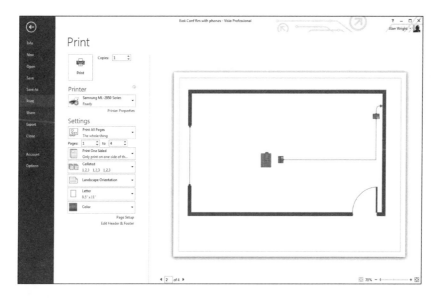

FIGURE 11.20

Layers that are not selected for printing are not seen in the Print Preview pane.

Gridlines

Gridlines are sometimes desirable features in a printed diagram. They provide guidelines and a sense of scale. Modifications can be easily noted and scaled.

To print gridlines, select the Page Setup link from the main Print Settings pane. Figure 11.12 shows both the Page Setup link and the Page Setup dialog box that this opens. Select Gridlines at the bottom of the Print Setup tab to enable this feature in the printed copy.

Get High-Quality Print Jobs

When you want to ensure that your print quality is maximized, one quick setting to check is the High Quality setting. Located in the Print Settings pane, this setting is included at the bottom of the Document drop-down list that is labeled Print All Pages by default. Notice the location in Figure 11.21 in the Drawing2 settings.

High Quality is a setting that changes the print output from the default optimized draft mode to a high-quality mode. You may not often see any difference, because the draft mode provides very sharp print quality. So what is the difference?

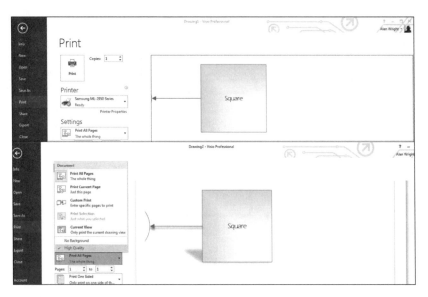

FIGURE 11.21

The High Quality option can include visual effects in your print jobs.

When Visio (and other Office products) prints a document, it does not include some visual effects that are seen in the drawing window unless you ask it to. Shadows are a good example. To print this effect takes extra time and slows down the printer. Visio removes these effects to improve speed. In Figure 11.21 you can see two Visio windows overlapped with the same content. Drawing2 in the lower window has High Quality enabled, and you can see that a shadow effect for the shape and connector is visible in the Print Preview window. This effect was removed in the Drawing1 document by default.

Other settings you can check using Printer Properties are unique to your printer. Make sure that you are using the equivalent of best or high in your printer's settings rather than draft or normal if the quality is not as good as desired. Also, some known techniques work well when you're dealing with certain quality issues. You will see a reference to this in Chapter 16, "Additional Visio Resources".

CAUTION Printer settings for quality and color should be weighed against the use of the printed media. Does it justify high-quality, full-color for handouts used in a status meeting? Not likely. However, the brochures that are printed for advertising would be another issue. Be aware of the default output and adjust it if warranted. The settings are right there and no one begrudges you for being green when you can be.

Color Printing

Last but not least is the capability to change your color settings quickly. In the Print Settings pane you find a button that allows you to choose quickly between the default Color or black and white (see Figure 11.22). This is a nice feature when printing handouts and for print jobs that do not need color, and it helps show you are eco-conscious and doing your part to keep operating costs down.

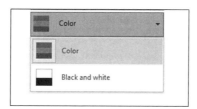

FIGURE 11.22

You can switch to monotone printing right from the Print Settings pane without digging into the Printer properties.

THE ABSOLUTE MINIMUM

Use CTRL+P to quickly jump to the backstage Print Settings pane.

Use the Print Preview to confirm your settings before you print; Visio uses a you-get-what-you-see Preview pane.

Make sure you have selected the printer you intend to print to; use PDF or XPS for testing the results.

Toggle the Page Break preview when your diagram is split up on several pieces of paper to ensure that your drawing will print correctly.

Use the fields for printable header and footer information to make printed materials identifiable.

Select output by pages or by zooming into a drawing and then using Print Current View.

Save ink and toner by not printing backgrounds.

PART III

ADVANCED

IN THIS CHAPTER

- How can I email a Visio diagram?
- How does SkyDrive help me keep my drawings available?
- Getting your diagrams out on the interweb.
- Save your diagrams into other formats without jumping through hoops.

12

SHARING VISIO DIAGRAMS

In the social world where we live, sharing has become a common part of our daily life. Whether it is a shared picture of someone's Mexican dinner plate or a status update on a friend's Facebook page, we have grown accustomed to sharing and being shared with. Visio provides lots of ways to share your work and even to make content that can be imported into other applications and media. This chapter considers how you can be a giver in sharing.

Share Drawings Using Email

I remember a person who would send me huge, bloated emails with PrintScrn screenshots that included the display from his multiple displays whenever he had a question. Although it is nice to see what others are seeing sometimes, this is not the most efficient way to share Visio drawings using email, especially if a drawing contains multiple pages.

Sharing your drawings in Visio is not only possible, but Visio gives you an intuitive interface to do so. After you create and save your drawing, you can open the File tab and select Share. Notice the options for Share: Invite People, Post to Social Networks, and Email. Select Email and you see the options displayed in Figure 12.1.

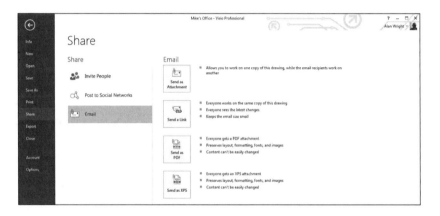

FIGURE 12.1

There are many ways to email drawings from Visio.

Four choices may be grayed out or enabled, depending on where you have saved your drawing:

- Send as Attachment opens a new email with your drawing attached as a VSDX document; the default subject line is the document name. Just add contacts to the To and CC fields and click Send. This is an independent copy, and any changes made after sending are not synced.

- Send a Link opens a new email with a link to your drawing; the default subject line is the document name.vsdx. Just add contacts to the To and CC fields and click Send. This link allows for the availability of a fresh, up-to-date copy.

- Send as PDF opens a new email with your drawing attached as a PDF document; the default subject line is the document name. Just add contacts to the To and CC fields and click Send.

- Send as XPS opens a new email with your drawing attached as an XPS document; the default subject line is the document name. Just add contacts to the To and CC fields and click Send.

 NOTE Sending a link does not mean that all recipients are able to open the drawing. It is common for corporate networks to restrict access to files located on a server to a minimum number of users. Permissions for some may be set to read-only access, which makes editing impossible. If you have questions about or trouble with a shared link to a file, consult with your network administrator to determine if permissions or rights need to be modified to access the drawing or if a different network location is recommended.

If your email recipients only need to see the drawing, consider sending it as a PDF or XPS formatted attachment. Both are common formats, and you can usually expect others to have the software needed to open and view. The format is preserved, and the recipient sees the drawing as it is meant to be seen.

If you need the recipient to make changes to or edit the drawing, a link or a copy of the VSDX file is the better choice.

Many email servers enforce size limits on attachments and may block the attachment from an email if it is too large. Also, sending large files to multiple individuals may be frowned upon in general because of the impact this has on network performance and email storage policies. Depending on the recipients and the reason for sending a copy, a link may be a better option.

Visio Viewer

Although it would be great if everyone had Visio, individuals and companies are forced to keep a close eye on resources and target Visio licenses to those persons who really need to work with Visio drawings on a regular basis. As a result, your generosity may put others into a difficult situation; if they don't have the Visio software, they won't be able to open a VSDX formatted file. Point them to Microsoft Visio Viewer 2013, a free application provided by Microsoft. Even if they have an older version, the newer version provides better results, and they need it for the new Visio file format. Search for the Viewer or use this link:

http://www.microsoft.com/en-us/download/details.aspx?id=35811

After downloading and running to install the Viewer, users must accept the Software License Terms and click Continue, as shown in Figure 12.2.

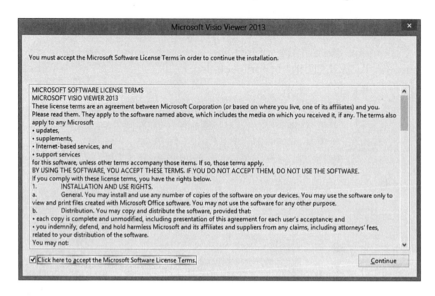

FIGURE 12.2

Visio Viewer 2013 is free; you just accept the terms of usage to install.

After installing Visio Viewer 2013, you are able to open Visio drawings and view them in Internet Explorer. You can navigate through tabbed pages, view comments, and selectively view layers. You can also select shapes and view shape properties. Visio Viewer installs to enable Visio files to be previewed in Windows Explorer and Outlook. Figure 12.3 shows how Visio Viewer is using Internet Explorer to show the drawing with the address bar and no tabbed ribbon interface.

SkyDrive

A new standard feature in Office 2013 and Windows 8 products is the prominence given to the cloud-based SkyDrive. Visio is no exception to this, and you benefit from examining how this service facilitates sharing.

Make sure the drawing you open is saved to a SkyDrive location. From the File tab, select Share and then select Invite People. You are able to choose from your contacts and select the level of access they are granted, as shown in Figure 12.4. You can type a message to include with the link to the file saved in your SkyDrive. Select Share to send the invitation to your recipients.

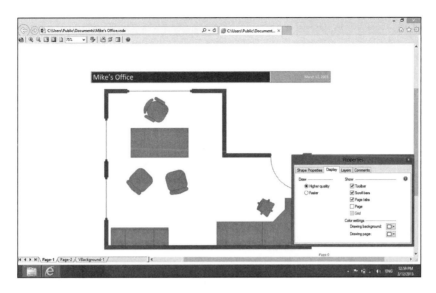

FIGURE 12.3

Visio Viewer 2013 allows you to see Visio drawings and inspect various elements of the drawing.

FIGURE 12.4

It is very easy to grant access to a file you have saved to your SkyDrive.

In the lower section you see Shared With, which shows who currently has access to this file and the level of access granted. To modify this, right-click a name and you can change or remove access, as shown in Figure 12.5.

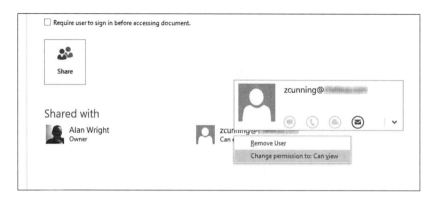

FIGURE 12.5

You can administer access to shared files from the Share backstage area in Visio.

 TIP SkyDrive allows you to easily share files with others; however, remember that SkyDrive allows you to access the same files from any computer or device with Internet access. As a result, you may find it useful to copy or save drawings and stencils to your SkyDrive for easy access from multiple computers you log in to.

Social Networks

Depending on where you have saved your drawing, you may see the option to Post to Social Networks included in the Share backstage area, as shown back in Figure 12.1 If you have added accounts from social network sites, you may be able to see options to post; if not, you are invited to add accounts to your LiveID, as shown in Figure 12.6.

When selecting Post to Social Networks, you are presented with the options to permit view or edit permission and include comments. You can select Post to send the drawing off to the indicated social network site (see Figure 12.7).

 CAUTION Be very careful when using this feature. When information is posted to a social network site it can be difficult to undo. There may be corporate confidentiality or intellectual property policies to take into consideration. Also, depending on how you have allowed these sites to share information you have posted, it may available to more persons than you had intended.

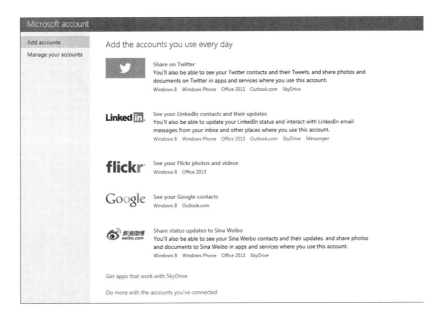

FIGURE 12.6

You can associate other social network accounts to your LiveID to enable more share options.

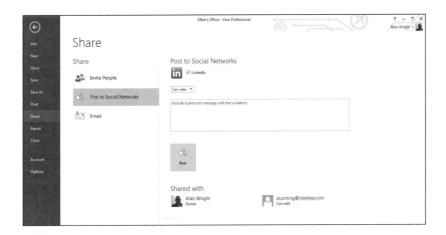

FIGURE 12.7

You can post your Visio drawings to some social network sites from Visio.

Creating a Web Page from Your Diagram

A nice way to use Visio is in the design of web content. The process for a department to get an intranet website designed and working usually depends on a number of factors. Visio enables you to not only design a mockup of a website for layout and planning, you can go as far as publishing web pages.

Notice how a simple employee benefits page can be set up using standard shapes with hyperlinks added and a background applied in Figure 12.8.

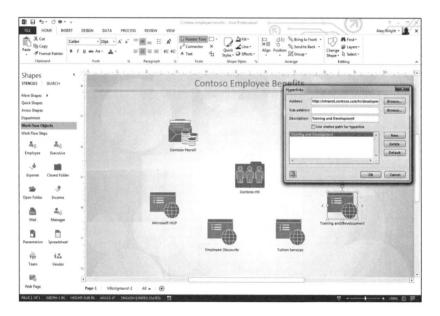

FIGURE 12.8

You can design diagrams and drawings for web pages using standard Visio shapes.

When you are happy with the drawing, open the File tab and select Export, Change File Type, and Web Page (see Figure 12.9). This enables you to create a web page that can be saved locally or at a network location. The final result is shown in Figure 12.10.

Web pages created from Visio have vector-based images, which means that you have no degradation issues when zooming in. Some obstacles and limitations exist when using Visio as a web page publisher that make it unrealistic as a website design platform; however, if you need to design specific pages that include diagrams or simple links with high-quality graphics, take time to experiment with Visio web page and publish tools to determine if these meet your needs.

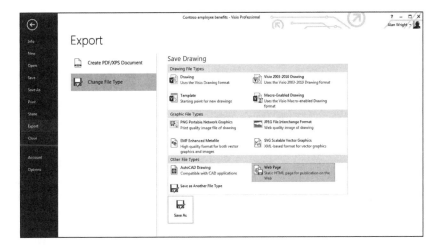

FIGURE 12.9

From Visio you can export drawings as web pages.

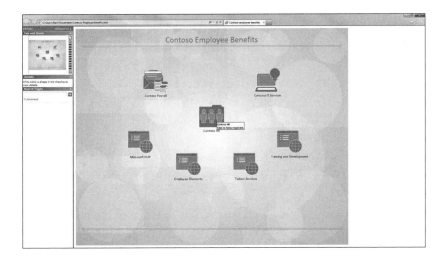

FIGURE 12.10

When Visio saves a web page, an instance opens automatically, allowing you to review the results.

Saving to Other File Formats from Visio

Chapter 3, "Working with Basic Diagrams," considered the importance of saving your diagrams, specifically using the new VSDX format. Although this default Visio drawing format is what you will likely use for day-to-day drawings, some situations might have you scrambling to save to a different format. This section considers some of the formats available and why you might use them.

Creating PDF and XPS Files

In Chapter 11, "Printing Visio Diagrams," you considered the advantages of printing to PDF or XPS formats so as to test results and minimize paper and toner waste. There are also other valid reasons to use these formats.

In this chapter when you looked at Share options, Send as PDF and XPS were two of your options. These formats allow you to create static, easily viewable copies of your drawing that maintain the appearance and formatting you have painstakingly put together. You can email and archive PDF and XPS files and refer back to them if things have changed in the actual drawings. Text remains text, and each shape can maintain one usable hyperlink.

To save a drawing into one of these formats, open the File tab, select Save As, and choose a location. In the Save As window, choose the format from the Save As Type, as shown in Figure 12.11.

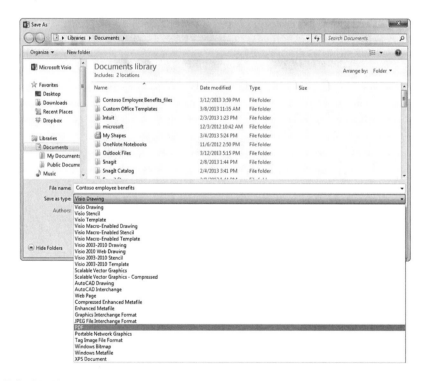

FIGURE 12.11

Use Save As to select a format when saving a Visio drawing.

XML Formatted Drawings

As late as Visio 2010, it was possible to save a Visio drawing using an XML format. That is no longer possible with Visio 2013. Because VSDX is XML-based, it was decided that a separate XML save option would lead to confusion. Files previously saved as VDX (drawing), VSX (stencil), and VTX (template) can be opened by Visio 2013.

Older Visio Formats

It is not possible to save to the Visio 2002 format (or older) from Visio 2013. If you are working with persons who are using older versions of Visio, you can use Save As to save your work to a 2003–2010 drawing format (VSD), as shown in Figure 12.11.

To make the 2003–2010 your default save format, open the File tab, select Options, and in the Visio Options window select the Save tab. Here you can change the drop-down option Save Files in This Format from Visio Document to Visio 2003–2010 Document, as shown in Figure 12.12.

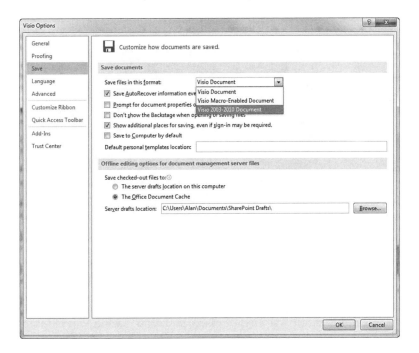

FIGURE 12.12

You can change the default save format if you regularly need to save work with the older VSD format.

Getting Visio Drawings into Other Applications

Visio provides the tools to make great visuals that can be used in websites, documents, presentations, and many other applications that you may work with. What is the best way to get your Visio content into these other forms of media? This section answer that question.

Office Applications

Visio is considered part of the Microsoft Office line of products; therefore, it shares the ribbon interface and many other common elements. This enables you to work with Visio content easily from other Office applications as long as Visio is installed on the same computer. Consider an example using PowerPoint 2013.

Notice in Figure 12.13 that you can insert an object into a PowerPoint slide. I have chosen a Visio drawing that I want to insert into the slide. In Figure 12.14 the diagram from Visio appears as one large selected object that I can move and resize.

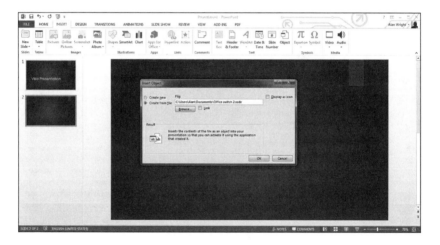

FIGURE 12.13

You can insert objects into Office products and choose Visio diagrams.

From PowerPoint you can double-click the selected Visio object; you are presented with the familiar Visio tools and ribbon, as shown in Figure 12.15. From here you can add content or otherwise modify the Visio diagram from within PowerPoint.

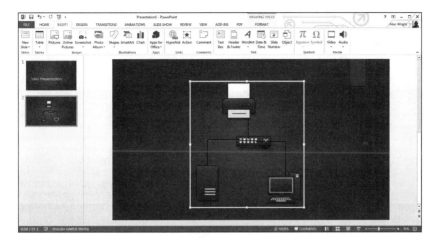

FIGURE 12.14

Visio objects can be moved and resized easily within other Office applications.

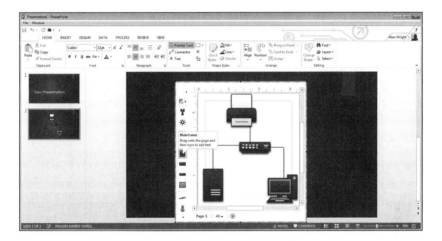

FIGURE 12.15

You can edit Visio diagrams from within other Office products.

NOTE Even if Visio is closed, when you edit a Visio object from within another Office application the Visio.exe process is running in the background. There may be an initial pause or performance hit because of this, depending on your system.

Maintaining a Theme

Because Visio shares many common elements with other Office products, it should be no surprise that the new themes in Visio can be complemented in other Office products. In the examples shown in the previous section, both PowerPoint and Visio had the same Ion theme applied, which makes for a nice combination if you could see the figures in color. Besides Ion, the themes Integral, Slice, and Organic are others you can share in the 2013 Office themes.

➜ To learn more about Themes, see page **72**.

TIP If you want to match the theme used in an Office application but are unable to find the same theme in Visio, try using variants in both applications until you find a close combination. Office 2013 introduced many new themes, and although many are not exact matches to the new Visio themes, the variants allow for some close matches.

Other Applications

The easiest way to bring Visio content into other applications is to copy and paste. Because there are so many applications, it is impractical to describe all the ins and outs of using the Copy and Paste features effectively.

A general rule is that Paste inserts a graphical copy of the source. So a shape or diagram from Visio is a bitmap picture that you may be able to resize into the target application.

Many applications have a Paste Special option that may allow you to retain some of the properties from Visio. Experiment a bit and see if you are happy with the results.

Exporting Drawings to Image Formats

You have seen already how Visio allows you to export drawings and save them into other formats such as PDF or XPS. Notice in Figure 12.16 some of the other formats available in the Graphic File Types section. To get to this screen, select the File tab, then Export.

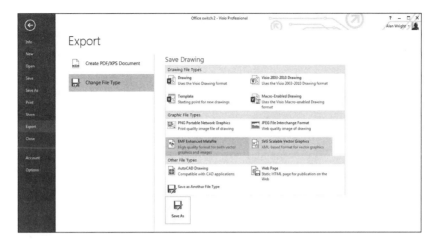

FIGURE 12.16

You can export drawings into several standard graphic formats.

Common graphic output formats are the following:

- **PNG**—This format is often favored for websites and is similar to JPEG. You can assign a color to be transparent (see Figure 12.17). It is a raster format that prints well.

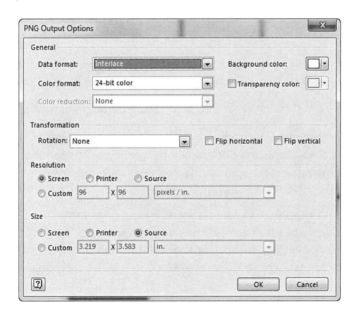

FIGURE 12.17

You can select how the image is saved as a PNG formatted image.

- **JPEG**—This has been a longtime standard raster format for photographs because it compresses the image into a small size with minimal loss of detail. It is also used for website images or graphics that are displayed on a screen.

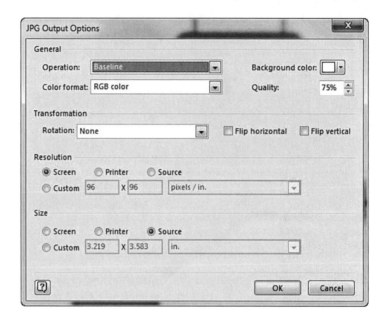

FIGURE 12.18

Similar to PNG image options, JPEG images allow for quality and color format choices.

- **EMF**—This format is vector based. It is favored for true color and quality printing.
- **SVG**—This XML format is a widely used, standard vector-based format.

Remember that raster-formatted images use a grid of pixels to re-create the image. Because of this they degrade when enlarged, becoming *pixelated*. Common image viewers open JPEG images easily; however, they might not recognize the PNG format as readily.

Vector-based graphics re-create images based on vectors that allow them to maintain sharp lines and colors. They are better suited for high-quality printing and play better with certain applications. If in doubt, consult the help section of the application you are using to see which format is recommended for importing graphics.

THE ABSOLUTE MINIMUM

Use the Share option to quickly create and prepare an email to send drawings from Visio. Remember that file size can be an issue when sending attachments, so consider the advantages to sending a link to a location your email recipients are able to access.

SkyDrive is a great feature that gives you access to your drawings or stencils saved there from other computers you use. Take the time to understand the options sharing a file from your SkyDrive presents.

Export from the File tab provides you with many options for converting your drawings. Consider how periodic PDF or XPS copies might be a way to chronicle changes made to flowcharts or diagrams that tend to evolve over time. Humans tend to be creatures of habit, so take a little time to understand how alternative graphic formats might serve you better when you need to import Visio work into another application.

13

IN THIS CHAPTER

- How will a touchscreen allow me to reach out and touch Visio 2013?
- How can I create my own templates?
- How can I avoid print nightmares when printing tiled Visio drawings?
- How can I avoid problems by looking before I print multipage drawings?

UNIQUE NEEDS: TOUCHSCREENS, CUSTOM TEMPLATES, AND COMPLEX PRINTING CONCERNS

It is increasingly common to use touchscreens when working with applications and software, but finding your way around the Visio touch interface is a unique situation. This chapter looks at the ways tools have been modified in Visio 2013 to facilitate touch.

Businesses and organizations have unique needs and standards. When preparing Visio content, you can save lots of time by preparing your own templates to reflect the colors, logos, and other standards that set your organization apart.

In this chapter, you look at how to print tiled print jobs with a minimum of fuss and consider other suggestions for simplifying your complex printing needs.

Touchscreens

Tablets and touchscreens are not new; however, it is only with Windows 7 and Windows 8 that you are seeing equipment that works well with true multitouch input devices. Some tablets can run Windows 8 Professional, which makes them a viable option in corporate environments where security has always been a concern and full professional versions of the Windows operating system now allow network administrators to manage tablets as they would any other computer. As a result of these factors, Office 2013 products have included special touchscreen interface tools.

Switching Between Touch Mode and Mouse Mode

If you have Visio 2013 installed on a touchscreen device, you likely have the Touch Mode enabled by default. This is a special mode that dramatically changes your tools layout to facilitate the touch interface. Notice Figure 13.1 has a normal layout.

FIGURE 13.1

Touch mode should be visible on your Quick Access toolbar; if not, enable the Touch/Mouse Mode control by selecting it.

To reveal the Touch mode, you may need to first select it in the Quick Access toolbar, as shown in Figure 13.1. It appears in the bar and enables you to easily switch between Mouse mode and Touch mode, as you can see in Figure 13.2. As you can see, the ribbon is bigger and the spacing between buttons is increased. This allows you to avoid selecting the wrong command when using your finger.

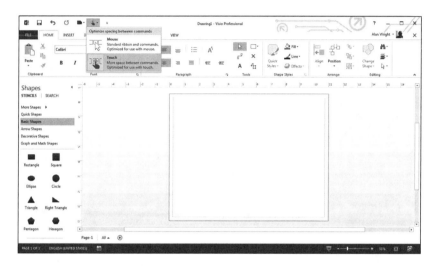

FIGURE 13.2

Quickly jump between Touch mode and Mouse mode from the Quick Access toolbar.

 NOTE When you jump between Touch mode and Mouse mode, the change affects all Office 2013 applications. Closing Visio 2013 does not toggle the mode, so it is important to understand the behavior. The same behavior is true if you switch modes in a different Office application, such as Excel 2013. Visio's interface switches as well.

Working with Shapes

Working with shapes is easy and intuitive when using a touchscreen. Touch to select a shape in your stencil and then drag it over with a finger to place on your drawing, as shown in Figure 13.3. You can draw shapes freehand and even fine-tune shapes when resizing, just as you would with a mouse. Many of the tools in Visio assist with moving and resizing with touch and provide visual cues and snap positioning.

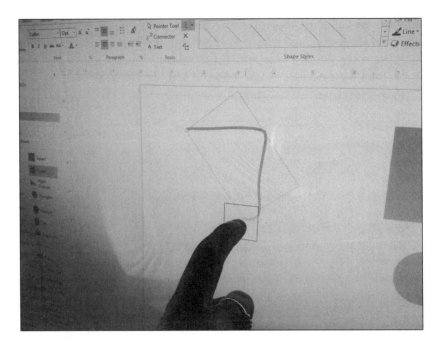

FIGURE 13.3

Using just touch, you can easily add shapes from stencils, draw freehand shapes, or resize shapes.

Selecting multiple shapes is easy if you hold the Ctrl key and touch multiple shapes and connectors, as shown in Figure 13.4. You can also touch and hold an object, and then select additional objects by touch while holding the first one.

General Touch Controls

Menus and controls are often sensitive to touch. If you open a context menu, sometimes called a minibar, using a mouse while in Touch mode, a standard menu appears because Visio knows a mouse click was used. However, if you open the same minibar using touch, the layout has the same generous spacing as seen in the tabs. Figure 13.5 shows how these context menus or minibars appear when triggered by a touch.

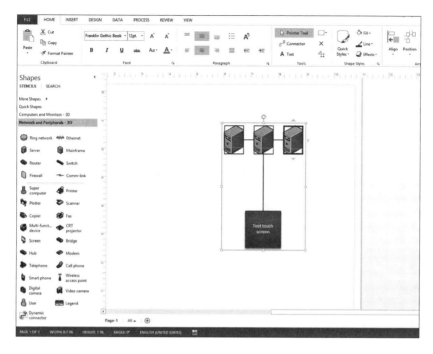

FIGURE 13.4

Hold the Ctrl key to select multiple shapes using touch.

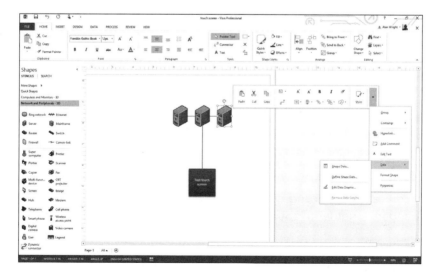

FIGURE 13.5

Don't worry about having large fingers; touch-sensitive menus have plenty of space between options.

Even menus that are opened from the ribbon interface behave this way. A mouse-click opens the normal tightly spaced interface, whereas Figure 13.6 shows touch-friendly spacing for selecting colors.

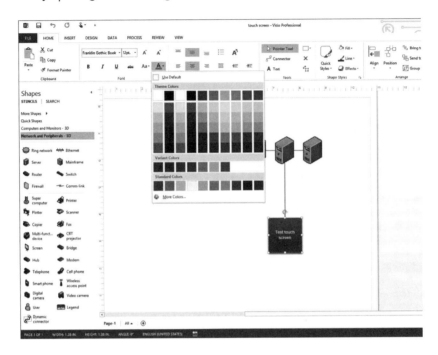

FIGURE 13.6

Menus that open after being selected by touch are easy to work with.

Working with text is easy, too. Select a shape with text, and touch again to enter Text mode. You see a control handle with a round blue circle below the text. Touch and drag the handle to highlight the text you want to edit, as shown in Figure 13.7. In the minibar that appears, you see basic text editing tools.

You can use other common gestures to interact with applications using a touchscreen; these actions also work in Visio:

- You can zoom in and out by using two fingers at the same time. Pinch two fingers together to zoom out; spread the fingers apart to zoom in.

- You can scroll by swiping up/down or left/right in a scrollable area.

- Tap to get the results of a single mouse click.

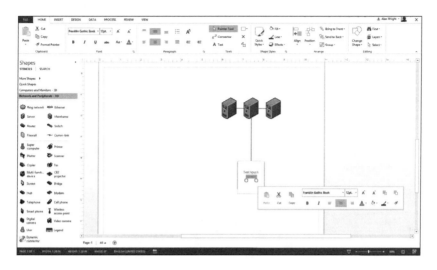

FIGURE 13.7

Use control handles to touch and drag to select text you want to edit.

- Double-tap is the equivalent of a double-click.

- To simulate a right-click with a mouse, press and hold a couple of seconds. A black square box can often be seen to let you know Visio displays right-click content when you remove your finger.

The Touch Keyboard

Windows has improved the touch keyboard with Windows 8. If you use or plan to use a touch keyboard occasionally when working with Visio, use the keyboard designed specifically for the operating system. Figure 13.8 shows the keyboard for Windows 8. Notice the button on the taskbar that brings up the keyboard as needed. In many situations the keyboard is present when text entry is expected. Another nice feature in Windows 8 is that it shifts your text field on the screen so that the keyboard does not obscure what you are typing. When you finish with the keyboard, you can tap outside of the text field, and the keyboard minimizes back to the taskbar. Otherwise, use the Close button (X) to close the keyboard.

FIGURE 13.8

Windows 8 has a very nice touch keyboard.

Creating Your Very Own Template

Chapter 3, "Working with Basic Diagrams," looked at templates and stated that they basically provide an advanced starting point for drawings. When creating new drawings, rather than starting from a blank page or using a close-enough template, you may find it easier to address your unique needs by creating and saving your own templates. This enables you to include content and other settings that fit with the distinctive standards of your organization. Custom templates save you time when you often use the same basic settings and tools and want these available when starting new drawings.

With a template you can save the following:

- Page size and scale settings

- Window size

- Shape stencils and styles

- Color palette

- Settings for snap, layers, and glue

- Print preferences

- Backgrounds and logos

When you want to create a custom template, follow these steps:

1. Open a drawing you have already created, or start a new drawing with one of the templates that you would like to modify. Any content on the pages becomes part of the template, so remove shapes and content you do *not* want to include.

2. Open any custom stencils that you have created, or open additional ones that you want to include in this template. Close any stencils you do not need (see Figure 13.9).

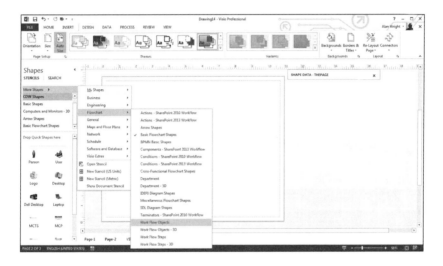

FIGURE 13.9

Add your own choices for stencils to your template.

3. Open the Page Setup dialog box and verify the settings you want to include in this stencil. Note especially the Print Setup and Layout and Routing tabs (see Figure 13.10).

4. Select a theme from the Theme gallery, or better yet, customize the color palette for this template to match your company colors.

5. If you want to include basic elements on your pages, create a background page. Add options like text fields, a company logo, or background image, as shown in Figure 13.11.

6. Open any task panes that you want to have available when working with this template.

7. Open the File menu, and click Save As.

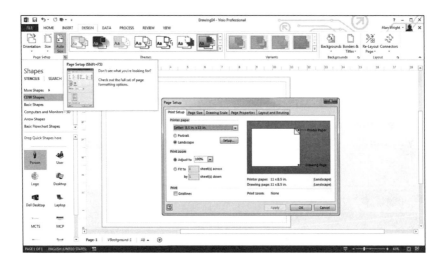

FIGURE 13.10

Make sure you have the correct properties selected for printing and layout in the Page Setup dialog box.

FIGURE 13.11

You can add elements to your background page that you want to include in pages by default.

8. Type a name for your template and make sure you change the Save as Type to Visio Template (see Figure 13.12).

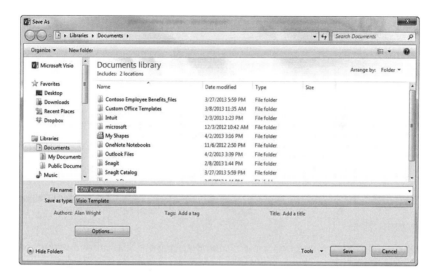

FIGURE 13.12

Choose Visio Template to save your creation to the VSTX template format.

9. Select the location where you want to save your template and then click Save.

To test your template, close Visio. When you next open Visio you likely see the template listed under Recent content. You can pin your new template to the Recent list by right-clicking and enabling the pin. Double-click to open the template file. Figure 13.13 shows the results of opening the template just saved in the previous steps.

➜ To learn more about templates, see page **42**.

➜ To learn more about creating a custom theme, see page **73**.

➜ To learn more about creating personalized stencils, see page **91**.

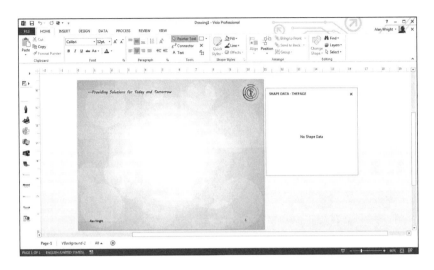

FIGURE 13.13

New drawings that you open from your template have all the groundwork done that you included in your template.

A Look at Complex and Multipage Print Jobs

Chapter 11, "Printing Visio Diagrams," covers most common types of single-page print jobs; however, at times you may need to print large diagrams across several pages (called tiled drawings), or you may have issues when you need to print multipage drawings that have different page orientations and settings. This section considers those unique scenarios as well as how to quickly combine Visio pages for printing.

Printing Tiled Drawings

I doubt anyone *likes* to print tiled drawings. It would be so much nicer to have a huge color plotter that could print laminated diagrams with a simple click to the Print button. Alas, that is not an option for most of us. Anticipating this situation, Visio allows you to manage tiled print jobs with a minimum of fuss.

Notice in Figure 13.14 that a large diagram has been created. It is practical when working on large print diagrams to ensure that page breaks are visible. Enable this visual aid from the View tab in the Show tool set. In this case it looks like some shapes were placed right where the pages split.

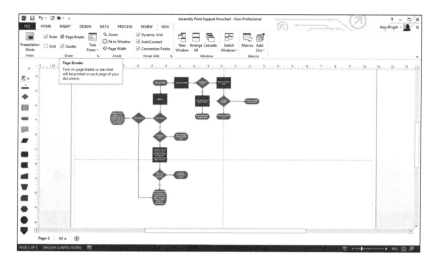

FIGURE 13.14

Enable Page Breaks from the View tab to aid you in planning your printed diagram.

Another aid is the Print Preview pane. To consult this, open the File tab and choose Print. You can see in Figure 13.15 that the shapes are indeed split up at the page break. Does this mean you need to rearrange everything? Or do you need to move shapes around to find the least-bad page split option?

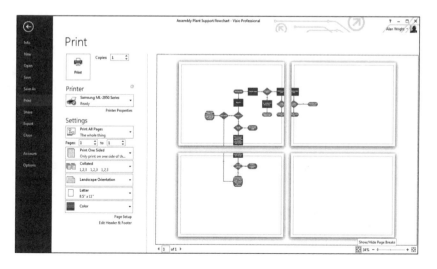

FIGURE 13.15

Check how the actual print job will look by consulting the Print Preview pane.

TIP   Don't panic if you see only dotted lines indicating page breaks and do not see separate pages when using Print Preview. Use the Show/Hide Page Breaks button that is unlabeled down to the left of the zoom controls at the bottom of the Print Preview screen. You can see this displayed in Figure 13.15. Click to toggle this visual effect.

You can fix this with a simple click. From the Home tab, expand the Position button, and select Move Off Page Breaks. Figure 13.16 shows how the diagram is automatically adjusted to avoid problems caused by page breaks.

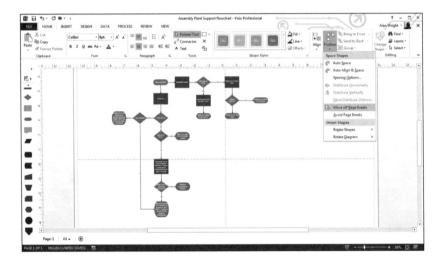

FIGURE 13.16

Correct the positioning of shapes in your diagram using the Move off Page Breaks tool.

Using Page Scale

If you need to change the size of a drawing for printing, you have a couple of ways to manually dictate the print scale without altering your drawing.

CAUTION   Be aware that using these techniques to print using a different scale will affect drawings that rely on scale. Plans may be rendered to show that each quarter inch is equal to a foot, for example. Changing the print scale to 90 percent of the drawing negates the accuracy of the drawing scale. A visual scale symbol or legend can, therefore, be a practical element to include in plans. You might also consider including a disclaimer in altered printed copies to avoid confusion.

To shrink a large diagram to force it to print on a single page:

1. Open the Page Setup dialog box by right-clicking the page tab from the drawing window, or select the Page Setup link from the bottom of the Print options.

2. In the Print Zoom area of the Print Setup tab, select Fit To; notice in Figure 13.17 that the default of 1 sheet across and 1 sheet down are filled in already. Notice also to the right that your drawing page has different dimensions than the printer paper. Click OK.

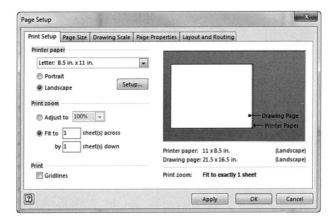

FIGURE 13.17

You can determine how many sheets are used in your print job from the Print Setup tab.

Consult your Print Preview to verify the results before you print. Because large diagrams are scaled down to fit onto a single page, you may not be able to read the text. You can select different values for sheets across and sheets down and use the previous suggestions for working with tiled drawings to fix any page break issue that you may see.

The second way to use scale is to select a scale percentage:

1. Open the Page Setup dialog box by right-clicking the Page tab from the drawing window, or select the Page Setup link from the bottom of the Print options.

2. In the Print Zoom area of the Print Setup tab, change the value of Adjust To from 100% to a larger or smaller value. You can select from a drop-down list or type in a value as shown in Figure 13.18. Notice that the Print Setup preview shows that page breaks are used. Click OK.

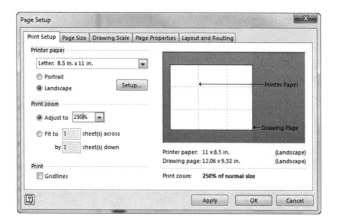

FIGURE 13.18

Use a scale percentage to fine-tune the size of the printed diagram.

Check your layout and use the suggestions for correcting page break issues noted previously in "Printing Tiled Drawings."

Using Avoid Page Breaks

When working with many diagram types, you might use the Auto Align or Auto Space options to clean up a diagram. If you plan to print the diagram, it is good to enable the Avoid Page Breaks tool. This ensures that these tools respect page breaks when doing their magic. Figure 13.19 shows the beginnings of a messy flowchart. Notice that the Avoid Page Breaks option has been enabled after selecting the Positions button. Figure 13.20 shows how the Auto Align feature fixes the alignment issues and avoids the page break.

➡ To learn more about using tools like Auto Space and Auto Align, see page **108**.

Printing Mixed Orientation Drawings

Visio manages the printing of drawings at the page level. This allows you to have a variety of pages in a single Visio file that can have very different settings. This is not all that unusual because many people include supplementary pages with close ups, secondary information for a large diagram, title pages, backgrounds, and titles and header fields all in the same Visio drawing file.

When printing, make sure that the print settings for each page give you satisfactory results. If all your pages are combined into a handout at a meeting, you may not want landscape and portrait orientations. Paper sizes may have been set differently for one page than the rest, and this may present additional problems if the printer you send this to cannot handle one or more paper sizes.

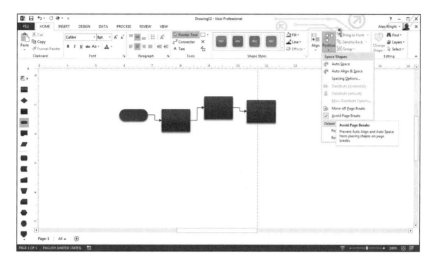

FIGURE 13.19

Enable Avoid Page Breaks to avoid issues later when printing your diagram.

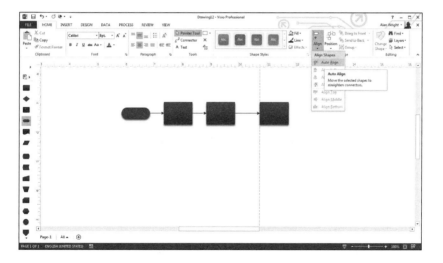

FIGURE 13.20

The Avoid Page Breaks tool adds awareness to the Spacing and Positioning tools which influences how tools like Auto-Align move shapes around a page break.

Besides consulting the page setup properties for each page, the Print Preview feature can be especially helpful because you can browse through your pages and even zoom in and out to verify that pages are set up correctly. The Settings area in the Print window reflects the settings for the specific page previewed. Figure 13.21 shows that page 3 has a landscape orientation, and the paper size indicated is A4. This is a problem because that printer handles only letter-size paper right now.

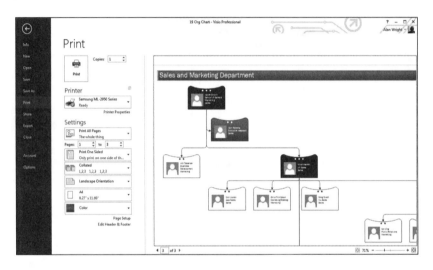

FIGURE 13.21

Use Print Preview to check your print values for each page before you print.

Combine Drawings into a Single Sheet

I have always liked the feature in Power Point that allows you to print master or handout notes so that you can keep presentation notes along with smaller versions of slides. I have also seen times when a page from one Visio drawing had content that would be nice to quickly add to another Visio file before printing. You can likely think of other times you have wanted to quickly combine pages or content into a single printed Visio page.

In Visio, there are a few ways to accomplish this. The most common method employed is usually copy and paste, which you may have used with good or bad results. It can be unpredictable at times, and you might wind up fighting with format and automatic alignment settings before you can print.

If you intend to print, you might be especially pleased with the results of exporting and inserting images. Figure 13.22 shows the results of using Export to save two

Visio drawing pages to the EMF Enhanced Metafile graphic file format. These were then inserted using the Pictures button located on the Insert tab. Notice that when selected, you see a contextual Picture Tools tab because these are image files. This format works well for resizing, and you can then position and add additional shapes or text before printing.

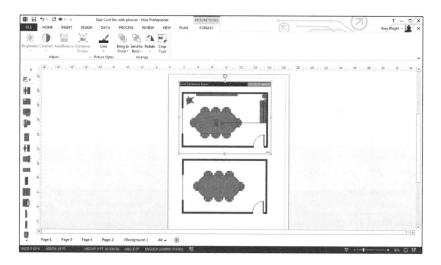

FIGURE 13.22

Use Export and Insert to combine images of pages of Visio content with minimal effort.

→ To learn more about Exporting to graphic file formats, see page **240**.

THE ABSOLUTE MINIMUM

Touchscreens are finally valid input devices, and you might be surprised how nice they can be to use with Visio. Make sure you know how to switch between Mouse mode and Touch mode. Sometimes a mouse still provides better control when you're doing delicate work, but don't feel like everything needs to be done with a mouse. Using gestures and the new menu layouts, it is very easy to do most common tasks by touch. Experiment and decide which works best for you.

Touch controls often need an initial touch to select an item and then a *second* touch to move or interact with a control handle. This can take some getting used to when a click-and-drag combination has been your custom, but you will quickly get used to the touch interface.

Templates are valuable tools allowing you to quickly get started on Visio drawings. If you have not done so already, take the time to create one or more custom templates if you do much work with Visio. Include custom stencils and background page content to standardize your drawings.

Page breaks can be a real problem when printing diagrams across several sheets of paper. Use Print Preview to ensure this does not cause unnecessary quality issues. Use the Move Off Page Breaks tool to quickly move shapes off page breaks.

Because so many issues can go wrong, printing can be a frustrating ordeal at times. Take the time to check your pages using Print Preview and compare the settings off to the left in the Print window to the capabilities of your designated printer.

USING DATA

SmartShapes have the potential to contain an amazing amount of data called, oddly enough, shape data. Data can include names, numbers, descriptions, sizes, quantities, and so on. Imagine how much more impact your Visio drawings can wield when you understand how to use this often-hidden data.

This chapter considers how shape data is accessed and how you can put it to work. You also look at how to create your own types of shape data that enable you to capture data relevant to you and your business. Finally, you look at putting this data at your fingertips using reports.

What Can I Do with Shape Data?

Chapter 10, "Shapes: More Than Meets the Eye," discussed SmartShapes and touched on the thought of data being contained in our shapes. This section delves deeper into this characteristic and considers how you can use this capability in your diagrams.

Exploring

Examine some of the predefined shape data fields from a couple of common diagram types.

1. Open a new Basic Flowchart template.

2. Add a Start/End shape and a couple of Process shapes.

3. If not open already, select the View tab, and from the Show section select Task Panes and enable Shape Data.

4. Select one of the shapes. Notice in the Shape Data pane that there are several fields for data, such as Cost, Process Number, Owner, and so on (see Figure 14.1).

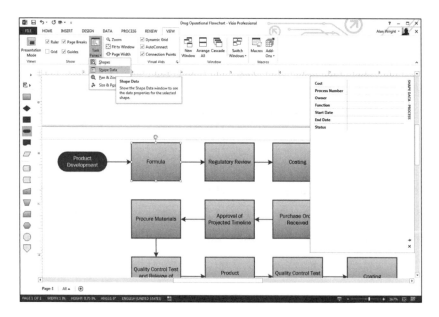

FIGURE 14.1

Shapes often have predefined fields for holding relevant data.

5. Open a new Basic Network Diagram–3D diagram template.

6. Add a router and a couple of server shapes.

7. As in step 3, select a server and look at the Shape Data pane (see Figure 14.2). Notice you can add data to many more fields that would be unique to a network server.

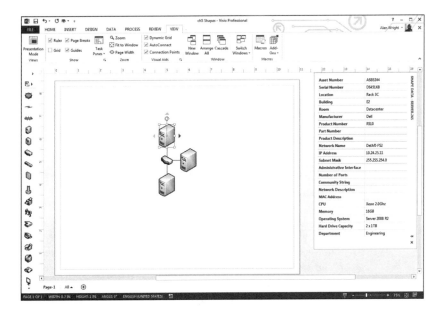

FIGURE 14.2

Shapes can have a few or many fields, depending on the anticipated usage of the diagram and shapes.

You can see in Figure 14.1 that the fields are blank. A flowchart can be used for many purposes, and some fields may be relevant and others not so much. You can manually enter the values that pertain to your flowchart, as was done in Figure 14.2. What is nice with Visio is that many fields have input controls that help you be consistent. In Figure 14.3, notice that the Status field offers five choices. You can type in text of your own choosing, but this is one way to ensure consistency. Date fields offer a navigable calendar for dates, and fields related to monetary units convert numbers into money.

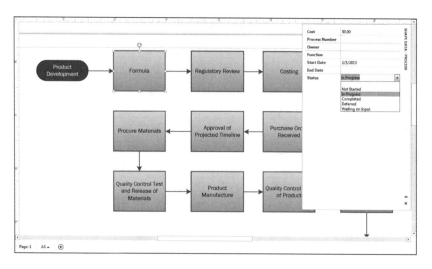

FIGURE 14.3

Many data fields have input controls to assist you.

 TIP You can select multiple shapes that are similar and edit the Shape Data fields for all selected shapes at once. For example, in Figure 14.1 a few processes might have the same owner. You could select all those shapes while holding down Ctrl and then modify the Owner field in the Shape Data pane. All selected shapes now have that owner when looked at individually.

Types and Uses

Depending on the diagram type and the shapes used, shape data can be static information that is held for reference, or it can influence the visual configuration of the shape in your diagram.

Notice in Figure 14.4 that shapes added to a floor plan have dimensional shape data revealed in the Shape Data task pane. Changing the dimensions immediately changes the size of the shape in your floor plan. This holds true for windows and doors. Most dimensional fields have input fields that reflect common standard sizes, which is again very useful.

How Can I Use Shape Data in the Real World?

If you thought in the past that Visio was a simple tool for making attractive diagrams, perhaps you start to see new ways to use Visio based on this capability to hold shape data. Building managers and office administrators often struggle with keeping track of assets. How does your company track cost, purchase dates, manufacturer, and other relevant details?

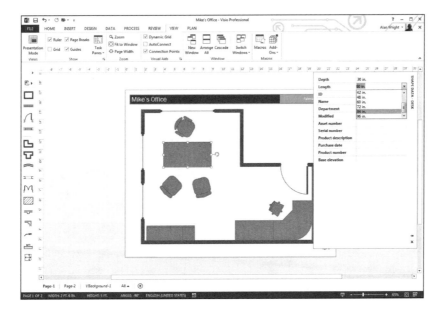

FIGURE 14.4

Shape data can also influence the way shapes are displayed in a diagram. Here, the change in shape dimensions changes the size of the desk displayed in the floor plan.

Overworked network administrators and engineers cannot memorize all the details about hardware and ownership for servers that populate their topography. Although many types of network management software exist for auditing and monitoring equipment connected to a network, this is not always an effective method for keeping tabs on company assets. Items such as part numbers, vendors, and contact information can be easily added to shape data.

Companies face the reality of losing key employees that take information that can be very time consuming to re-create. Visio enables administrators and managers to use many ways to centrally manage information that might otherwise be fragmented and lost.

Creating Shape Data Fields

Although it is nice when you find shapes that have everything predefined, at times you may have a special project or need that is not, and no SmartShapes seem to work. You can create your own Shape Data fields easily. Consider some ways to do this.

Add a Simple Data Field

Create a shape that allows you to track paint colors. It is a simple shape you can drop into a room that contains details for the room.

1. Create a new Blank Drawing.

2. Create a basic circle shape using the Home tab and drawing tools.

3. Right-click the circle and select Data, Define Shape Data as shown in Figure 14.5.

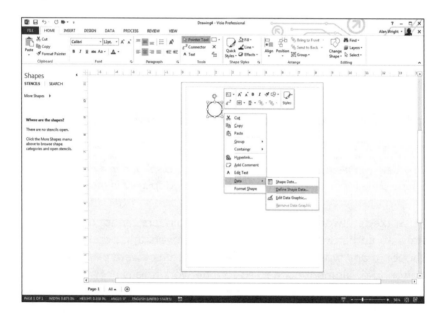

FIGURE 14.5

You can add or create new Shape Data fields using the Define Shape Data dialog box.

4. In the Define Shape Data dialog box, change the Property1 Label to Wall Color (see Figure 14.6).

5. The Type remains String; Format can be Normal; and you can input a Prompt, if you would like. Prompts present hover text when inputting information.

6. Select New and replace the Label Property2 with Gallons. The Type is Number, and Format can be General Units.

FIGURE 14.6

Customize the Shape Data fields with Label, Type, and Format choices.

7. Repeat step 6 a few more times, adding Brand, Trim, Cost, and Date Labels with appropriate type and format fields until you have something like Figure 14.7.

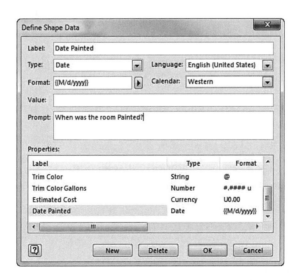

FIGURE 14.7

Add several new labels to a shape to collect the precise data you want to refer to later.

8. Select OK when you're finished, and select the shape. Make sure that the Shape Data pane is visible and you see something like Figure 14.8.

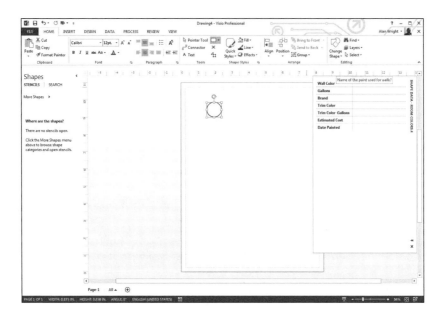

FIGURE 14.8

Work with the Define Shape Data window until you see the desired results in the Shape Data pane.

This shape can be added to a custom stencil and dropped into floor plans to hold information later, as shown in Figure 14.9.

→ To learn more about adding shapes to stencils, see page **91**.

Selecting the Correct Data Type

The type of data you use is an important selection to make because it determines the format of the shape data. As shown in Figure 14.10, you can choose from eight types of data.

- String data refers to text; it can be formatted as normal, uppercase, or lowercase.

- Number data can be a whole number, a number with units of measurement, or decimal points; fractions can also be included in the formatting.

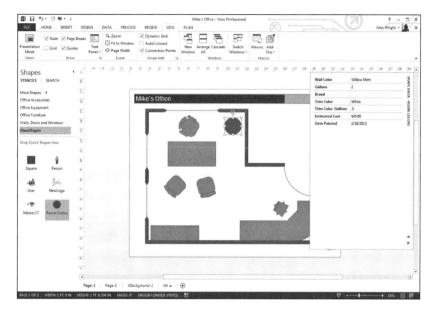

FIGURE 14.9

Shapes that you have customized can be added to diagrams from your custom stencil sets.

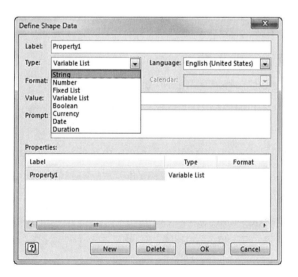

FIGURE 14.10

It is important to select the correct type of data you want to add to your shape.

- Fixed List refers to a drop-down list that you establish with no choice for indicating anything outside of the list.

- Variable List includes a drop-down list with the option to type in a custom entry.

- Boolean offers a simple true or false choice.

- Currency provides a few variations based on currency currently selected for the computer system.

- Date offers a calendar; however, you can type in a date and Visio presents it in the indicated format. Format can include day and time aside from the normal variations of date.

- Duration allows formatting for weeks, days, hours, minutes, seconds, and a combination of hours, minutes, and seconds.

Adding Lists and Format

Adding lists is relatively easy, and it can save time later when you know that selections for a data field fall most likely into one of a few possible options.

Use the Wall Color field that you created earlier for maintaining a log of paint colors. Imagine this is used in a set of offices that have limited colors to fit a corporate standard.

To add a fixed list, follow these steps:

1. Select the shape you created in the last example (or create a new one).

2. Right-click and select Data, Define Shape Data to open the Define Shape Data dialog box.

3. For the wall color, change the Type from String to Fixed List.

4. As shown in Figure 14.11, add the list contents to the Format field. Type list items separated using semicolons and no spaces.

5. Click OK. Notice that now the shape offers a fixed list of colors for the Wall Color field, as shown in Figure 14.12.

If you want to allow for additional choices, use the Variable List option and follow the same steps described previously. You can still have a list in the Format field, but there is the option to type in data that you could not anticipate.

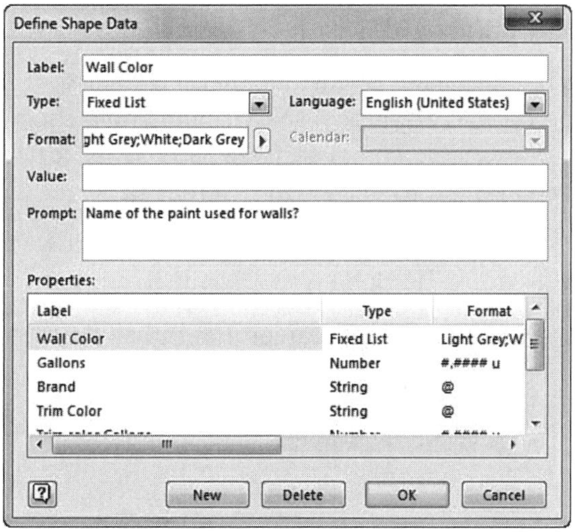

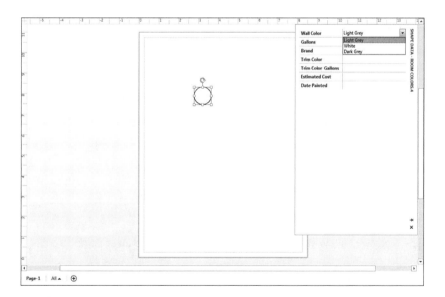

FIGURE 14.11

Add list contents to the Format field.

FIGURE 14.12

Fixed lists can save time when you are able to predetermine possible choices for shape data.

Saving a Set of Shape Data Fields

After you have created a set of custom Shape Data fields, you can save and apply the set of shape data to additional shapes. Imagine a shop that fabricates custom cabinets. A list of available colors and sizes and styles for cabinets could be created and then applied to units with different sizes.

Stick with the paint list that you created earlier and apply it to a different shape to illustrate how this would be done.

1. Select your circle shape from earlier that has all the data fields you created, and make sure the Shape Data pane is visible.

2. In the Shape Data task pane, right-click and select Shape Data Sets, as shown in Figure 14.13.

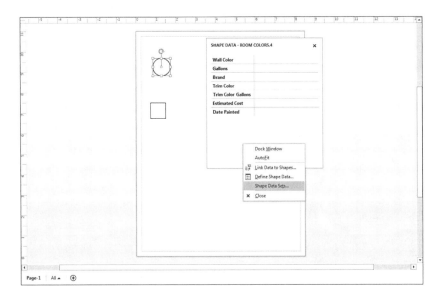

FIGURE 14.13

Shape Data Sets allow you to apply custom sets of Shape Data fields to other shapes.

3. In the Shape Data Sets pane, select Add.

4. In the Add Shape Data Set pane, type in a name for this set of data fields. Notice you are copying from the selected shape (see Figure 14.14). Click OK.

5. Create or select a different shape, and in the Shape Data Sets pane select the new set that you just created (see Figure 14.15).

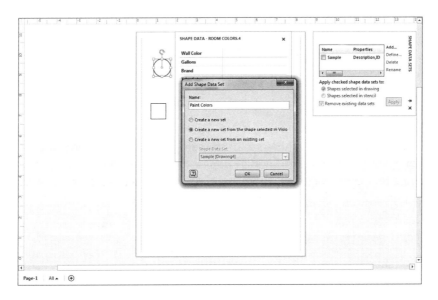

FIGURE 14.14

Add a set of shape data fields to a Visio session through the Add Shape Data Set pane.

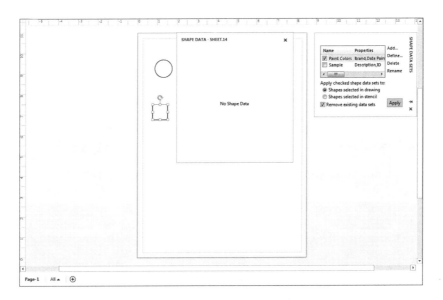

FIGURE 14.15

Shape data sets can easily be applied to other shapes, even replacing existing fields.

6. Notice the other options that are selected by default in the Shape Data Sets pane, Apply checked shape data sets to. Shapes selected in the drawing, and the Remove existing data sets. Click Apply.

7. Select and compare the original shape and the new one. They both have the same data fields.

If you close Visio, the shape data sets are not saved for the next session. You need to open a shape that has the set of shape data you created and add this set again if you want to apply to additional shapes. For this reason it is a good idea to add shapes to a custom stencil where the data fields are retained for use elsewhere. The data set can be pulled from a saved drawing as well.

Displaying Text in Shape Data Fields

Now that you know how to add data to a shape, you might find it useful to display this hidden data. For example, if you plan to print a floor plan and you would like to see the wall color choice you created earlier in this chapter, you can enable that choice easily.

1. Select a shape with shape data.

2. Select the Insert tab and select Field from the Text tool group. This will open a Field dialog box.

3. In the Category: column, select Shape Data.

4. In the Field name: column, select the data field you wish to display. In Figure 14.16, the field "Wall Color" is selected.

5. Click OK. In Figure 14.16, the shape displays the words "Willow Mint," which is the value that is held by the Wall Color field in this example.

➜ To learn more about inserting Text Fields, see page **160**.

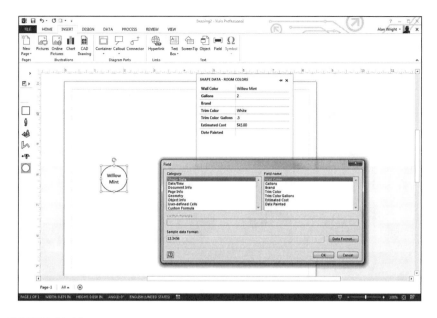

FIGURE 14.16

It is easy to display custom shape data fields as text.

Creating Reports

Visio has the capability to generate reports that summarize shape data information. This can be very useful for inventory tracking.

Using the Report Definition Wizard

To illustrate how these reports work, use the Paint Color shape from earlier in this chapter. In Figure 14.17, you can see that this shape has been added to a basic set of floor plans. Information has been filled out for each room. Now you generate a report in one place that tells you how much paint was used and the colors.

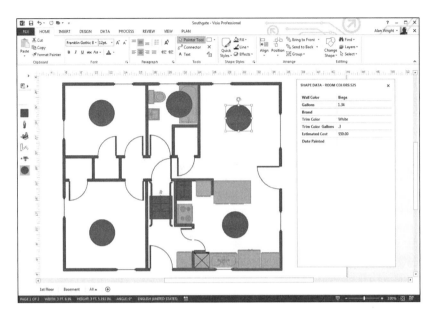

FIGURE 14.17

Visio allows you to create reports from shape data. For example, you can get a report for paint colors and costs.

Start by creating a new report using the Report Definition Wizard.

1. Open a drawing and add the Paint Color shape from earlier to a new page. A new page named Paint Report was added to the floor plans in Figure 14.18.

2. Navigate to the Review tab and select Shape Reports. In Figure 14.18 you can see the Reports dialog box that opens.

3. Select New to open the Report Definition Wizard.

4. Select Shapes on the current page. Before clicking Next, select Advanced to refine the shape data that is included in the report.

 TIP As shown in Figure 14.19, you can define reports to look at a single page from a drawing, all pages, or only selected shapes. Use the Report Definition Wizard to create or modify reports accordingly.

FIGURE 14.18

Use Shape Reports to run existing reports or create new reports to meet your needs.

5. In the Advanced dialog box, expand the drop-down labeled Property. As shown in Figure 14.19, you want to change the Condition to Exists and the Value to True for any Shape Data fields you want to include in the report. Use the Add button to add them to the Defined criteria field. Click OK when finished. If you do not refine the criteria, Visio includes many common bits of shape data criteria, and the report leaves a blank row for those properties, which needlessly clutters up the final report.

TIP   The Condition and Value fields in Figure 14.19 allow for a very flexible array of definition criteria for your report. Experiment based on the need for the report. For example, if you only want data included that has value in excess of a certain monetary amount, you select a Condition of Is Greater Than and input a Value to use for the baseline value.

6. Click Next to indicate the properties you want to see as column titles in the report. Select all the values that you want to include (see Figure 14.20).

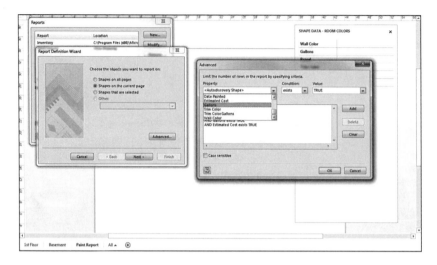

FIGURE 14.19

It is a good idea to use the Advanced dialog box to refine the report definition criteria.

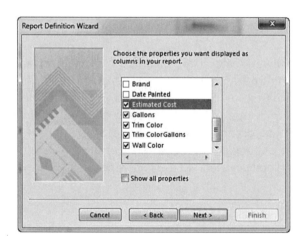

FIGURE 14.20

Select which columns of data appear in your report.

7. Type in a name for the Report Title and click Next. As shown in Figure 14.21, the next window asks you to type in a name for the saved report definition. Use the same name you typed in for the report title, and leave the option button selected for Save in this drawing. Click Finish.

FIGURE 14.21

Give your new report a name that enables you to remember its purpose.

Generating Reports

Now that you have a definition created, run the report to see how it works.

1. Go to a page in the Visio drawing and from the Review tab, select Shape Reports again. This time, select and run the report just created by clicking the Run button. In Figure 14.22 the report is named Paint Report.

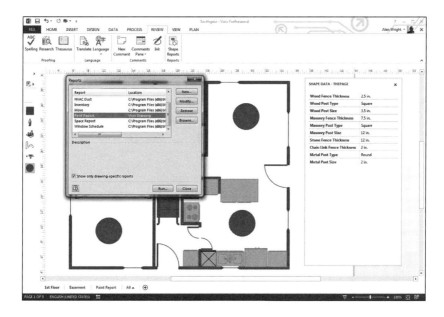

FIGURE 14.22

From the Review tab, use Shape Reports to select from available reports in the Reports dialog box.

2. In Figure 14.23 you can see that a few output options exist in the Run Report dialog box. In this case, select Excel and then click OK. (Selecting Visio Shape creates an embedded Excel spreadsheet that becomes part of the page.)

FIGURE 14.23

You can choose from several output options for your report.

3. Figure 14.24 shows the final result in an Excel spreadsheet.

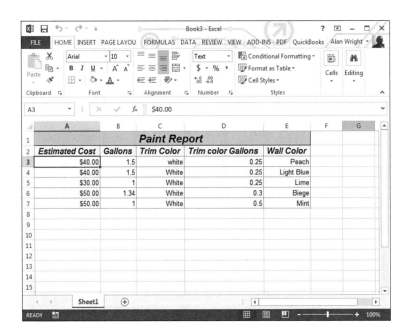

	Estimated Cost	Gallons	Trim Color	Trim color Gallons	Wall Color
	\$40.00	1.5	white	0.25	Peach
	\$40.00	1.5	White	0.25	Light Blue
	\$30.00	1	White	0.25	Lime
	\$50.00	1.34	White	0.3	Biege
	\$50.00	1	White	0.5	Mint

Paint Report

FIGURE 14.24

After a report has been generated, it can be saved or shared easily.

TIP   There are many ways that data that can be assembled using reports, and this flexibility provides you with many ways to present and use data generated in a report. You might want to include the report right in the same page. This can be useful when printing. Select your output as Visio Shape in step 2 and Link to Report Definition to get an embedded Excel spreadsheet. (An example of an embedded report is shown in Figure 14.25.)

Reports are really snapshots of shape data that you have chosen to view or that are predefined based on shapes that are in your drawing. Changes to data after a report has been run require you to rerun the report to get a new snapshot.

Adding Totals and Subtotals

Reports may be more useful when you add totals and quantities to them. You can do this easily using the Report Definition Wizard. You can modify existing reports or include this in new definitions. In Figure 14.21 you see a Subtotals button in the left pane. This opens the Subtotals dialog box shown in Figure 14.25. By adding Count and Total properties, the embedded Excel spreadsheet also shown in Figure 14.25 has calculated additional information.

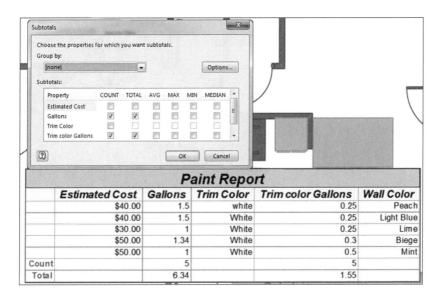

FIGURE 14.25

Visio shape reports can provide calculations based on many criteria.

THE ABSOLUTE MINIMUM

Take the time to experiment and consider how shape data can be created to capture information that is useful to you. Create shapes that fill that need and add them to your custom stencil sets so that they are available when working on similar drawings down the road.

When creating your own shape data fields consider using lists to make data entry as easy as possible. Unfortunately, harried administrators and managers tend to do the minimum when updating data, and if a list allows them to enter something quicker than typing in data, you are more likely to see compliance.

Use the Shape Data pane when working with shapes. It is a very handy way to monitor and modify shape data.

Reports are an extremely useful feature in Visio. Admittedly, it may take you some time to grasp their value. Consider the types of drawings you work with and what you want to communicate. Inventory reports, quantities, material lists, cost of assets, model numbers, and reports on business states are examples of some of the types of reports that can be generated. They can be run on flowcharts, org charts, building plans, and so on. Your imagination is the limit.

IN THIS CHAPTER

- How can I make my time count using linked external data?
- How does Automatically Link with External Data save me even more time?
- How does Refresh with My External Data save so much time I create time paradoxes?
- How can I get fancy with data graphics?
- How will customizing data graphics make my diagrams really pop?

15

WORKING WITH EXTERNAL DATA AND DATA GRAPHICS

The material in this chapter is focused on features that Visio 2013 Professional and Visio Pro for Office 365 include in the Data tab. If you have Visio 2013 Standard, you may be justifiably disappointed that these features are not included, so maybe you shouldn't read this chapter because it may create a strong desire to upgrade. If you are still curious, please continue.

Linking to external data and using data graphics are certainly capabilities that take Visio to a new level. You will be fascinated by the potential these tools bring to your diagrams, and we encourage you to experiment with these tools in your drawings. Besides saving you time, they empower individuals without Visio to influence Visio diagrams.

This chapter gives you examples of how to bring assembled data into your drawing with minimal effort on your part. You also see some ways you can use data graphics to liven up drawings and create dashboard-style elements for a diagram.

Linking Shapes to External Data

Chapter 14, "Using Data," considered a few of the ways that you can use shape data, adding data to existing fields and even customizing the fields to accept data that you want a SmartShape to hold. You also learned how you can display shape data in your drawing. This works well for many situations, but there are a few obvious issues to consider. Manually entering in this data into a Visio drawing and keeping it up to date can be tedious. In many cases, data is already prepared in a spreadsheet or database, so you could find yourself reinventing the wheel when manually adding this data to your shapes. Finally, not everyone is set up to modify Visio content on his or her computer.

Visio has enabled you to link shapes to external data for a few years now, and if you have Visio 2013 Professional, this is a great feature that you appreciate after you see how to use it. Linking can be done with several types of source data.

 NOTE The Data tab and Link to External Data tools are limited to Visio 2013 Professional versions, but both Standard and Professional include additional tools that enable you to work with external databases. The tool you use is found in the View tab— open Add-Ons from the Macros section, select Visio Extras, and then select Database Wizard. The process to set this up is quite a bit more complicated and is beyond the scope of this book.

Also, a few templates are specifically designed to work with external data, and they have wizards to help guide you through setting up the external data. Org charts are an example of this, using a wizard to simplify the importing of external data from Exchange servers or Excel spreadsheets.

Look at Your External Data First

To link data you need to look at your data source and possibly do some preparation so that the data will import easily into Visio. It is a good idea to prepare your data source with the shape data field names in mind, because this saves you time later and possibly avoids confusion. A unique key or identifier is used to match your external data to a shape data field in Visio.

To demonstrate how to use an external data source you will see examples in the following pages using data that has been prepared for a branch office. Office assignments are kept up to date in an Excel spreadsheet and stored on a network drive. This is linked with a floor plan for the branch office that was created in Visio. Figure 15.1 shows the Excel spreadsheet that has been prepared using column names that match the shape data fields in the Space shapes for a Visio floor plan. Follow the next few sections to see how to bring the data over from the spreadsheet, rather than type in all those phone numbers, names, departments, and so on.

FIGURE 15.1

Prepare your data source to match Shape data fields.

Using Link Data to Shapes

In Figure 15.1, you can see the Data tab. This section focuses first on the section labeled External Data; later in this chapter, you look at the Display Data buttons.

Follow these steps to link your data starting from the Data tab:

1. Click the Link Data to Shapes button to open the Data Selector dialog box. Select the type of data you link to, as shown in Figure 15.2. In this case, you connect to an Excel workbook. Notice some of the other data sources that can be used. Click Next.

2. Also shown in Figure 15.2, browse to the location of your data source and click Next.

3. If the worksheet or range is incorrect, use the Select Custom Range button to correct it. In this case, the Excel worksheet Space Data was identified correctly by Visio. (Compare Figure 15.3 and Figure 15.1.) Click Next.

FIGURE 15.2

Select the type and location of external data to link to.

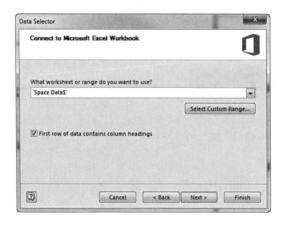

FIGURE 15.3

Select the specific worksheet to use for an external data source.

4. Next, verify which columns and rows you want to link to. Click the Select Columns or the Select Rows button to refine your choices, or leave the defaults to link to all columns and data. Figure 15.4 shows how to uncheck columns or rows that are not needed. Click Next when done here.

5. Configure Refresh Unique Identifier is where you point to the Name column shown in the spreadsheet back in Figure 15.1. Use a value you do not expect to change, because this is used as a key to cross-reference the data in the spreadsheet with the shape data fields. (These fields do not need to have the same name; it just worked out that way here.) Click Next.

6. You see a final window congratulating you for successfully importing your data. Click Finish.

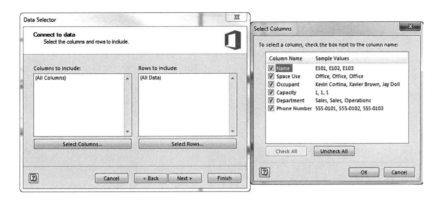

FIGURE 15.4

In the Data Selector dialog box, you can use all data or be more selective.

7. By default, your drawing window adjusts to include an external data window across the bottom. (This window can be hidden when you want to maximize the visibility of your diagram by unchecking the External Data Window checkbox from the Data tab.) You can drag an item from the external data window onto a shape in the drawing window. The results are shown in Figure 15.5. Notice that one row of data now shows a link; in fact, the office labeled E101 has shape data that was entered automatically from the spreadsheet.

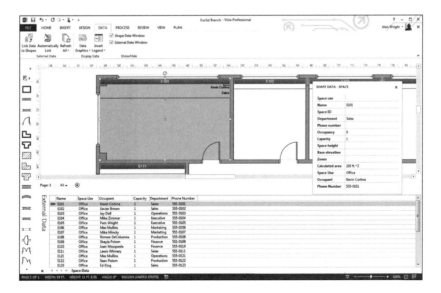

FIGURE 15.5

Drag and drop to manually establish a link between a shape and external data.

8. Right-click a row in the external data window, as shown in Figure 15.6, and you can see that there are many additional tools that affect how the data is linked to your shapes. You cannot edit data from here.

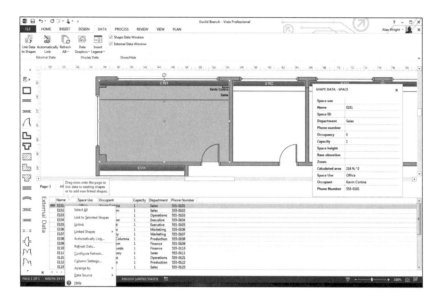

FIGURE 15.6

From the external data window, you can tweak some link settings with the context menu.

The capability to bring in external data can be useful for many scenarios. Assets, network resources, HR, part numbers, pricing, and other sales information are a few examples of how data can be maintained in a spreadsheet or database and then brought into Visio as linked external data.

 TIP You can use the drag-and-drop method for linking data manually even when you do not have shapes set up ahead of time with any key identifier fields. For example, in Figure 15.5, the office can be unnamed and the results are the same. In some cases you may have established shape data that serve for identifiers in a diagram, and in other cases it may be a work in progress.

 NOTE If you have external data brought into Visio for linking, Visio matches column names to the labels for shape data fields that are used by shapes. If your external data has columns that were selected that do not match any labels in your shape, Visio creates additional shape data fields to hold this data.

Using Automatically Link Data

You could drag data to shapes and perform your links as we have just seen, but the Automatically Link tool makes this even easier. This works smoothly if you have prepared your data to match your shape data fields and have a unique identifier for each shape in your Visio drawing that matches a field of data in your external data. The office numbers shown back in Figure 15.5 that occupy the Name field in the Space shapes are an example of this.

To automatically link multiple rows of external data follow these steps:

1. From the Data tab, click the Automatically Link button.

2. The first window offers you the option to automatically link to All Shapes on the page or just selected shapes. In Figure 15.7, All Shapes has been selected. Click Next.

3. Here you want to point again to the corresponding values from your data source and the shape data field. In this example, Name has been used for both values (see Figure 15.7). Select the appropriate values and then click Next.

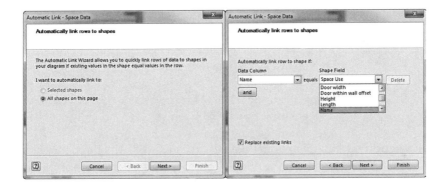

FIGURE 15.7

Use the Automatic Link Wizard to make quick work of linking multiple shapes to an external data source.

4. Click Finish if the selected criteria is correct.

5. Figure 15.8 shows the results; all fields have now been labeled, and you can see the reassuring links in the external data window.

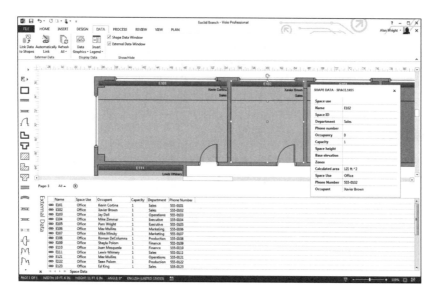

FIGURE 15.8

Automatically Link can quickly sync data to all your shape data at once.

NOTE When using Automatically Link, any shapes that do not match the key identifier that has been selected remains unaffected by the linked data. For example, in the office floor plan used in this chapter, an office that had no "name" would be skipped. Also, additional office names that were not captured in the external data would be skipped.

You can add additional external data sources as well. They appear as tabbed sources in the external data window. You can use the same steps outlined earlier to link these data sets as well.

How would you use this feature? Perhaps you are the office administrator for the branch office in these examples, and you keep the office assignments on an Excel spreadsheet on your computer that includes name, department, and home phone numbers. The building's facilities department has its own database that indicates office phone numbers and other details about each office without reference to the occupant. By bringing these two data sets into Visio, you can link the data to show relevant data from both sources all in one place without any additional typing on your part. You just found time for another coffee break!

Refresh Link Data

By now you may have noticed another button on the Data tab labeled Refresh All. As the name implies, this tool allows you to refresh data that was brought in from your external data source. Suppose that there have been updates to phone numbers, personnel, prices, and so on. As long as the source data has been updated, you can select Refresh All to update your Visio shape data.

You can also adjust specific settings for the refresh:

1. From the Data tab, select the drop-down from the Refresh All button and then select Refresh Data.

2. Select the appropriate external data source, and click Configure.

3. In the Configure Refresh window, adjust your data source, unique identifier, or set an interval for Automatic Refresh. You can use the optional Overwrite User Changes to Shape Data to replace differences between shape data with data in the external source that were typed in manually (see Figure 15.9).

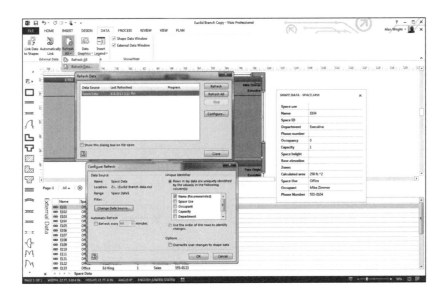

FIGURE 15.9

You can configure how your external data source is used after linking data.

Setting Up a Master to Use Link Data

You can create your own shape master with custom shape data fields that match data you already assembled elsewhere with the idea of linking external data to a custom shape. In Chapter 14, you saw how to create shape data fields.

Chapter 5, "Working with Shapes," showed you how to create shape masters from new shapes or copies of existing shapes. By combining these two techniques, you can create a shape master that is already set up to link to external data with fields that correspond exactly to the data you are concerned with. Add to this the elegance of refreshing linked data to catch any updates to your data source, and your Visio diagram becomes a long-term tool that remains relevant in a very dynamic environment.

Imagine doing this with shapes on a floor plan for a store. By linking to data related to inventory or sales and refreshing your data every few hours, you can create a visual floor plan that tells you where you are out of stock or are running short on merchandise, complete with linked SKU numbers, color, pricing size, and more.

→ To learn more about creating Shape Masters, see page **90**.

→ To learn more about creating custom shape data fields, see page **269**.

What Are Data Graphics?

Data graphics are another awesome feature in Visio that provide you with a variety of ways to display data. In addition to text, you can also use colors or shapes to communicate status information based on shape data.

How to Create a Data Graphic

Although there are many practical ways you can use data graphics, for the sake of simplicity the office floor plan from earlier in this chapter is used. You can see how to add a data graphic to the conference room shown in Figure 15.10 that will alert you if there are too many people in the room. Notice that you already have shape data indicating Occupancy and Capacity in the Shape Data task pane.

To add Data Graphics we'll follow these steps:

1. From the Data tab, select Data Graphics and Create New Data Graphic.

2. In the New Data Graphic window, select New Item.

3. In the New Item window, identify the data field for Occupancy. It is not listed in the initial drop-down; you can select More Fields to bring up the Field window shown in Figure 15.11. Select Shape Data for the category and then scroll down to locate the Field name: Occupancy. Click OK.

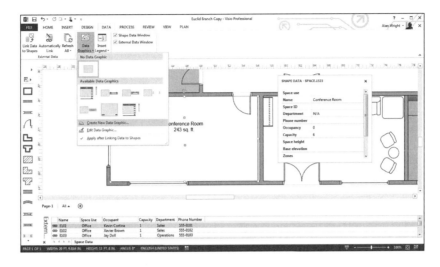

FIGURE 15.10

You can create custom Data Graphic settings in your drawings using the Create New Data Graphic tool.

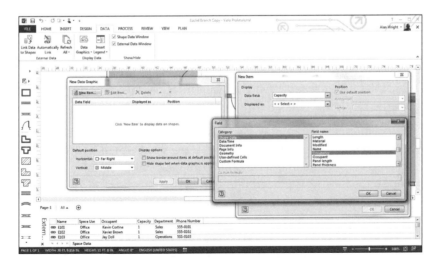

FIGURE 15.11

You can be very specific when assigning data graphics to shape data fields.

4. For Displayed As use an Icon Set and select an appropriate set of icons from available Styles. Because you know that this conference room has a capacity of six, you can use that with some basic equations to indicate which icon is shown based on occupancy. Finally, notice in Figure 15.12 that the position

of the data graphic can be precisely located by choosing from Horizontal and Vertical drop-down lists. Click OK.

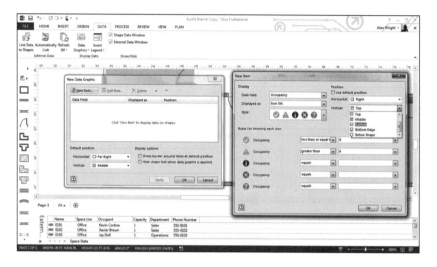

FIGURE 15.12

Select your preferences for how and where the data graphic is displayed.

5. In the New Data Graphic window, you see summarized your settings for Data Field, Displayed As, and Position. Click OK.

6. Click Yes when asked, "Do you want to apply this data graphic to the selected shapes?"

7. The conference room now displays a round green circle with a check mark because the occupancy is still 0. To show what would happen if the occupancy value changes to something greater than six, Figure 15.13 shows what happens when 12 is placed into the Occupancy field. A yellow triangle with an exclamation point immediately appears.

TIP You can also create formulas to perform calculations based on values placed in shape data fields. This can be useful when you do not know the value, or if you are using a value from linked external data. Figure 15.11 shows the Field dialog box. Selecting the category Custom Formula allows you to create basic equations that are used as the data field.

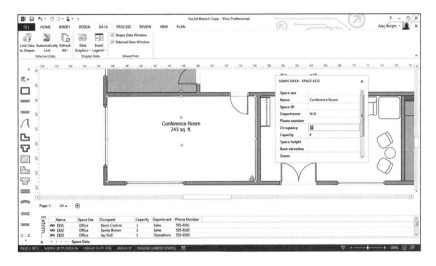

FIGURE 15.13

Changes to the Shape Data field can trigger different data graphics.

 TIP It is useful to include a legend that explains what the colors or symbols mean that are used as data graphics in a diagram. Use the Insert Legend button on the Data tab to add a legend that explains what each enabled data graphic means, even if it is not currently displayed in the diagram.

Customizing Data Graphics

To further illustrate how data graphics work and some of the many things you can enable them to do, consider the following example of a sales department. Management wants you to show the status of the divisional sales figures with a simple data graphic to motivate sales personnel. This is posted to a SharePoint site, and all employees are able to see how the divisions are performing.

In Figure 15.14, you can see that an org chart has been linked to an external data source. Because the linked data did not match existing shape data field labels, new Shape data fields were created. Incidentally, this data was automatically displayed using data graphics with default Position settings when it was linked. The shape spacing had to be manually adjusted in this case to accommodate the data graphics that display to the far right of each org chart shape.

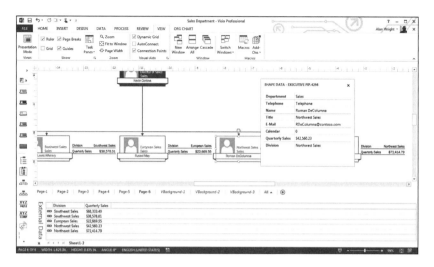

FIGURE 15.14

Adding external linked data can create data graphics automatically.

 NOTE Visio does not treat data graphics as separate shapes, so some overlap may occur if the data graphic displays outside of a shape. Using tools to rearrange or position shapes may help; otherwise, you may need to change the Position settings for the data graphic to display inside your shape.

The data displayed in Figure 15.14 is kind of dry. You can change how this is displayed and use a more attention grabbing appearance. From the Data tab, select Data Graphics to modify existing data graphics. Figure 15.15 shows how you can hover your mouse over an available data graphic to preview how this would appear.

For the sake of this example, assume that management likes the data graphic speedometer, but they want you to tweak the position of the pointer on the gauge.

1. From the Data tab, select Data Graphics and then choose the option Edit Data Graphic shown in Figure 15.15.

2. In the Edit Data Graphic dialog box shown in Figure 15.16, select the Data Field Quarterly Sales and click Edit Item to change the settings for the data bar.

3. In Figure 15.16, adjust the Minimum Value and the Maximum Value. Use a range of 15,000 to 80,000 to narrow the range for the values you are working with in this scenario. Also change the Value Format to Currency.

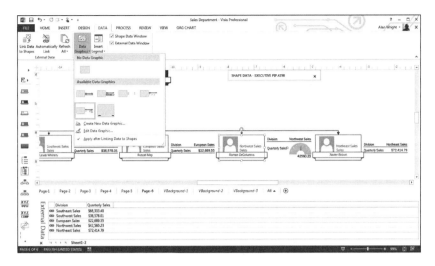

FIGURE 15.15

You can preview some basic variations for a data graphic right from the Available Data Graphics gallery.

FIGURE 15.16

Modifying existing data graphics is easy and very customizable.

4. Figure 15.17 shows the new data graphic applied to the divisions with an easily understood visual. The European sales division needs to step it up! Anytime the linked data changes *and is refreshed*, the data graphic adjusts accordingly.

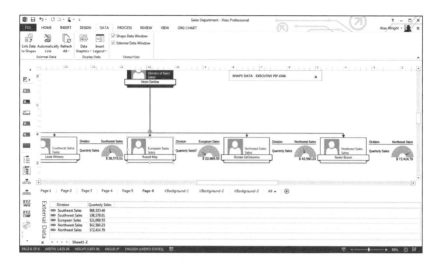

FIGURE 15.17

Linked data combined with shape graphics provides a powerful way to communicate information.

THE ABSOLUTE MINIMUM

Shape data is a powerful feature in Visio; it enables you to make diagrams that reflect real-world changes.

Linking data sources that you have assembled or that belong to your organization will save you time and effort in the long run. Consider the advantage to using an automatic refresh interval. It is a good idea to document the interval so that viewers know how up-to-date the information is that they are viewing.

When adding data graphics to your diagrams, select data fields that contain data that truly deserves the attention. Stock, inventory, availability, and monetary values are all examples of data that you want to see included in a dashboard display.

Combine linked external data and effective data graphics to cement your reputation as a Visio expert.

IN THIS CHAPTER

- How can I help others to view my drawings?
- How can I get help with my questions?
- Where can I learn more about Visio 2013?
- Who are Visio MVPs and how can they help me?

16

ADDITIONAL VISIO RESOURCES

This book has considered many aspects of Visio with the intention of providing you with a solid understanding of the tools and features of Visio 2013. As you progress from an absolute beginner to an experienced user, it is natural to ask, "What's next?"

This chapter is offered as a reference to reliable online resources that you can consult and rely on for tips, suggestions, and help with problems. Besides valuable built-in help tools, Visio provides online resources. Microsoft has created many resources for end users such as yourself that you should be aware of. Additionally, Microsoft has officially recognized experts in the Visio community; you can trust them to provide solutions that work.

Visio Viewer

Visio Viewer is an important resource that you should be aware of. Not all users have Visio installed on their computers, which could be a problem when you want others to look at your Visio drawings. If this happens to you, just point customers, co-workers, and friends to this free viewer that allows them to see your Visio drawings (see Figure 16.1). They may look to you to walk them through installing and using this tool. Chapter 12, "Sharing Visio Diagrams," provides steps that you can refer to when helping others install Microsoft Visio Viewer 2013 as well as a few other practical suggestions related to sharing your drawings.

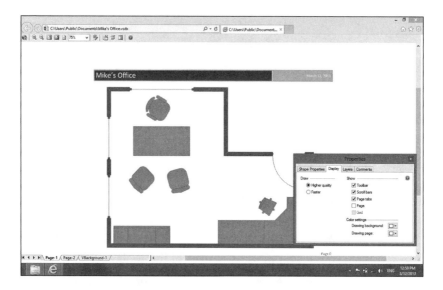

FIGURE 16.1

Visio Viewer allows people without Visio to view drawings in their web browsers.

→ To learn more about installing and setting up Visio Viewer, see page **229**.

Resources and Tools

Visio has internal resources that you might overlook or be unaware of. Help features, for example, have proven to be inadequate in the past, and perhaps you do not consult them very often. You will find Visio Help to be very useful, and we encourage you to make good use of this resource. This section shows you some of the many resources and tools available online, which can be freely downloaded.

Visio Help

You might overlook the built-in help features for Visio when you're working. As with all Office products, the upper-right corner of your Visio window has a question mark icon that opens the Visio Help dialog box shown in Figure 16.2. This allows you to browse through categories or type in a few keywords to search both local help content and online help information. Help content provides detailed explanations, steps, screenshots, and links to related subjects.

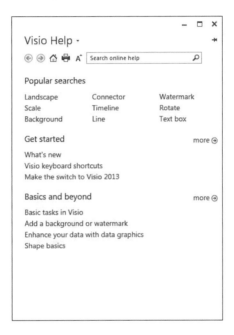

FIGURE 16.2

The Visio Help dialog box is an abundant source for additional information.

As you work with tools in the ribbon tabs, you occasionally see commands that have a prominent Tell Me More help link like the one shown in Figure 16.3. Click the link to open the Visio Help dialog box for information specific to that command or tool, as shown in Figure 16.4.

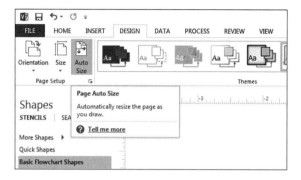

FIGURE 16.3

Visio offers Tell Me More links to view additional help information for some commands.

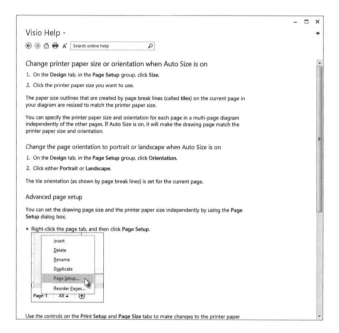

FIGURE 16.4

Visio Help provides detailed information and helps you understand better how and when to use tools.

The Official Visio Blog

An excellent source of information on Visio 2013 is the official Visio blog, which is maintained by the team behind Visio 2013. New articles pop up and present tips and explanations that guided the development team working on Visio (http://blogs.office.com/b/visio/).

Figure 16.5 shows a recent blog post recapping dozens of posts related to the new Visio 2013. This is a site worth visiting from time to time, just to get insights into the features you use now and information on features that you may not have tried yet.

FIGURE 16.5

The official Visio blog provides great background information from the Visio development team.

Office.com

Office.com is a Microsoft website devoted to supporting all the Office applications. Many built-in search features refer to Office.com, such as searching for templates or inserting online pictures. Another way to search online resources is to navigate to the website in your web browser and search for templates directly. Many templates designed for older versions of Visio still work fine with Visio 2013 (http://office.microsoft.com/en-us/templates).

How could you use this? Follow these steps to download and open a template:

1. Open your web browser and navigate to the path provided in the previous paragraph, or type **office.com** into the address field and select the Templates link.

2. In the search field, type in the keywords **event planner** and press Enter. Figure 16.6 shows several results for various Office applications. The third result shown is for Visio 2003.

FIGURE 16.6

Office.com has many older templates that can still be used in Office 2013.

3. Select the Event planner for Visio 2003 and notice the detailed information shown in Figure 16.7. Select Download and accept the Microsoft Service Agreement that appears. Save the file to your computer, and follow the directions to save and extract the template file.

4. Navigate to the template file you extracted, and double-click it to open it in Visio.

5. As shown in Figure 16.8, this template includes its own document stencil and shapes that you select, such as the chair shown that has shape data fields ready to accept seating assignments and other details that have been thoughtfully included in the shape.

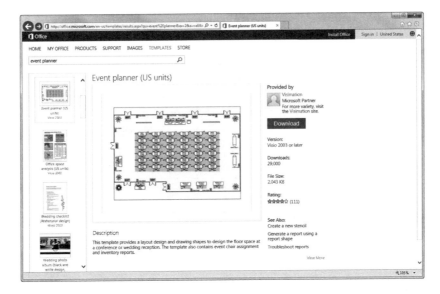

FIGURE 16.7

Additional information and thumbnails are offered before downloading a template.

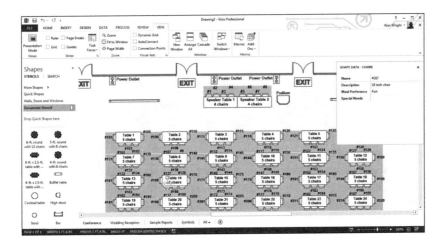

FIGURE 16.8

Visio 2013 can make good use of older stencils and shapes in your drawings.

Microsoft makes available more great online resources for Visio users:

- Forums like answers.microsoft.com (http://answers.microsoft.com) enable you to ask questions regarding Visio 2013 and read through questions and answers provided by other users.

- Training is offered through the Office.com (http://office.microsoft.com/en-us/training/) website for Visio and other Office products.

- Downloads can be found in the Download Center website. Search using keywords like **Visio 2013** to find additional gems. For example, a recently added stencil is shown in Figure 16.9 that includes hundreds of new icons related to Office and new server technologies and server roles. The stencil name is FLEX_Stencil_121412.vss (the download link is http://www.microsoft.com/en-us/download/details.aspx?id=35772).

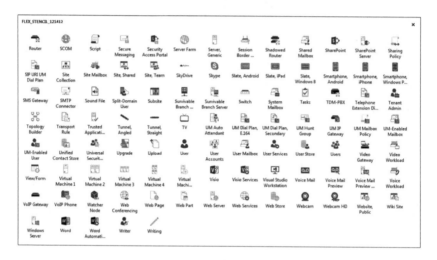

FIGURE 16.9

Shapes from the FLEX stencil that include many new icons.

  TIP   For best results using shapes in the FLEX_Stencil_121412. vss, make sure that the shapes do not have a theme applied.

Additional Reading

As your abilities with Visio grow, it is logical to look for more information that can help you develop and deepen your knowledge and skills using Visio 2013. Although much information is available online, it is hard to beat a good book that you can refer to as you explore deeper into the workings of Visio. Depending on your interests, consider a few books that have proven to be solid reference books on the subject:

- *Using Visio 2010* (Chris Roth; Visio MVP, Que Publishing) provides more detailed information that you can refer to when working with shape data concepts and a brief introduction into developing for Visio with a chapter devoted to creating a custom SmartShape. Still a great read, and the concepts presented are very compatible with tools present in Visio 2013.

- *Visio 2010 Step by Step* (Scott Helmers; Visio MVP, Microsoft Press) focuses on basic to advanced concepts, with emphasis on flowcharting, network diagrams, and business process diagrams. Scott also introduces some deeper information by introducing you to Visual Basic for Applications. It includes good examples presented by an expert in the field.

- *Microsoft Visio 2010 Business Process Diagramming and Validation* (David J. Parker; Visio MVP) is a much deeper dive into concepts that guide the development of validation rules and Business Process Management. This feature is built into Visio Professional 2013, and the principles and examples used here are still practical for aspiring developers.

- *Developing Microsoft Visio Solutions* (Microsoft Press) has long been considered a solid book that lays the groundwork for advanced Visio concepts and programming. Although it's out-of print, the content can be found online and still makes for good reading.

Websites Worth Checking Out

Visio experts tend to be very helpful and enthusiastic about Visio. Many individuals who are not employees of Microsoft have been singled out and recognized officially by Microsoft for their support to users and contributions to the advancement of Visio by awarding them with the Most Valued Professional (MVP) award. Many Visio MVP awardees maintain websites and blogs. It is not uncommon to see them actively participate in Visio forums where they can provide you with suggestions and assistance when you have problems and questions.

Although many individuals offer advice and suggestions for Visio, the following is a list of established and active websites devoted to Visio and maintained by individuals and groups with a proven track record of supporting end users such as yourself.

- Chris Roth is a Visio MVP and his Visio Guy blog provides lots of tips and how-to information. Chris worked for Visio Corp, and he created many of the shapes. While the site is aimed more at developers and those that want to find out what is possible when working with Visio, look around on his website to find additional shapes and stencils as well as detailed information related to practical uses of Visio: http://www.visguy.com/.

Searches on this website include the forum, which is another great source for Visio know-how. This public forum (http://visguy.com/vgforum) is available to you as well, and it has a lot of users—so don't be surprised to get a quick response to your questions. This site has been here for several years, and there is a lot of information, as shown in Figure 16.10, so be specific when searching. If you ask for help in the forum, provide as much information as you can to get prompt results.

FIGURE 16.10

Search for tips and suggestions using keywords. Shown here, "print" reveals a lot of content, so be prepared to add keywords related to version or year.

- John Marshall is a Visio MVP—the first person to be singled out with this honor, in fact. John continues to be very active in supporting the Visio community. He runs Visio.MVPS.org which is a great website for third-party shapes and help on managing Visio with VBA. His blog provides in-depth information on a variety of topics. To see his latest comments on Visio, use this link: http://johnvisiomvp.wordpress.com/category/visio/.

- David Parker is a Visio MVP, and his website contains information related to additional training and resources that have been developed for businesses and customers: http://www.bvisual.net/.

- John Goldsmith is a Visio MVP, and his website includes many insightful blogs that help you dig deeper into Visio. A recent blog shown in Figure 16.11

deals with modifying a Visio master shape. The topic is nicely explained and includes easy-to-follow steps and several screenshots. His website can be found at http://visualsignals.typepad.co.uk/.

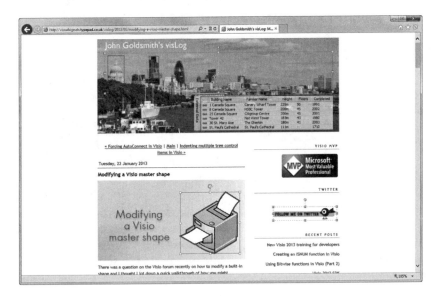

FIGURE 16.11

John Goldsmith's visLog has plenty of useful information, such as this blog post on modifying a master shape.

- Another website worth checking out is the MVP website, which has content and information compiled by Visio MVPs. The site can be found at http://visio. mvps.org/.

- Chris Hopkins is part of the Visio development team, and his blog is aimed more at developers. It is a great source for SharePoint administrators who want to use Visio Services and need a concise explanation of what works and what doesn't. Check out his blog at http://blogs.msdn.com/b/chhopkin/.

- VisioCafe has been around for many years. Their site provides free third-party stencil collections and does a good job of keeping updated content. Figure 16.12 shows the VisioCafe home page. News and updates are provided, and suggestions are given for creating network and rack diagrams. Stencils created for rack diagrams by manufacturers of servers and networking equipment can be downloaded for free. They also have a considerable collection of unofficial stencils that have been made available for free download. Their website can be found here: http://www.visiocafe.com/.

FIGURE 16.12

VisioCafe is a nonprofit website with up-to-date stencils focused on rack diagrams.

THE ABSOLUTE MINIMUM

Microsoft Visio Viewer 2013 is a free tool that you will want to share with others who need to look at your Visio drawings when they do not have Visio installed. It is good for you to know how to find it so that they can easily see your drawings.

As you continue to advance your Visio skills, don't overlook the tools that are readily available. Core help tools are built into Visio, and they leverage online help resources that will continue to provide you with explanations and tips to use Visio tools effectively.

Check out the official Visio blog for great tips and information on features that make Visio 2013 stand out.

Don't discount older Visio templates as being irrelevant because of their age. Templates that have been designed for older versions have stencils and shapes that continue to be useful and can be used in your drawings and diagrams.

Visio experts want to help you get the most out of Visio. Take advantage of their generous spirit and their wealth of experience by checking out their blogs, and use the forums to get quick answers to questions you have.

COLLABORATING WITH VISIO

As you work with a Visio diagram, you can collaborate with others in a variety of ways. Visio 2013 has made it even easier for you to gather input from other people through commenting and instant messaging features that work well with SharePoint. Co-authoring tools are an important new SharePoint 2013 feature, and this chapter shows you how to use them.

Tools such as Ink and Track Markup that have been traditionally used for collaboration are still available in Visio 2013. Finally, sharing files is a big part of collaboration. This chapter shows you how to use Visio tools to prevent sharing unnecessary or confidential information with your files.

SharePoint

SharePoint is a special web based software platform that has been an important tool for businesses and organizations that want to encourage collaboration. Documents are saved to servers and can be made available all the time while ensuring that security concerns are met when accessing documents. This chapter focuses on the collaborative tools that are used with Visio; after all, collaboration is at the heart of SharePoint.

SharePoint uses libraries to organize documents. Figure 17.1 shows a library named CDW Visio Documents with a Visio drawing selected. You can see information about location, date last modified, and even who has been granted access to this file. Edit and Share options can be selected, and you can see an ellipsis (SharePoint uses these a lot) to indicate that additional menu options are available.

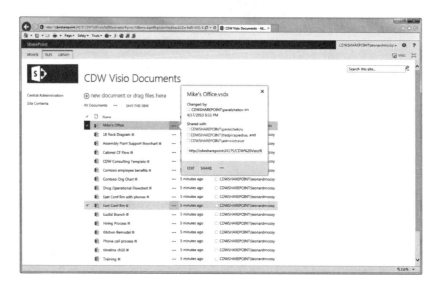

FIGURE 17.1

SharePoint enables you to make documents available for easy collaboration.

From the SharePoint library, you can select a Visio drawing to open it using Visio Web Apps in your web browser. This means that you can open a Visio drawing without Visio installed on your computer (see Figure 17.2). Notice that you are not able to edit the drawing in this view, but you can select shapes and view shape data by selecting Shape Info. Select Comments to view and add your own comments to selected shapes.

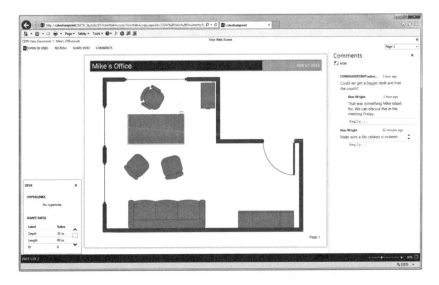

FIGURE 17.2

SharePoint allows you to view drawings and add comments using Visio Web Apps.

Saving and Editing in SharePoint

For many years, SharePoint has used a checkout feature to provide you with the option to check out documents for editing and to have exclusive editing control. If a document has been checked out of the library by another user, a message like the one shown in Figure 17.3 appears. If you need to open a file that has been checked out by someone else, you can open a read-only copy or create a second copy.

FIGURE 17.3

SharePoint prevents others from editing a drawing that has been checked out.

To check out a Visio drawing from a SharePoint server, follow these steps:

1. In your web browser, enter the path to a document library that contains the drawing you plan to work with. This may have been shared with you as a link in an email.

2. You are likely presented with a prompt to provide a username and password. These may be your network username and password. If needed, login information is usually included when a link has been provided.

3. Figure 17.1 shows how the library appears from a SharePoint 2013 server after the link has opened. Locate the drawing file and select the three dots (...) to the right of the filename to open the menu shown in Figure 17.1. Select ... again to open the menu shown in Figure 17.4. Notice the options listed here.

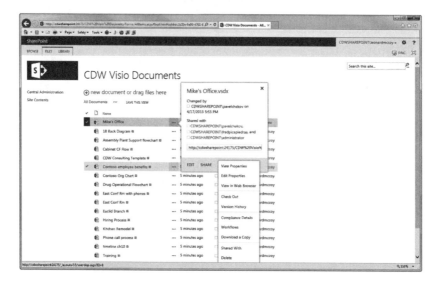

FIGURE 17.4

Open menus to reveal options available to you for a document, such as Check Out.

4. Select Check Out from the menu shown in Figure 17.4. Notice that the file icon has changed in the SharePoint library. It now indicates it is checked out, and if you hover your mouse pointer over the icon it reveals the information shown in Figure 17.5.

5. Select the filename to open it in Visio Web Access, as shown in Figure 17.2.

6. Select Open in Visio above the drawing and to the left to open the drawing in the Visio application. A dialog box may pop up to warn you about opening files that could contain viruses. Click Yes to open the file.

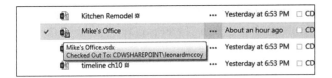

FIGURE 17.5

SharePoint uses the document icon to inform you if a document is checked out.

7. Open the File tab and look at the Info tab for this drawing. Figure 17.6 shows a document that is checked out. The checked-out document remains highlighted in yellow to remind you that you have locked this document and no one else will be able to modify the drawing. (Others who attempt to open your checked-out drawing see a warning like the one shown in Figure 17.3.)

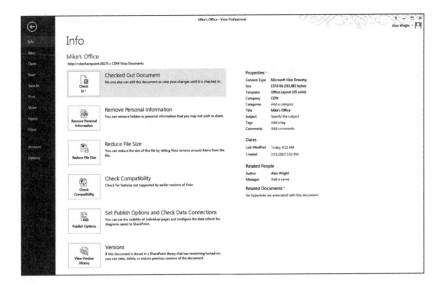

FIGURE 17.6

Visio reveals status information for SharePoint documents, such as this Visio drawing that is currently checked out.

8. Edit the document and then save changes. Don't forget to check the document back in so that others can work with it and see your changes. Visio reminds you of this when you close the drawing.

NOTE SharePoint has many settings that can be enabled or disabled by your SharePoint administrator. One of these is to require checkout for documents that are opened. Depending on such configuration settings, you may be prompted to check out a drawing automatically. It is worth mentioning here that requiring checkout disables co-authoring, which is discussed in the next section.

Versioning is another valuable setting that is often enabled in SharePoint. It allows you to track when changes are made to a drawing and who made those changes. Figure 17.7 shows four versions of a document with timestamps and the person who last edited the drawing. Select the timestamp information in the modified column to reveal a drop-down menu. Using this menu you can view older versions, restore the current version from an older version, and delete versions that are no longer needed.

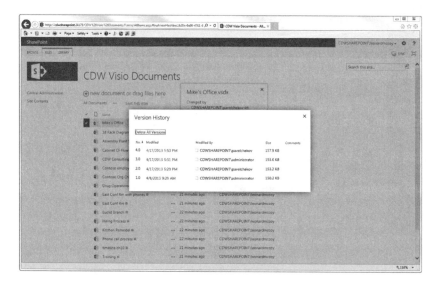

FIGURE 17.7
Version History enables you to see when changes were made and by whom.

Co-Authoring

An exciting new feature that SharePoint 2013 provides for users of Visio 2013 is co-authoring. This enables multiple individuals to work on the same document simultaneously and make changes that can be saved without interfering with each other. Co-authoring avoids other problems that can frustrate collaboration, such as tracking down the person who forgot to check a document back in to the library or merging several copies of the same original drawing.

If you try to check out a document that is already open, you see a message like the one shown in Figure 17.8 alerting you that you are denied exclusive access. You can open the document and edit it as if you had checked it out while your co-workers continue to be productive using the same drawing.

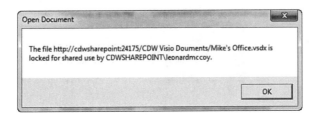

FIGURE 17.8

A drawing open in Co-author mode is considered locked for shared use.

Co-authoring comes in handy when

- A large drawing needs to be updated. It can be worked on by an entire group using the same file rather than having several copies that all need to be merged later.

- Several people are invited to review a drawing. Their comments and additions are all saved in the same drawing on the SharePoint server.

You see notifications on your status bar if others have a Visio drawing open, and shapes they are working on will be marked by a small icon, as shown in Figure 17.9. Their work is cached until they save their work, which then releases those edits, and their changes become visible to others. You are alerted on your status bar that changes have been saved to the SharePoint server by the appearance of Updates Available. Click this text or save your work, and the drawings are updated from the SharePoint server to reflect changes others have made.

You can even work on the same shape. If both happen to change the same property, such as the text field, the last to save overwrites the other. This type of conflict is rare, and a little coordination and communication can avoid this problem altogether.

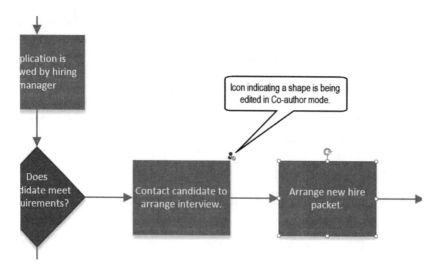

FIGURE 17.9

Visio drawings that are in Co-author mode alert you to shapes that are currently being edited by others.

You communicate with others while using Co-author mode by following these steps:

1. Open a Visio drawing from a SharePoint library. Ask a co-worker to open the same drawing, select a shape, and make a change.

2. In your Visio drawing, look for the small Person icon that is shown in Figure 17.9. It appears above the shape near the top-right corner.

3. Click the small icon to reveal the person's name. Hover over the name with your mouse pointer to reveal contact information, as shown in Figure 17.10.

4. Select an icon to use phone, email, or instant messaging to communicate with your co-worker. If no options for a particular mode of communication are available, that icon appears grayed out. In Figure 17.10, only email contact information is available.

 NOTE Co-authoring can also be used with drawings saved to SkyDrive.

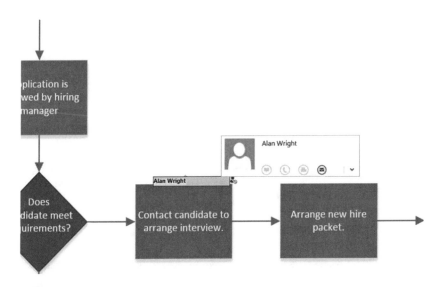

FIGURE 17.10

When you need to identify and communicate with a co-author, select the small Person icon to reveal contact information.

Markup and Review in Visio

Visio provides powerful tools that allow you to collaborate with others while preparing a diagram. You may have used these tools in other Office applications and understood their value. Unlike the use of callouts for commenting—a habit that many people still retain—these special tools can be easily hidden and even removed from a drawing, which only adds to their value.

Adding Comments

Comments have been reworked in Visio 2013 to make them more useful by attaching them to shapes. Comments will show a timestamp and author. They can be expanded or contracted to allow for easy navigation of long chains of comments. The presence of comments are revealed by small balloon icons that are located at the top-right corner of shapes to provide a visual cue that comments are attached to the shape. To view these comments, click the icon. Figure 17.11 shows a Visio drawing where comments have been opened.

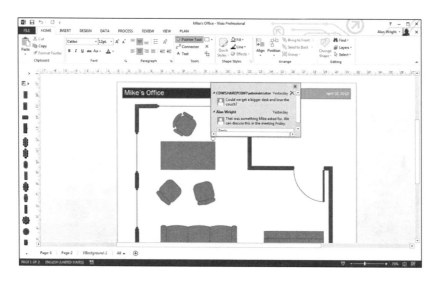

FIGURE 17.11

Commenting can provide valuable feedback when collaborating with others.

You add comments to a shape by following these steps:

1. Open a Visio drawing, or create a new drawing that has at least one shape located in the drawing window.

2. Right-click a shape and then select Add Comment from the context menu.

3. A small comment icon appears with a field that awaits your comments. Type in a comment, as shown in Figure 17.12, and press Enter. A small icon remains to let you know that there is a concealed comment associated with that shape.

4. Select the Review tab and notice the group of tools labeled Comments. Select the Comments pane drop-down to show the Reveal Tags option. Select the check box to enable and disable this option, and notice how the drawing window is affected. Figure 17.13 shows how comment tags can be hidden completely.

5. Select the Comments pane to add this task pane to the drawing window. It appears docked to the left side, as shown in Figure 17.14, and displays all the comments included in the drawing.

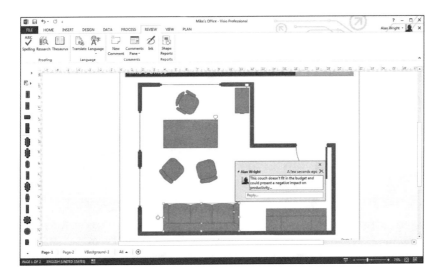

FIGURE 17.12

Add comments to shapes to target your remarks.

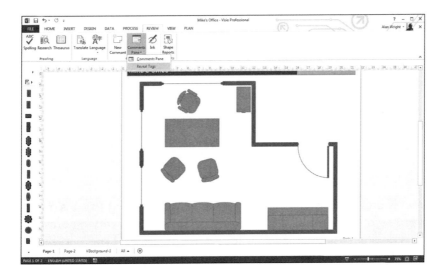

FIGURE 17.13

Hide commenting visual cues with a simple click using the Reveal Tags tool.

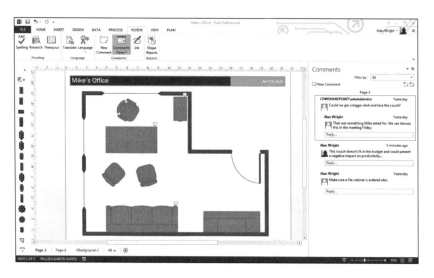

FIGURE 17.14

Use the Comments pane to review comments that have been added to a drawing.

When you select a shape with a comment, the related comments are highlighted in the Comments pane. You can also select a comment in the Comments pane, and the small icon balloon appears highlighted to indicate the shape this comment is attached to. Because comments can multiply so easily, the Comments pane includes a filter to narrow the results in a few ways, including by person, page, or recent comments.

You can select the New Comment button from the Review tab when you want to add a general comment to the entire page.

Using Ink

Ink tools provide another useful way to add commenting to a Visio drawing. Using Ink tools, you can create hand-drawn shapes and handwritten notes when looking over a diagram using tablets and touchscreen devices. Lines and shapes you draw can be left as Ink shapes or converted to Visio shapes that can be edited using standard shape drawing tools. Like other Visio shapes, you can copy, move, and resize ink shapes; these shapes can then be added to your custom stencils to make them available for other drawings. Visio even attempts to convert letters you draw freehand to text.

To use Ink tools, open the Review tab and select the Ink button. Figure 17.15 shows the Ink Tools menu.

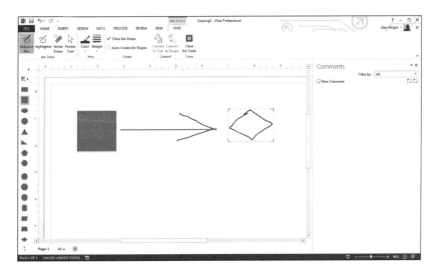

FIGURE 17.15

Ink tools can be used to add freehand comments to a drawing.

The tools found on this tab include the following:

- Ballpoint Pen is a straightforward drawing tool that allows you to draw freehand-style lines (called *strokes*). These lines combine to form part of the same ink shape until you click the Close Ink Tools button or select the Pointer tool. As an example, Figure 17.15 shows three strokes that form an arrow.

- Highlighter is essentially the same as the Ballpoint Pen tool; it draws strokes that have the appearance of a highlighter, including a degree of transparency.

- Stroke Eraser enables you to selectively remove strokes from an ink shape.

- Pointer tool changes the mouse pointer to the default Pointer tool, and Visio combines any strokes you have drawn into an ink shape.

- Color and Weight provide basic drop-down menus to change those properties of the Ballpoint Pen or Highlighter tools.

- Close Ink Shape provides you with another way to indicate you are done adding strokes to an ink shape. Select this and the next stroke starts a new ink shape.

- Auto-Create Ink Shapes closes ink shapes after a long pause. You can enable or disable this feature using the check box.

- Convert to Text and Convert to Shape converts the selected ink shape to text or a Visio shape. After converting to text, you can edit and format by using standard text tools.

Auto-Create Ink Shapes is enabled by default, and many people like this feature. If you want to adjust the time allowed to automatically close an ink shape, follow these steps:

1. Select the File tab, and select Options from the vertical tab list.

2. When the Visio Options dialog box opens, select the Advanced tab from the side bar.

3. In Ink Tool, under Editing Options, use the slider to increase or decrease the time allowed before this tool closes an ink shape (see Figure 17.16).

4. Click OK.

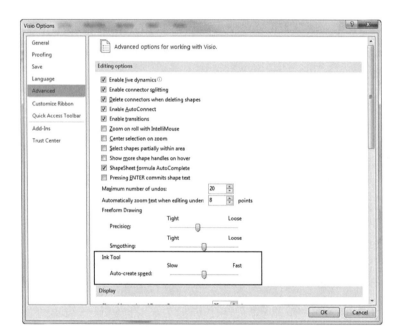

FIGURE 17.16

You can adjust the time allowed between strokes before a new ink shape is started.

Ink has been around for years and has been a valuable tool for tablets that use a pen for an input device. Newer tablets and all-in-one computers that use multitouch touchscreens can still use Ink effectively. Visio 2013 includes additional tools that make working with touchscreens even more enjoyable.

➜ To learn more about working with a touchscreen in Visio, see page **246**.

Using Track Markup

If you used Visio in the past, you may be wondering where the Markup tools went. With the improvements to the Commenting tools, Markup tools have been removed from the Review tab. You can add them back easily enough if you prefer to keep them readily available.

Track Markup has been used by teams to create an overlay where comments and shapes can be added without changing the original drawing. The Markups can be displayed or hidden easily, and a drawing can have several Markup overlays. Using the tools to remove private information described at the end of this chapter, Markup overlay content can be removed easily.

To add the Track Markup tool to the Review tab, follow these steps:

1. Select the File tab and select Options from the vertical tab list.

2. The Visio Options dialog box opens; select the Customize Ribbon tab from the side bar.

3. In the Choose Commands drop-down list, select Commands Not in the Ribbon.

4. Scroll down the list and select the Track Markup command.

5. Under Customize the Ribbon, select Review, and then click the New Group button.

6. Select the new group, click the Rename button, and type a name for this tool group. (Figure 17.17 shows the name Markup has been used.) Click OK.

7. Select the Add button between the lists to add the Track Markup command to your new group on the Review tab as shown in Figure 17.17. Click OK.

8. Select the Review tab. You now have a new tool group, and the Track Markup tool is available.

Figure 17.18 shows how easily you can add shapes and comments to an overlay after enabling Track Markup. The drawing area has a colored border, and shapes added share this color. A Reviewing task pane also shows up; this tracks the changes made to the overlay and provides a way to control how overlays are displayed. Select Track Markup again to exit markup mode, and return to the original drawing.

FIGURE 17.17

Add the Track Markup command to the Review tab using the Visio Options dialog box.

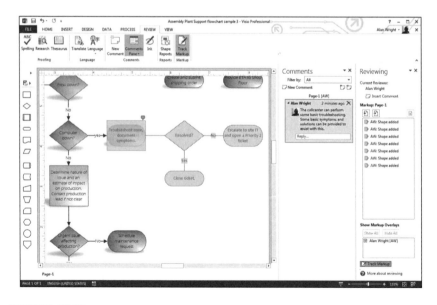

FIGURE 17.18

While Track Markup is enabled, shapes and comments are added to an overlay and do not affect the original drawing.

After leaving Markup mode, you can use the Comments pane to see comments, and the Reviewing pane allows you to show or hide any markup overlays associated with the page by using the corresponding check box under Show Markup Overlays. Figure 17.19 shows a markup overlay; you can see tabs along the right edge of the drawing that indicate the markup layer at the top and a tab at the bottom indicating the original drawing. You can use these tabs to jump back and forth if you want to examine shapes on these layers. Shapes may be visible from multiple overlays, but you can select shapes only if the tab they are on is selected—and this includes shapes in the original drawing.

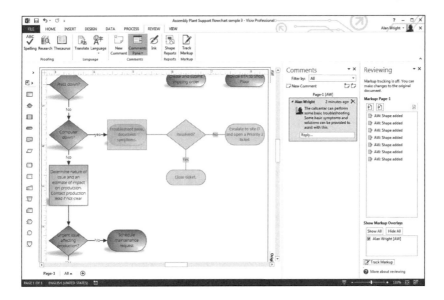

FIGURE 17.19

Markup overlays can be used to communicate ideas without altering the original.

Don't Share Too Much

Although you might be understandably focused on sharing the drawings you create, it is wise to consider what is being shared. Your drawing may have grown in size, and sensitive data may be embedded in your document. A couple of handy tools can be found in the Info tab to help you remove unnecessary data to reduce file size and remove sensitive data.

Check information in the document and remove personal information by following these steps:

1. Open a Visio drawing that you saved, and then open the File tab. Make sure the Info tab is selected, as shown in Figure 17.20.

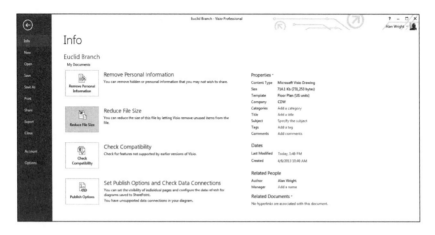

FIGURE 17.20

Use Info to see file properties and access tools to remove sensitive information.

2. Select the large button labeled Reduce File Size to open the Remove Hidden Information dialog box. Click the File Size Reduction tab, as shown in Figure 17.21

FIGURE 17.21

Reduce file size by stripping unused elements from a drawing.

3. Remove any items by selecting them and then clicking OK.

4. Select the Remove Personal Information button also shown in Figure 17.20. The same Remove Hidden Information dialog box appears with the Personal Information tab displayed as shown in Figure 17.22.

FIGURE 17.22

Using the Remove Hidden Information dialog box enables you to keep confidential information private.

5. Select both check boxes that start with Remove to remove the indicated data types. Check the box that starts with Warn Me if you plan to do further edits before sharing the document. Click OK.

6. Notice the file size and information displayed in Figure 17.23. The file size is a little smaller; of course, this varies depending on the file. Perhaps more important, you can see right away that personal information was removed.

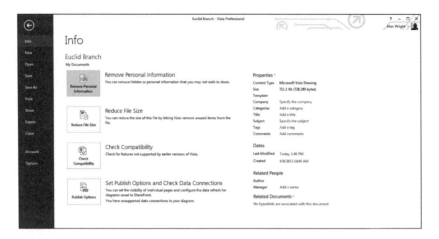

FIGURE 17.23

Visio drawings can be sent safely without accidently providing confidential information after using Remove Personal Information.

What Is Removed

As shown in Figure 17.23, many types of information are stripped from your drawing. Consider why you might want to remove some of these items:

- You likely think of file properties when working with Office documents. You may not want author, manager, and company names revealed through this drawing.

- Because you might not have commenting visible in a drawing, you could forget that reviewer comments and markups are present. This information may contain embarrassing or confidential details aside from being information that does not need to be shared.

- Paths indicating the file locations for stencils and templates might present a security risk as they reveal information about your file structure.

- Drawings that use external data also retain file path information and expose confidential information.

File size is reduced by removing unneeded master shapes and themes that may have been used at one point during the creation of a drawing, as shown in Figure 17.22. It is easy to forget that a drawing retains this information until it is removed. To further improve file size reduction, you might consider resizing inserted image files.

→   To learn more about resizing inserted image files, see page **192**.

What Is Not Removed

Drawings retain shape data and text that has been added to text blocks. Therefore, confidential information that was entered in this way is still there. Extra pages temporarily added and callouts used for commenting are not removed. Just to be safe, make it a practice to look through pages to ensure that you (or a co-worker) have not added private or confidential information before a document is shared.

THE ABSOLUTE MINIMUM

Make good use of SharePoint servers that are available to you. Encourage collaboration in your team, and if possible use the co-authoring tools to heighten productivity and improve communication.

Use the Comments tools in the Review tab to collaborate with co-workers and customers. Take time to experiment with adding comments to shapes and using the Comments task pane.

If you like using markup overlays, add the command to the Review tab (or any custom tab). Be prepared to walk others through the steps to find this command and add it to a tab in their copy of Visio if they will need to see the markup tools.

Take time to remove extraneous information by using the Remove Hidden Information dialog box. This reduces file sizes and ensures that no private or confidential information is sent via a drawing.

TIPS FOR FLOWCHARTS, PROCESS, AND BLOCK DIAGRAMS

Visio has many very specialized templates, some with new or updated features for 2013. This chapter looks at a few specific templates and provides some pointers and tips to help you get the most out of the tools provided.

Process and Flow Chart Diagrams

Although flowcharts tend to be pretty straightforward creations, the following sections present a few tips that might make diagram creation go smoother for you.

Auto Resize and Flowchart Shapes

Flowchart diagrams should be as streamlined as is realistically possible. It is a good practice to avoid jumbled and inconsistent shapes and layouts that detract from a well-laid-out flowchart. Most flowchart shapes have a feature that allows them to automatically grow vertically to contain long text entries. Figure 18.1 shows one normal default Process shape and two Process shapes that have been resized. The second shape autoresized to contain the text, and the third was resized using the control handles. The context menu is shown for each.

It helps to understand how Auto Resize works because it may not always appear to be enabled. By default, these shapes resize vertically. The capability can be disabled by selecting Set to Default Size. Also, after a shape has been resized manually, the Auto Resize feature is disabled. To enable this, look for the Resize with Text option when right-clicking the shape. In the case of the horizontally resized shape in Figure 18.1, the shape expands vertically with text and does not lose the extra horizontal real estate.

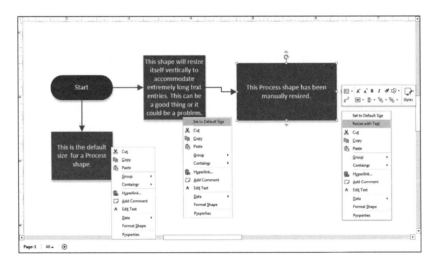

FIGURE 18.1

You can use the Auto Resize feature or disable it when working with flowchart shapes.

Decision Shapes

Visio includes many options when you use Re-Layout Page on the Design tab. Whereas most results are predictable and more desirable than manually throwing a flowchart together, flowcharts tend to get flustered when encountering Decision shapes and dynamic glue. Notice in Figure 18.2 how the flowchart on the left is converted to the flowchart on the right using the Re-Layout tool. Both Yes and No options are now run out of the same point using dynamic glue. The result is not as clear as you would expect, and it is not a very useful flowchart.

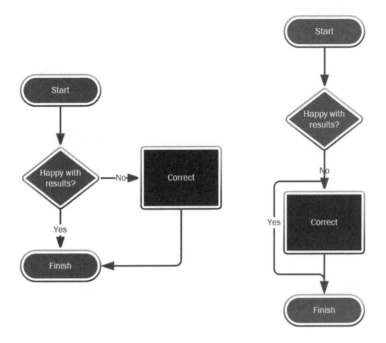

FIGURE 18.2

Dynamic glue and Decision shapes can have issues when you use the Re-Layout tool.

The solution in a case like this is to use point-to-point glue. Notice in Figure 18.3 that the same flowchart on the left now has point-to-point glue for the Yes and No connection points on the Decision shape. After using the same Re-Layout Page tool, the results are comprehensible and the chart is usable.

→ To learn more about the Re-Layout Page tool, see page **118**.

→ To learn more about dynamic and point-to-point glue, see page **129**.

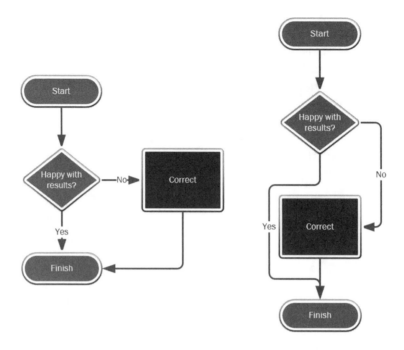

FIGURE 18.3

Using point-to-point glue on Decision shapes might save you grief later.

Using Subprocesses

Subprocesses enable you to simplify a complicated flowchart by focusing on the higher-level process steps and relegating subsections of the flow to secondary pages where they can still be consulted when needed. As an example, Figure 18.4 shows a typical flowchart for handling support tickets.

This could be simplified in this example by making the entire phone call process a subprocess. In Visio 2013 Professional, you can do this easily by selecting the appropriate shapes and navigating to the Process tab. In the section labeled Subprocess, select the button labeled Create from Selection (see Figure 18.5).

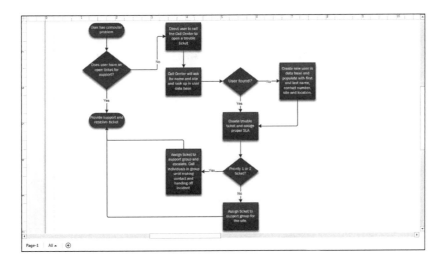

FIGURE 18.4

Flowcharts can contain lots of details. Use subprocesses to keep the focus on the main processes.

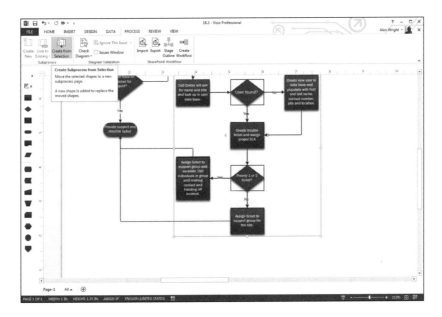

FIGURE 18.5

Use Create from Selection to replace selected shapes with a Subprocess shape.

Select this to see your selected shapes replaced with a single Subprocess shape. Just name the new page containing your subprocess; it's a good idea to name the shape to match the page it is related to. As shown in Figure 18.6, use Ctrl+click to open the new page from the Subprocess shape to review the relocated steps.

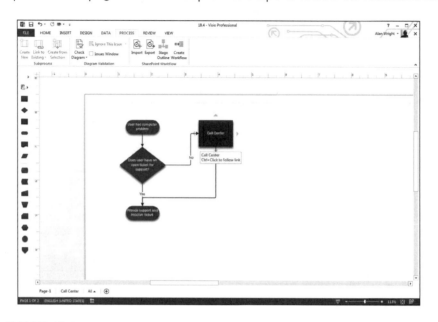

FIGURE 18.6

You can jump to a subprocess from a higher-level flowchart using the hyperlink.

Alternatively, you can manually do the same thing by cutting and pasting the shapes into a new page. Drag a Subprocess shape into the drawing to replace the shapes that were cut out. Repair the connectors, and attach them to the new Subprocess shape. Right-click the Subprocess shape, select Hyperlink, and using a Sub-address, browse for the new page. Click OK, and you have essentially done the work of the Create from Selection tool.

➜ To learn more about working with hyperlinks and shapes, see page **188**.

Swimlanes and Phases in Cross-Functional Flowcharts

Chapter 8, "Making Advanced Diagrams," talked about containers and considered how they are used in the case of swimlanes. Swimlanes are containers that are generally used in cross-functional flowcharts to indicate ownership of process steps. Usually a swimlane indicates a person, position, or business unit that is responsible for steps or processes.

In Visio 2013, the default configuration of this template is a horizontal orientation. Some prefer vertical swimlanes, but consider how the horizontal orientation makes better use of wide-screen displays. As shown in Figure 18.7, vertical swimlanes are still an option in the stencil, and the ribbon allows you to change orientation behavior.

 TIP If you often work with cross-functional flowcharts and prefer a vertical orientation, you should make that your default orientation. From the cross-functional flowchart ribbon tab, select Orientation and then select Set Default. You can then establish your preferred orientation as Horizontal or Vertical. Click OK to make this the new default when opening new flowcharts.

Adding Swimlanes

Adding swimlanes is easy. You can drag them over from the stencil, insert from the Ribbon tab, or right-click to insert. You can also hover between two existing swimlanes at either end of the container; a small triangle appears that allows you to insert a swimlane at that point.

→ To learn more about working with swimlane containers, see page **148**.

Phases are another feature of cross-functional flowcharts. They are used to further segregate tasks and processes by stages. They can be added by dragging into the flowchart from the stencil or inserting from the contextual Ribbon tab. In Figure 18.7 you can see that a phase has been added. A nice feature with phases is that they behave as a container. You can see that moving the phase in this example brings the shapes in the swimlanes along for a ride. Phases can be resized or moved after being positioned. Resizing causes other shapes to adjust their position within their swimlane rather than be absorbed by a phase.

Resizing Swimlanes

Resizing swimlanes and phases is a straightforward action. Hover over the border you want to move, and you see the cursor change to two parallel lines with arrows indicating the directions of movement. Click and drag to effect the resize. The top-most swimlane in Figure 18.7 has been resized.

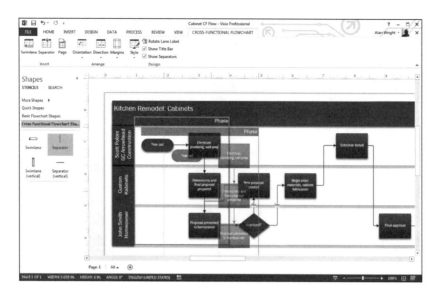

FIGURE 18.7

Phases act as containers when moved.

One limitation to bear in mind when resizing swimlanes or phases is that they do not become smaller than their contents and the minimum space established in the Margins property for the page. You can adjust the Margins value from the contextual Ribbon tab to modify the minimum space surrounding shapes in a swimlane or phase.

The Cross-Functional Flowchart Contextual Ribbon Tab

When working with cross-functional flowcharts, you see that they have their own ribbon, shown in Figure 18.8.

FIGURE 18.8

Cross-functional flowcharts have their own contextual ribbon.

From here you can do the following:

- Insert swimlanes, phase separators, and pages.

- Arrange horizontal or vertical orientation, and toggle direction from left to right or right to left.

- You can establish the minimum space required to surround shapes on the page with the Margins feature.

- Apply several style variations unique to this type of flowchart.

- Use Rotate Lane Label to change the orientation of the text for the swimlane title.

- Show or hide the title bar.

- The Show Separator check box will delete phase separators when unchecked. A warning pops up to let you know that this is a one-way edit. To bring the phases back, you need to re-add them.

Validating Your Diagram

Visio 2013 Professional now includes tools to validate most types of flowchart diagrams. In Figure 18.9, you can see that validation has been run on this cross-functional flowchart by using the Process tab and selecting Check Diagram. Two errors were detected in this example, and you can see that Rules can be selected and even imported to run against your diagrams.

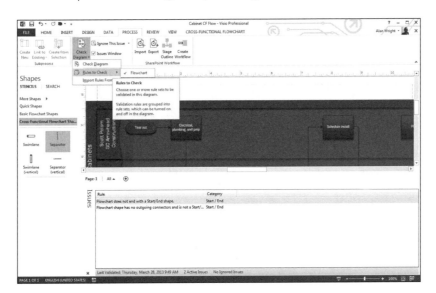

FIGURE 18.9

Visio 2013 Professional includes diagram validation tools.

In the Validation section of the Process tab, you can Ignore This Issue, or expand to review ignored issues, Ignore Rules altogether, or Stop Ignoring Issues and/or Rules.

NOTE Validation is not a new feature, however; it was previously available only in the in Visio 2010 Premium version. With adjustments to the lineup of Visio versions released for 2013, validation tools are now included with Professional, and hopefully this will encourage more companies to further develop and take advantage of this useful feature.

Business Process Diagrams (BPMN 2.0) and SharePoint Workflows

BPMN and SharePoint Workflows are considered advanced flowcharting styles and are included in Visio Professional 2013.

BPMN Diagrams

Business Process Model and Notation (BPMN) flowcharts have received better tools including updated validation rules and over 350 new shapes and shape variations that support the BPMN 2.0 standard, which is considered a big upgrade from the BPMN 1.2 standard supported in Visio 2010. (Don't worry, Visio 2013 still works with the BPMN 1.2 drawings you may have created in the past.)

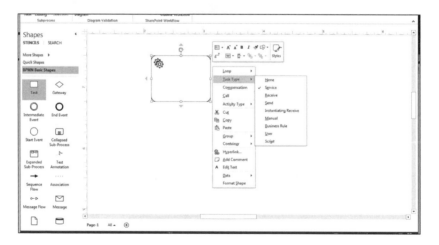

FIGURE 18.10

BPMN flowcharts allow basic shapes to be modified into dozens of variations using context menus.

SharePoint Workflows

Both Microsoft SharePoint 2010 Workflow and Microsoft SharePoint 2013 Workflow templates are included with Visio 2013 Professional. With SharePoint 2013, new validation rules were needed, and they are supported in Visio.

This type of flowchart is intended to map a SharePoint workflow, and the results can be exported to Microsoft SharePoint Designer for configuration. With SharePoint 2013 Workflow, a new start point and many more shapes have been added to the three stencils. Because this template uses a new Stage container, you see the Container Tools contextual tab appear when working with Stage containers, as shown in Figure 18.11. Finally, SharePoint Designer 2013 can open VSDX files without any export process. Just save your workflow to the default Visio drawing format, and you are good to go.

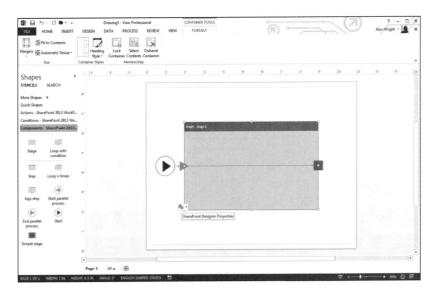

FIGURE 18.11

The default start point when opening a Microsoft SharePoint 2013 Workflow template.

 NOTE The SharePoint 2013 Workflow template supports .Net 4.0 workflows, and aside from the new Stage container, loops and steps can also be used to group elements of your workflow. When in SharePoint Designer 2013, you also have access to the Visio interface to effect any edits before publishing.

Block Diagram Tips

Block diagrams are not new, and in Visio 2013 you have 2D and a couple 3D variations to choose from. They are often used to capture a variety of design, process, and flow modeling. Block diagram shapes have a few unique qualities that are pointed out here to help you get the most from your block diagrams.

Blend Block Shapes

One key element when working with block diagrams is to blend shapes together. You find a few shapes in the block template stencils that have been designed to allow blending to take place.

Notice in Figure 18.12 how arrows have been blended into a box shape. These arrow shapes have the capability to have either an open or closed end, which makes this visual feat possible. The context menus are displayed for two shapes that allow you to open or close sections for blending. This feature works in both 2D and 3D shapes.

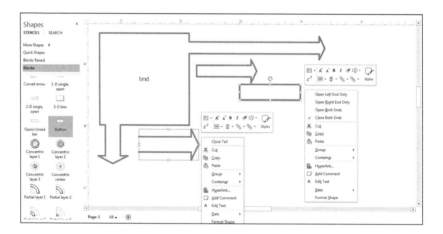

FIGURE 18.12

Use open-ended shapes to blend two or more shapes together.

 TIP If you have trouble getting shapes to look right when you try to blend, make sure that you are not using a theme with gradients or shadows. The blend is essentially an illusion because the shapes remain separate, and they have separate shadows as a result. This effect can be disabled on an individual shape using the Format Shape pane. Another problem might be the Z-order because the open-ended shape must be on top of the shape you are blending to. Use a context menu to choose Bring to Front if this is the problem.

3D Perspective Block Diagrams

The Block Diagram with Perspective template is a special 3D block diagram that uses a vanishing point (VP) to achieve a unique 3D effect on your block diagram. This type of diagram requires a bit of finesse to get everything just right, but it has a very pleasing appearance when used properly.

The rendering is done by treating the top of the shapes as being on the same geometric plane. Most individuals use this presentation to illustrate relationships using the Depth setting shown in Figure 18.13. This can be revealed by using the context menu and selecting Set Depth. Notice the visible difference in these shapes achieved by simply altering the Depth percentage.

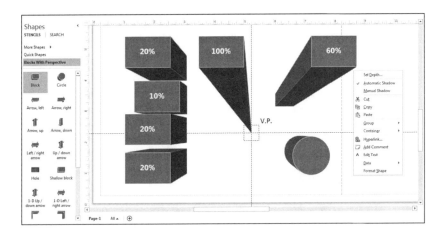

FIGURE 18.13

Block diagrams with perspective provide captivating visuals.

If the VP is moved, prepare to do some housecleaning. In Figure 18.14, the only change from Figure 18.13 is the positioning of the VP. Some shapes need to be moved, and some need a Z-order change.

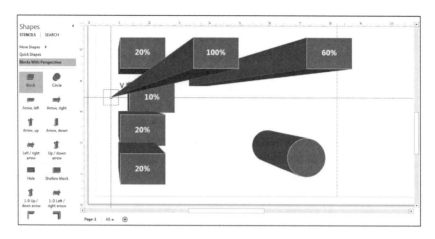

FIGURE 18.14

Using Perspective can be frustrating at times; expect to spend some time tweaking the results.

CAUTION If you have any shapes selected when moving the vanishing point, only those shapes are affected by the move. You are actually moving a point that is unique to those selected shapes. The VP for the page continues to be indicated by the purple crosshairs. If you do not want to have multiple vanishing points in your drawing, make sure nothing is selected when moving the VP.

THE ABSOLUTE MINIMUM

It is good to be aware of ways to override automatic format settings because these might occasionally have undesirable results. Flowchart shapes can be reset or allowed to expand to accommodate text.

Make sure that you understand how and when to use subprocesses in your flowcharts. It is not unusual for flowcharts to be printed and referred to in meetings and training. A well-laid-out and concise flowchart speaks well of your organizational abilities.

When working with Decision shapes, it is a good practice to use point-to-point glue to ensure coherent results later.

Make good use of the special tools bundled into the cross-functional flowchart contextual tab. Change the default orientation of swimlanes if you find yourself changing back to the vertical orientation.

Take time to look through the new shapes and behavior in the updated BPMN and SharePoint Workflow templates.

Use the Diagram Validation tools from the Process tab to ensure that processes are set up correctly in your flowcharts.

IN THIS CHAPTER

- Can I use Visio to map my logical network… just like Mr. Spock?

- How can I painlessly create rack diagrams?

- How do I save time when creating timelines without creating paradoxes?

- How can I make org charts that catch the eye (and the rest of the face)?

- How do I keep my plans looking like they were planned?

TIPS FOR WORKING WITH OTHER DIAGRAM TYPES

Visio has so many templates to choose from that Chapters 18 and 19 are dedicated to briefly present tips and examine some of the unique features and special contextual tabs that set a few of these diagram types apart.

Administrators, technicians, and even help desk personnel often rely on logical network diagrams for planning and troubleshooting. Rack diagrams are valuable aids for documenting equipment that is currently deployed in datacenters and network closets and for planning future deployments. Timelines are widely used by many individuals for a variety of purposes.

With Visio 2013, it's time to face the fact that faces are expected to appear in your org charts. You will enjoy the new tools and content to help liven up your organization. Finally, we all use floor plans, plot plans, utility plans, and maps from time to time. Don't think that you need to be an engineer to work with these types of diagrams, because Visio makes it easy.

Working with Network Diagrams

Many network engineers and administrators love the easy-to-understand diagrams that can be created using the various network diagram templates included in Visio. Visio 2013 Standard includes only the Basic Network and Basic Network 3D stencils, but Visio 2013 Professional includes AD, LDAP, Detailed Network, Detailed Network 3D, and Rack templates.

 NOTE With Visio 2013, new shapes have been added to the Network stencils to reflect modern equipment that is found on networks: smart phones, VOIP phones, tablets, as well as enhanced server shapes to reflect task-specific roles such as mail servers.

Logical Diagrams

Intended to help viewers understand how network resources are interconnected, logical diagrams are *not* meant to be physical representations of how cables connect computers and servers together or where computers and servers might be physically situated in a location. (Nor is this a *Star Trek* reference, although Spock would logically use Visio when creating diagrams.) When creating a logical network diagram, you likely need to make a couple of basic changes to help your diagram accomplish its purpose (see Figure 19.1).

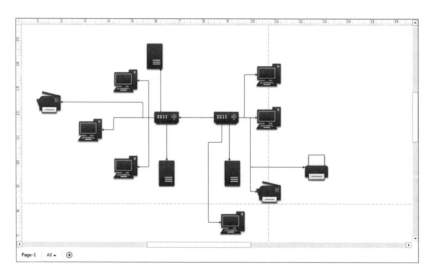

FIGURE 19.1

Logical diagrams such as this basic network diagram should be tweaked to better capture the relationship between networked resources.

In Figure 19.2, you can see several network resources arrayed around two routers that might be located in different cities. Straight connector styles are a better choice than the spaghetti that the dynamic right-angle connectors created in Figure 19.1. Also the default arrow-ended connectors were replaced with no arrow ends using the Format Shape pane.

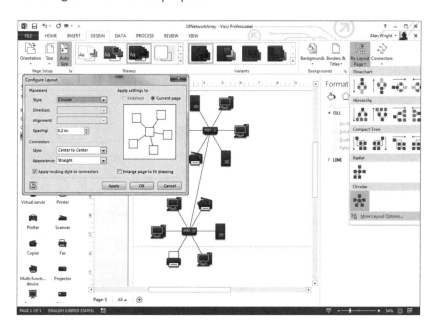

FIGURE 19.2

Use the Configure Layout dialog box to fine-tune a layout for a page or selection of shapes.

An easy way to effect this transformation is to use the Re-Layout Page tool and More Layout Options from the Design tab. In Figure 19.2 you can see the Configure Layout dialog box, which enables you to choose Circular in the Style drop-down menu. The 0.2 choice in the Spacing drop-down menu forms a tighter grouping, and the Center to Center choice in the Connector Style drop-down menu works well with the Straight choice in the Appearance drop-down menu. When using these settings, keep in mind that the changes can be applied to an entire page or just a group of selected shapes.

Rack Diagrams

Unlike logical diagrams, rack diagrams are intended to *accurately* document the hardware mounted in a server rack or cabinet located in a data closet or data center. For this reason, the shapes tend to be very detailed and match the appearance of standard rack-mountable components, as shown in Figure 19.3.

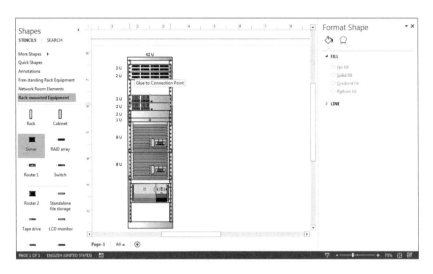

FIGURE 19.3

You should be able to accurately capture the contents of your rack or cabinet in a rack diagram.

 NOTE Rack diagrams are included with Visio 2013 Professional and Visio Pro for Office 365.

Finding Shapes

Many of the shapes that are intended for rack diagrams are found in the stencils that open when you open the rack diagram template. Because these diagrams are widely relied on for planning and documentation, many manufacturers provide Visio stencils to match their rack-mounted equipment. Additional stencils can also be downloaded from Microsoft that include common branded components from Sun, IBM, HP, and other established manufacturers. A quick Internet search for Visio stencils includes up-to-date shapes from many other companies.

→ To learn more about finding stencils and other online resources, see page **304**.

Placing and Attaching

When rack-mounted shapes are dragged to a chassis or cabinet shape, they snap to glue points automatically and by default indicate the amount of rack units they occupy with a visual 1U, 2U, or more. Notice in Figure 19.4 that two glue points are highlighted as a shape snaps into a 42U rack. You can see the vertical dots that indicate rack mount points. To accurately capture how your rack or cabinet is set up, you might want to zoom in and use the rack unit measurements as a reference. When glued, they move with a cabinet or rack when it is moved.

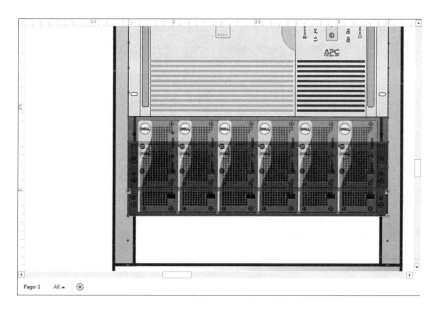

FIGURE 19.4

Rack diagram shapes snap to predefined glue points and become part of the rack or cabinet they are glued to.

Timeline Tips

Timeline stencils include three basic shape types: Timeline, Milestone, and Interval. These can be combined to create schedules, historical overviews, projected timelines, and so on. As shown in Figure 19.5, you can use and combine many variations of these three basic shapes.

 NOTE The Timeline template is available in all versions of Visio.

Many settings can be adjusted using context menus; a few examples are compiled in Figure 19.6. Notice that timelines, intervals, and milestones all allow you to change type using the context menu. It is also easy to correct dates, orientation, and even hide elements all from the context menus.

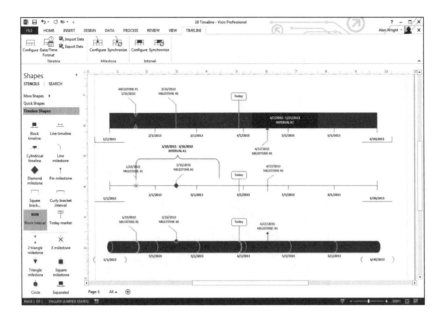

FIGURE 19.5

You can create timelines to suite any taste.

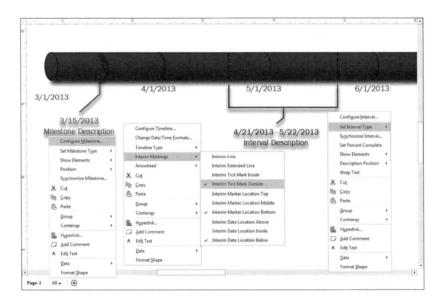

FIGURE 19.6

Timelines make extensive use of the context menu to fine-tune the appearance and data.

Timelines have their own contextual ribbon, as shown in Figure 19.5. Using the ribbon you can use the Configure button to edit the time endpoints, scale, and time format. The Date/Time Format button is a bit more granular, allowing you to edit format options for all visible time reference fields. There are buttons to synchronize milestones and intervals. These can be useful when scheduled events influence other events.

Finally, you have tools to import and export from Microsoft Project files. (Note that you must have Project installed to perform this.) When importing, you can select the task types you want to import: All, Top-level tasks only, Milestones only, Summary tasks only, or Top-level tasks and Milestones. You can then assign the Visio style of shapes to be used for Timeline, Milestone, and Interval shapes.

Org Chart Tips

Organization (org) charts have been shaken up a bit with Visio 2013. Emphasis has been placed on creating fresh and exciting visual alternatives to the standard boxy org chart that everyone has grown accustomed to. Ten new styles and dozens of new shapes have been introduced; the new Pip style is shown in Figure 19.7.

USE PHOTOS IN YOUR ORG CHARTS!

With Visio 2013, shapes include the use of photos. This is a nice feature and one that most organizations like because everyone likes to put a face with a name. When adding and editing photos, you have access to a Picture tools tab that allows you to perform basic editing and cropping.

You can import photos from an Exchange server so that the same familiar photo used in Outlook appears in the org chart. You can also import photos from a folder that has filenames that match the field used in your org chart, such as name, employee ID, or email.

Finally, you can manually add photos from the Org Chart tab or use the context menu. When doing so, you are able to perform minor edits and even crop the image from the contextual Picture Tools Format tab. (See Figure 19.11 later in the chapter.)

If you are creating an org chart for a spy organization and do not want to use pictures, you can hide this feature altogether to protect their identities. Select the shapes you want to remove pictures from, and use the Show/Hide button on the Org Chart tab to hide this feature.

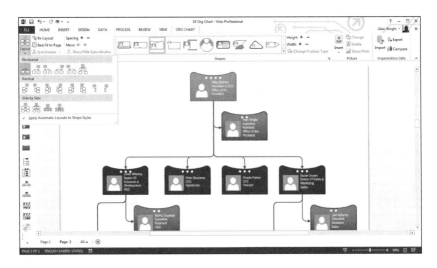

FIGURE 19.7

New styles can jazz up those old fashioned org charts.

 NOTE The new org chart styles are designed to work with the Embellishments feature. This new feature provides a few more variations in the overall appearance of shapes designed to respond to this setting. To change the Embellishment setting, navigate to the Design tab and expand the Variants section to reveal Embellishment. You can choose among High, Medium, or Low settings. This setting is then applied to the entire page and cannot be applied to selected shapes.

➜ To learn more about the Embellishment feature, see page **76**.

Org charts have their own contextual tab, which includes a nice layout tool that can be seen in Figure 19.7. Besides the general layout options, you can change spacing and sizing.

A prominent section of the Org Chart tab is the shape styles gallery labeled simply as Shapes. This allows you to apply a different style to your org chart. Because of the intense rendering that takes place, there is not a hover preview of a style change. Some styles drastically alter the layout of an org chart. Change styles from Pip to Petals, for example, and you see a jump to a broad, airy layout, which makes it harder to see everything in one place until you zoom out. To control this default behavior, expand the Shapes gallery to reveal Apply Automatic Layouts to

Shape Styles and uncheck it (see Figure 19.8). This can also be toggled on and off from the Layout button in the same Org Chart tab. You can use this for comparing styles, but as Figure 19.9 shows, the final chart is likely to need to have a layout that works with the style used.

FIGURE 19.8

You can stop layout changes from occurring automatically when changing shape styles.

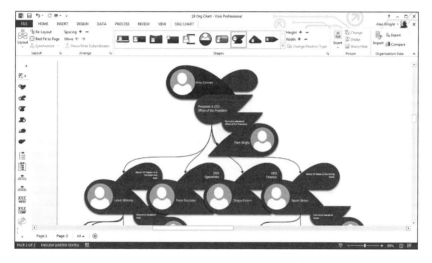

FIGURE 19.9

The Petals shape style is very distinct and needs a better layout than this one.

Create Org Charts Manually

If you want to create an org chart from scratch using Visio shapes, you should be aware of some characteristics and handy tools. Hierarchical connections are expected when working with org charts, so to add a subordinate position, simply drop one shape on top of another, and the new shape is connected automatically. (You can be less precise now than in the past; a slight overlap is enough to trigger this connection.)

In Figure 19.10 you can see several options that can be accessed using the context menu. The Shape Data pane also can be invaluable for updating or correcting data in your org chart. Org charts accept updates either in the text fields or directly in the Shape Data pane. In either case, the entry is synced. Use Insert to add images to your shapes. As shown in Figure 19.11, and explained further in the sidebar "Use Photos in Your Org Charts," photos are an important element in modern org charts.

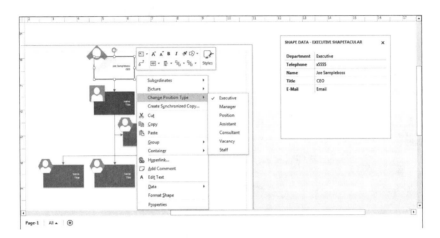

FIGURE 19.10

Use the Shape Data pane and the extensive context menus to tweak your org chart shapes.

FIGURE 19.11

You can add pictures to your shapes and even edit them without leaving Visio.

Using the Organization Chart Wizard

Visio works well in rendering prepared information from Excel spreadsheets or other sources. This will save you time since Visio can easily extract common fields such as name, phone number, department and title all from a spreadsheet using a wizard. To test the creation of an org chart from a spreadsheet using the Organization Chart wizard, use the sample spreadsheet named ORGDATA.xls that was installed on your computer when you installed Visio. It is found in the path C:\Program Files (x86)\Microsoft Office\Office15\Visio Content\1033 on 32-bit English installs. Of course, if you have a spreadsheet already prepared you can use that file in the following steps.

1. Open an org chart template. When the Organization Chart wizard opens, select Information that's already stored in a file or database and click Next.

2. Select A text, ORG PLUS (*txt), or Excel file when choosing where your information is stored, and then click Next.

3. Browse to the location of the file that contains your data and click Next (see Figure 19.12).

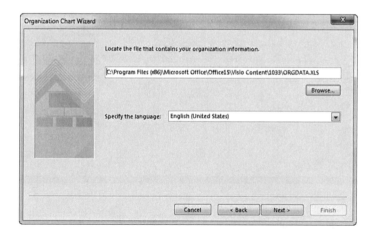

FIGURE 19.12

Use the Organization Chart Wizard to convert prepared data into an org chart.

4. Select the column names in the spreadsheet that are relevant to the org chart and click Next. (If using the sample file, you can leave the default choices of Name and Reports_To.)

5. Add any data file columns to the Displayed Fields column to include those fields in the actual display on the shapes and click Next.

6. Add fields that you want to include in the shape data. This does not make them visible in the org chart; it simply includes them in the Shape Data pane. They may include the same choices as step 5. Click Next.

7. You can include pictures from an exchange server or folder. If you're using the sample spreadsheet, leave the default selection as Don't Include Pictures and click Next.

8. Leave the default selection to allow the wizard to divide your chart across pages, and then click Finish.

9. Compare displayed data to the Shape Data pane as shown in Figure 19.13. It reflects choices you made in steps 5 and 6. Notice that you have more than one page, and scroll down on Page-1 to see all the individuals included.

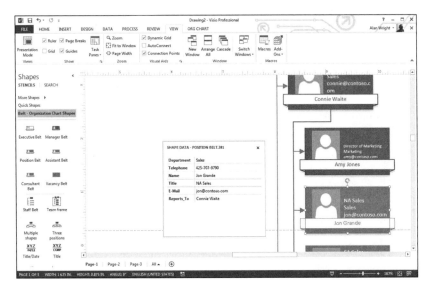

FIGURE 19.13

Org charts display data that you choose, and shapes can contain even more data.

You can also create a chart on-the-fly using the Organization Chart wizard. Rather than choosing Information that's already stored in a file or database, select Information That I Enter Using the Wizard. This can be a formidable task if you're starting from scratch because the information you need is stored in a spreadsheet or a delimited text file, which is then used to create the chart. Type in a name and select a location to get started.

If you choose delimited text file, you will see a notepad open asking you to enter data using the format "Name,Reports_to,Title,Department,Telephone," and a couple of lines of sample data is provided to assist you. Make your additions and then save the file. Visio then converts this data into an org chart that you can work with.

Office and Space Plans

When you're working with plans, you need to be aware of a few unique characteristics. Wall shapes tend to autoconnect to other wall shapes, and shapes glued to walls tend to move with walls. Walls have a single side that is referred to as a reference line. Using the context menu for walls, you can flip the side used for the reference line, add a guide line, or add a dimension. Guide lines can be handy visual reference points. To remove a guide line, select it and press Del.

Some shapes found in Floor Plan templates have been designed to provide many layout variations with a single shape. As shown in Figure 19.14, you can use the context menu to reverse the direction and orientation of door shapes, for example. Further changes can be made from the Shape Data pane for these shapes, such as dimensions and degree of opening to show in the drawing window.

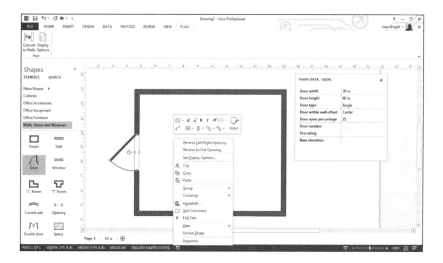

FIGURE 19.14

Use the context menu to work with special floor plan shapes like doors and windows.

NOTE Visio 2013 Standard includes the Maps and Office Layout templates. You need Professional or Pro for Office 365 versions for more advanced plans, including HVAC, Electrical and Telecom, Home Plan, Plant Layout, and many more.

Creating Plans Using Shapes

Depending on the plan template you selected, you may be working with interior floor plans. If you need to include exterior walls, make sure the Wall, Shell, and Structure stencil is open. Rather than using a room shape, consider using a space shape and converting it to exterior walls. You can start with the basic rectangular space shape, or use the L- or T-shaped space shapes. Use the Convert to Walls tool and select exterior walls. If you select an individual wall and view the Shape Data pane, you see a Wall Thickness field. Here you can select from standard measurements to convert exterior or interior walls or set a custom thickness.

Besides the shapes, you can use drawing tools to provide the shape you want to start with, as shown in Figure 19.15. From the contextual Plan tab use the Convert to Walls tool to turn a rough sketch into walls that you can work with. In Figure 19.15, you can also see the Convert to Walls dialog box that lets you select interior or exterior walls, whether to show dimensions or guide lines, and what to do with the original lines you drew. In Figure 19.16, you can see the results of the sketch in Figure 19.15.

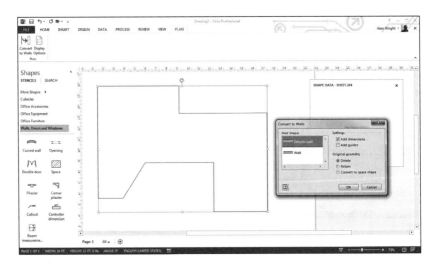

FIGURE 19.15

Create your own walls with the Convert to Walls tool.

TIP Depending on how you create a shape using line tools, dimensions may be presented on the inside or outside of the final shape after you have run the Convert to Walls tool. Working in a counterclockwise direction produces dimensions on the outside (as shown in Figure 19.16). Creating lines in a clockwise direction results in dimensions being displayed inside of the finished shape.

The Plan tab also includes a tool to let you select how much of the wall, door, and window shapes are visible. The Door tab can be seen in Figure 19.16.

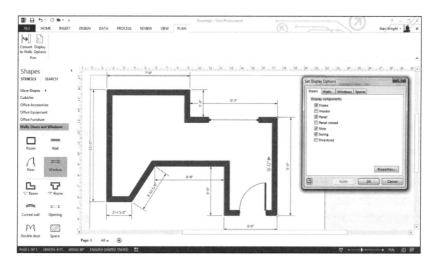

FIGURE 19.16

You can customize the appearance of walls and other shapes using the Set Display Options dialog box.

Space Shapes

If you have never used them before, Space shapes can be very useful. Drop a Space shape into a room, right-click, and select Auto Size. You see the shape resize to fit into the room it was dropped into. Notice in Figure 19.17 that a few rooms have the cross-hatching that indicates a Space shape is present. You can see a context menu for the Space shape as well.

If the area you want to work with is only a portion of a room or even an exterior area, you can right-click and select Edit, which allows you to customize the size of the Space shape by putting you into Edit mode. You can select and move points to adjust the Space shape, and the area updates as you make adjustments. Press the Esc key to exit Edit mode when you're finished.

FIGURE 19.17

Space shapes provide some very practical ways of displaying shape data in your plans.

The Shape Data pane allows you to type in additional shape data entries, which can be displayed. From the context menu select Set Display Options to select up to four Shape Data fields you want to show. This is a practical way to display extra information for a room like names, department, phone numbers, and so forth. By default, the area is calculated, and you can choose from various units of measurement.

A Space shape has two important points to be aware of. In Figure 19.17, you can see a Basepoint for the Space shape. The second has been pulled off to the right of the shape and is a locator for the displayed text. Either point can be selected and moved, providing you with lots of versatility in this special shape.

Working with Dimension Lines

When working with plans, it is important to use a dimension line to display key reference measurements. Although Visio may know the dimensions, and they may be revealed in the shape data, visual dimensions remain useful elements for floor and building plans. If you plan to print, it becomes even more important to include these.

As mentioned earlier, if you right-click a wall shape, you have the option to choose Add a Dimension. This is simply adding a dimension line shape for you. You will find open stencils dedicated to Dimension shapes appropriate to your plan when you open a template. In Figure 19.18, the stencil is named Dimensioning–Architectural.

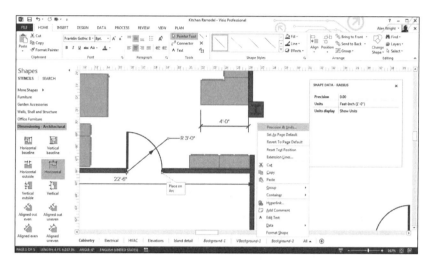

FIGURE 19.18

Use Dimension Line shapes to enhance the information communicated in your plans.

Notice in Figure 19.18 that a few Dimension shapes have been added to a floor plan. The 36-inch doorway has a Radius shape added; the control point labeled Place on Arc dictates the measurement displayed as R 3'-0". Notice the Shape Data pane provides options to control what is displayed and the unit of measurement used. Also visible is a cabinet that has a Horizontal Dimension shape added. You can adjust the size and location of the displayed measurements fairly easily by selecting and dragging control handles. The context menu is also displayed, which allows you to fine-tune units of measurement and display options. You can also establish new page measurement defaults or reset the selected shape to the current default page properties.

THE ABSOLUTE MINIMUM

When working with logical network diagrams, make good use of the Configure Layout dialog box to fine-tune the spacing and overall style for selected clusters of shapes.

Rack diagrams can be easily customized by downloading stencils from vendors for Visio.

Timelines basically use three components. Use the context menus to adjust styles and time values.

Take the time to verify you have data prepared and updated to create your org chart. An org chart says a lot about the people in it, so take advantage of the new styles and variations available. It is a good investment to take the extra time to get pictures of your people. Naming the picture files properly can save you a lot of time later when importing to the org chart.

Spend some time working with the tools and stencils available for creating plans. Many context menu items are unique to floor plans. The Shape Data pane is a very useful tool to keep open when tweaking your plans.

Index

D

J-K

L

M

Q

R

T

X-Y-Z

FREE
Online Edition

Your purchase of **Visio® 2013 Absolute Beginner's Guide** includes access to a free online edition for 45 days through the **Safari Books Online** subscription service. Nearly every Que book is available online through **Safari Books Online**, along with thousands of books and videos from publishers such as Addison-Wesley Professional, Cisco Press, Exam Cram, IBM Press, O'Reilly Media, Prentice Hall, Sams, and VMware Press.

Safari Books Online is a digital library providing searchable, on-demand access to thousands of technology, digital media, and professional development books and videos from leading publishers. With one monthly or yearly subscription price, you get unlimited access to learning tools and information on topics including mobile app and software development, tips and tricks on using your favorite gadgets, networking, project management, graphic design, and much more.

Activate your FREE Online Edition at
informit.com/safarifree

STEP 1:   Enter the coupon code: LGPUFWH.

STEP 2:   New Safari users, complete the brief registration form.
           Safari subscribers, just log in.

If you have difficulty registering on Safari or accessing the online edition,
please e-mail customer-service@safaribooksonline.com